HOW TO ACCESS YOUR EBOOK, VIDEOS,

GW00370760

TEACHERS

Email us at info@brighterminds.ie if you haven't received your special teacher login.

STUDENTS

TO LOG IN

- If you have already completed registration and chosen a username (see below),
  go to www.brighterminds.ie, click on EBOOK LOGIN and enter your **username** twice.

- If you don't yet have a username, complete the **one-time registration process** shown below.

STUDENT REGISTRATION PROCESS - one time only, when you receive your book

1. Go to www.brighterminds.ie and click on EBOOK LOGIN at the top of the page.

2. When prompted for a username, enter the **Unique Book Code** shown in the box below.
   (Note - the unique book code contains lower-case letters only, and no numbers)

3. Follow the on-screen instructions and **enter your details in the registration screen**.

4. Enter an easy-to-remember **username**. You may use upper- and lower-case letters and numbers, but in order to log in later, you must enter your username exactly as chosen.

5. When your registration has completed, **write your new username into the box below**.

6. **Log in** by clicking on EBOOK LOGIN and entering your new chosen username twice.
   You should now see your JC Engineering ebook, videos and quizzes.

   If you have any difficulties, email us at support@brighterminds.ie

Your **Unique Book Code** for Registration

> jedwqdb

Write your chosen **Username** here

Published by Brighter Minds, 2020

Our thanks to the authors, reviewers, Philip Campion for the artwork,
and Phil Daly Art at facebook.com/philyarts for the engineering room Health & Safety drawing.

Information for Teachers

This book is divided into **12 Units of Learning**:

- **Units 3-11** contain **practical projects**
- In the practical units, the **theory** is predominantly **related to the project**
- All units contain **activities** to promote **engagement** and reinforce learning

Each unit of learning covers the three strands:

- **Processes and Principles**
- **Design Application**
- **Mechatronics**

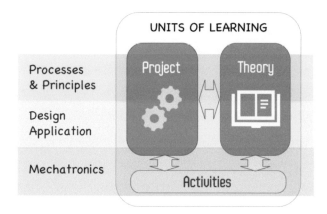

Progression of Projects and Units

Projects increase in complexity in a **progressive** way, beginning with **drawing** exercises and single-piece **manufacturing** projects, and leading to more complex **mechatronic control systems**.

All units have **ample opportunities for student design**. The 12 units of learning deliver all NCCA **learning outcomes**. Below is a suggested **timeline** for the units:

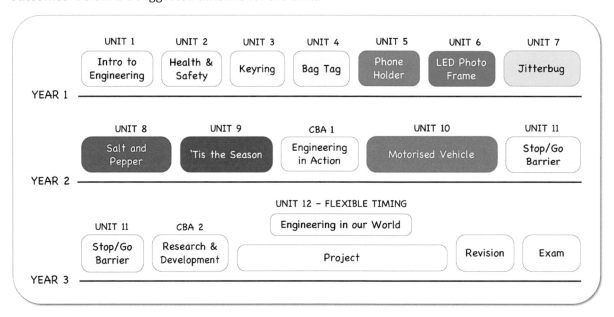

Navigating between Project and Theory, Completing Activities

Work on the **projects** is guided by a **storyboard of activities** at the **beginning** of each unit.

As students work through the project activities, **you can refer to the relevant theory contained later in the same unit**.

The **theory** sections also contain their own **activities** to enliven and revise theory topics.

The theory sections also include **additional theory** to prepare students for later projects and examinations.

Revision questions are provided at the end of each unit.

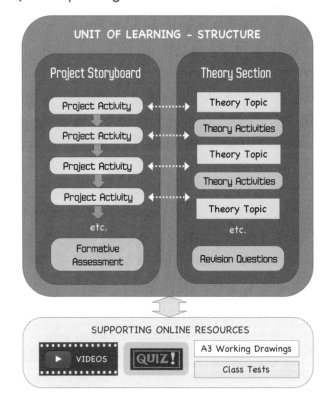

Supporting Teacher Choice

The content of the units in this book can be applied in an **adaptive** way to support different cohorts and mixed-ability classes. Teachers can **choose which activities to carry out**, and **how much design work** to allocate to students. Teachers can **substitute other similar projects** instead of the provided projects. The workbook-style **activities** can be filled out by **students individually** during class, or instead used as **group work**, **class discussions**, **homework**, or any combination.

Online Resources – Students

The book is supported by **online resources** such as the **ebook** and supporting **videos** and **quizzes,** which are accessed by logging in with your unique username at **brighterminds.ie**. The videos and quizzes are especially useful for learning and revision as they are different, **engaging and interactive**. The online resources can be viewed both at school and at home without the need for any special software.

Formative Assessments

At the end of each project, there is space for students to **self-reflect** and formatively **self-assess** their own work. Space is also provided to record **teacher formative feedback**, and student **peer** feedback if desired.

Evidence of Learning

The **workbook nature** of the book allows it to be used to record **evidence of student learning**.

Learning Outcomes

The **Introduction** to each unit sets out the objectives, contents, **learning outcomes** and suggested timeframes for each unit.

Online Resources – Teachers

Further resources for teachers will be available at brighterminds.ie, such as a starting **scheme of work**, units of learning breakdowns, working drawings, posters and a **teacher's document** outlining how this book and e-package supports national educational objectives and programmes.

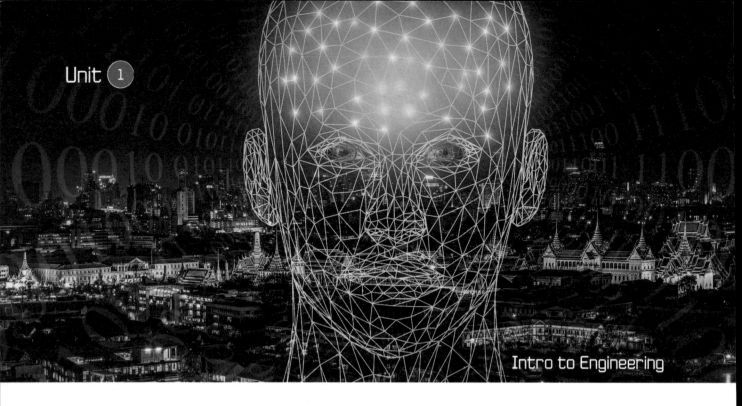

Unit 1 – Introduction to Engineering

Unit Objectives

- Gain an **overview** of the field of engineering, and an overview of and **enthusiasm** for the **Junior Cycle Engineering** course
- Understand some relevant **terminology** and get some 'tasters' for the rest of the course

Content

- What **engineering** is all about - what engineers do, what skills are involved
- **Benefits** of studying engineering
- Possible **careers** - where engineering might lead you in the future
- Contents of the **Junior Cycle Engineering** course – the kinds of things you will do and learn
- What the **three strands** of learning involve:
  - ○ **Processes and Principles** – examples and activities
  - ○ **Design Application** – examples and activities
  - ○ **Mechatronics** – examples and activities

Learning Outcomes from this Unit

PROCESSES AND PRINCIPLES	DESIGN APPLICATION	MECHATRONICS
1.6, 1.8	2.2, 2.3, 2.4	3.1, 3.2, 3.4

Suggested Timeframes

START TIME	YEAR 1	First week of term		DURATION	1 week

What is Engineering?

Note: the goal of these optional activities is not to get the 'right answer'. It is to promote thinking.

Activity 1

In your own words, try to **explain** what you think **engineering** might mean or involve, and what you think engineers **do**:

_____

_____

_____

_____

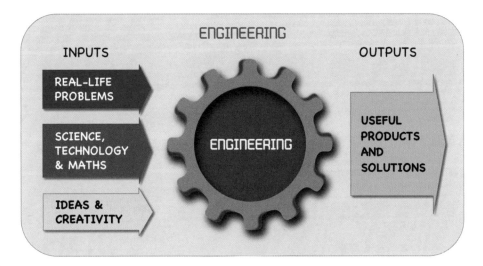

Engineers design and build a wide variety of things: e.g. **structures, machines, systems, materials, devices, computers, processes** and **organisations**.

Engineers apply **science, technology, maths** and their own **creativity** to **solve problems** and **design and build useful things**

Where can I see Engineering?

Engineering can be seen **everywhere**. Almost everything you see around you has been **designed by engineers**. Here are some examples:

- Every **product** in your home and school
- The **buildings** you live, work and study in
- The **cars, buses, trains** and **bikes** you take to school
- The **airplanes** in the sky, and all the **equipment** that controls them in the air and on land
- The **machines** and **structures** that generate and distribute your **electricity**
- The **materials** that you see around you like **metals** and **plastics**, and even some aspects of your **clothes**

Why become an Engineer?

- There are so many things that need to be **designed**
- Engineering projects are **interesting**, **challenging** and **fun**
- You get the opportunity to **solve problems**, and to be **innovative** and **creative**
- You get the opportunity to **use science, technology and maths** in a **practical** and **useful** way
- You can **improve the quality of people's lives** - for example, with better-designed buildings, transport, energy, communications, medical products, and labour-saving machines
- Engineers are **sought-after** and **well-paid**, and you can choose to **work anywhere** in the world
- You can work in a **very large range of interesting areas and industries** - see below

Career Opportunities

The picture below show a selection of the large number of different areas in which engineers can work.

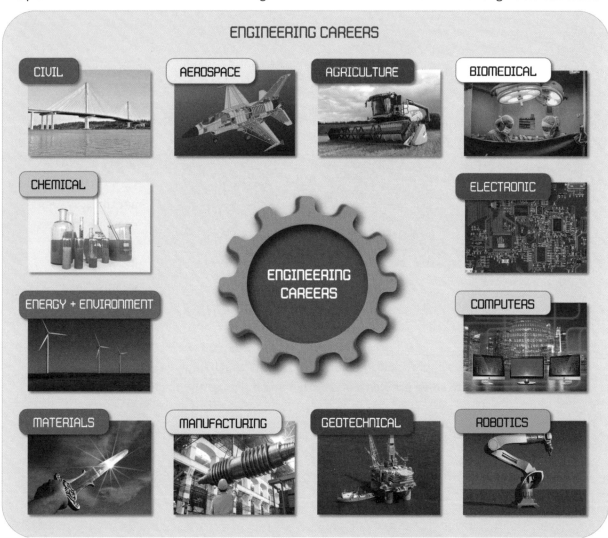

> **WHAT'S LEFT TO INVENT?** Don't think that most of our problems are already solved, and all the good ideas have all been thought of! We need **engineers and good ideas** more than ever.
> For example, to help develop **solutions for climate change**, to design more **sustainable energy** and **food production** systems, to design better **transport, buildings**, and **healthcare solutions,** to help us respond to **pandemics** better, and much more.

What will you Learn in Junior Cycle Engineering?

In Junior Cycle Engineering, you will:

- **build working projects** using different **materials** and **technologies**
- learn engineering **tools**, **processes** and **skills**
- learn the process of **design** and get opportunities to practice design
- learn how to build **mechatronic control systems** using **electronics** and **mechanisms** and **programming**

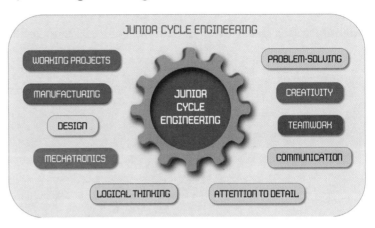

You will also learn valuable **general skills** that are **transferable** to school subjects, life and careers - such as **problem-solving**, **decision-making**, **innovation**, **time management**, **teamwork** and **communication**.

Three Strands of Learning

There are **three strands** of learning in Junior Cycle Engineering, which are summarised in the table below.

1. PROCESSES & PRINCIPLES	2. DESIGN APPLICATION	3. MECHATRONICS
• Materials	• The Design Process	• Mechanisms
• Tools & Equipment	• Factors in Design	• Electronics
• Manufacturing Processes	• Evaluating Designs	• Computers and ICT
• Manufacturing with Precision and high-quality Finishes	• Designing Projects	• Control Systems
	• Project Management	• Working with Mechatronics

Units of Learning

You will follow **Units of Learning** that teach all 3 strands in parallel. Most units of learning consist of:

- a **practical project**
- **supporting theory** for that project and unit
- lots of short **activities**

The projects **increase in complexity** and **skills** as you work through them, beginning with understanding drawings and materials, and progressing to **designing** and **building** your own mechatronic projects.

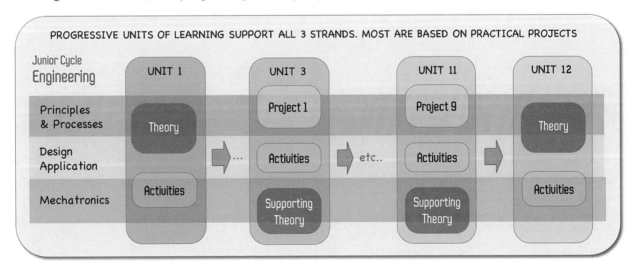

Introduction to Strand 1 - Processes and Principles

In this strand, you will learn about **engineering materials and equipment**, and primarily develop your **manufacturing skills**. In manufacturing, the focus is on **accuracy**, **precision** and **high-quality finishes**.

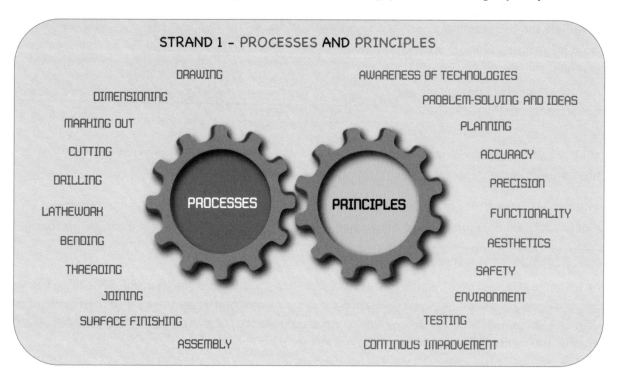

STRAND 1 - PROCESSES **AND** PRINCIPLES

DRAWING
DIMENSIONING
MARKING OUT
CUTTING
DRILLING
LATHEWORK
BENDING
THREADING
JOINING
SURFACE FINISHING
ASSEMBLY

PROCESSES

PRINCIPLES

AWARENESS OF TECHNOLOGIES
PROBLEM-SOLVING AND IDEAS
PLANNING
ACCURACY
PRECISION
FUNCTIONALITY
AESTHETICS
SAFETY
ENVIRONMENT
TESTING
CONTINOUS IMPROVEMENT

Activity 2 – Processes & Principles

In your own words, **explain** what you think is meant by an **engineering process**:

_____

_____

Can you **identify** and name **four engineering processes** that **remove material**?

1. _____ 2. _____

3. _____ 4. _____

Activity 3 – Processes & Principles

In your own words, **describe** what you understand by the following **engineering principles**:

Accuracy: _____

High-Quality Finish: _____

Activity 4 – Processes & Principles Taster

Identify a **material** you think might be suitable to make the **key ring** shown here.
Justify (give a reason for) your choice of material.

Material: _____

Justification: _____

Can you **identify four different engineering processes**
that you think might be required to make this key ring:

Process 1: _____

Process 2: _____

Process 3: _____

Process 4: _____

Introduction to Strand 2 - Design Application

In this strand, you will learn about the **design process** and the different **factors** you need to consider when designing. You will have lots of opportunities to **practice design**, to **choose materials** and to evaluate and **improve existing designs.** You will explore the **impact of design** on **function**, **environment** and **society**. You will also learn about **project management** and how to plan and track your time.

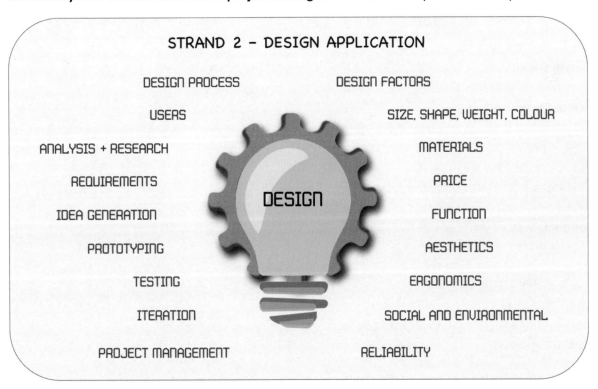

STRAND 2 - DESIGN APPLICATION

DESIGN PROCESS   DESIGN FACTORS

USERS   SIZE, SHAPE, WEIGHT, COLOUR

ANALYSIS + RESEARCH   MATERIALS

REQUIREMENTS   PRICE

IDEA GENERATION   DESIGN   FUNCTION

PROTOTYPING   AESTHETICS

TESTING   ERGONOMICS

ITERATION   SOCIAL AND ENVIRONMENTAL

PROJECT MANAGEMENT   RELIABILITY

Activity 5 – Design Application Taster

This girl is using a chair that is not designed well for her needs.
Explore the **good and bad design features** of <u>YOUR</u> **school chair**.
(Hints: height, size, back, stability, movability, comfort, weight etc)

<u>(A)</u> Identify three **good design features** of your chair:

1. _____

2. _____

3. _____

<u>(B)</u> Identify **three poor design features** of your chair:

1. _____

2. _____

3. _____

Activity 6 - Design Application Taster

Compare and contrast the older and newer **shaving designs** below, under the factors listed:

Effectiveness:		
Speed of Shave:		
Price:		
Safety:		
Environmental Impact:		
Other Advantages:		
Disadvantages:		

Activity 7 - Design Application Taster

Research a number of **inventors** and **record** their **names** and **inventions** here:

	Name	Invention(s)
Female Inventor 1:		
Female Inventor 2:		
Male Inventor 1:		
Male Inventor 2:		
Young Inventor 1:		
Young Inventor 2:		

Introduction to Strand 3 — Mechatronics

A **mechatronic system** uses **electronics** and **mechanisms** to **control its outputs** based on its inputs

- A **system** is a **set of parts that work together** to carry out a certain function

- A **control system** uses a set of **inputs** to control a set of **outputs**

The word "**mechatronics**" combines the "mecha" from **mechanisms** and the "tronics" from **electronics**.

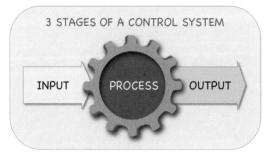

- Typical **inputs** to mechatronic systems are **switches**, levers and **sensors**

- Typical **outputs** from mechatronic systems are **movement**, **light**, and **sound**

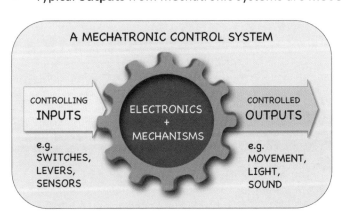

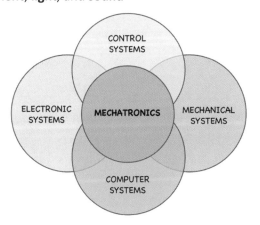

Mechatronics refers to **control systems** that combine **electronics**, **mechanisms** and **mechanical systems**. Mechatronic systems also usually use **computer systems** and **software programming**.

Activity 8 – Mechatronics Taster

Explore your engineering room with your teacher's guidance and **identify 3 machines** that you think are **mechatronic** systems. **Justify** why you think each machine is a mechatronic system.

	Machine Name	Why do you think this is a mechatronic system?
Machine 1:		
Machine 2:		
Machine 3:		

Activity 9 – Mechatronics Taster

Choose **one mechatronic device** from your classroom, home or garden and **describe its operation** in terms of **inputs**, **outputs** and **process** *(i.e. how does it convert its inputs to its outputs)*

Name of Device:

INPUTS	PROCESS	OUTPUTS

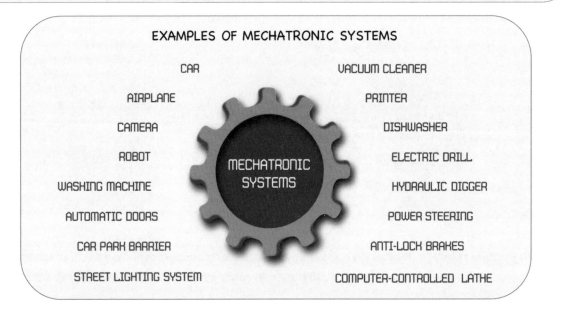

EXAMPLES OF MECHATRONIC SYSTEMS

CAR
AIRPLANE
CAMERA
ROBOT
WASHING MACHINE
AUTOMATIC DOORS
CAR PARK BARRIER
STREET LIGHTING SYSTEM

MECHATRONIC SYSTEMS

VACUUM CLEANER
PRINTER
DISHWASHER
ELECTRIC DRILL
HYDRAULIC DIGGER
POWER STEERING
ANTI-LOCK BRAKES
COMPUTER-CONTROLLED LATHE

Unit 2 – Health & Safety

Unit Objectives

The objective of this unit is to ensure that students are aware of the **hazards** within the engineering room, and are trained in the appropriate **safety signs, safety precautions** and **safety behaviour**, before embarking on any practical activities within the engineering room.

Content

- **Hazards** in the engineering room
- Difference between a **hazard** and a **risk**
- **Safety signs** and **personal protection equipment**
- What to do **if an accident occurs**
- Develop a **set of rules** to follow in the engineering room

*Later units in this book provide **additional safety information** on **specific tools and processes**.*

> The information in this unit is important for your personal safety.
>
> It will also help you answer safety-related **examination questions**.

Learning Outcomes from this Unit

PROCESSES AND PRINCIPLES	DESIGN APPLICATION	MECHATRONICS
1.3		

Suggested Timeframes

START TIME	YEAR 1	Early September		DURATION	1 week

Identifying Hazards and Risks

> A **hazard** is anything that **could cause you harm**

Hazards can be dangerous objects or dangerous situations. Examples of hazards are **bare electrical wires**, **chemicals**, **sharp edges**, **power tools**, **loud noises**, and **fumes**. Note that all hazards do not have the same likelihood of causing you injury – i.e. they have different **risks**.

> **Risk** is the **likelihood** a hazard will result in an **injury**.
> Risks can be categorised into **high**, **medium** or **low**.

Activity 1 – Hazards and Risks

Categorise the following **hazards** in terms of **risk**. Write **high**, **medium** or **low** in the boxes below:

HAZARD	RISK
(dangerous object or situation)	(likelihood of an injury occurring)
A person climbs up one step on a ladder:	
A person climbs a ladder that is on wet ground:	
A person climbs a metal ladder connected to mains electricity:	

Activity 2 – Identifying Hazards

Record **three hazardous objects or situations** in your engineering room:

	Name the HAZARD (i.e. a dangerous object or situation)	WHY IS THIS HAZARDOUS? (Think about how someone could be injured)	RISK (High, Medium or Low)	Write down a SAFETY PRECAUTION (i.e. an action that could be taken to make this safer)
1				
2				
3				

Safety Precautions

A **safety precaution** is an **action** that can be taken to make a task or situation **safer**

EXAMPLES OF SAFETY PRECAUTIONS

- Wearing **personal protective equipment** such as **safety glasses, safety gloves** and **ear defenders**
- **Tying up** long hair before using machinery
- Ensuring your workpiece / material is **clamped** tightly before working on it
- **Tidying** away schoolbags and books so they can't be tripped over

Types of Injuries

When identifying hazards and their safety precautions, it is useful to think about the **different ways in which people can be injured**.

Injury Type	Details	Typical Causes	Safety Precautions
DAMAGE TO EYES	• **Particles** in your eyes • Very dangerous	• Drilling • Cutting • Hammering • Filing	• Wear **safety goggles** • **Do not touch** your eyes
INJURIES TO BODY	• Injury from **moving parts** • **Cuts** from **sharp edges**	• Drills • Hammers • Chisels	• Wear protective **gloves** and **clothing** • **Clamp** your work • Follow the **safety instructions for the machine or process** • Be fully **trained** on every tool and **equipment** you use
	• **Burns** from hot metal or plastic, flames	• Soldering Iron • Hot Glue Gun	
	• **Chemical burns** • **Toxic** substances absorbed through skin • **Skin** bonded together	• Glues	
DAMAGE TO LUNGS & BRAIN	• Breathing in **toxic fumes**	• Gluing • Soldering • Varnishing, Painting	• Wear a **face mask** • Work in a **well-ventilated area**
DAMAGE TO HEARING	• Exposure to **loud noise**	• Drilling • Grinding • Lathework	• Wear **ear protection**

Activity 3 – Identifying Hazards and Safety Precautions

1. Identify the hazards in the picture below, by **drawing a circle** around them. Write a **number** beside each circle. Then, **fill out the columns** below for each hazard you have circled.

Hazard No.	What is the danger?	What safety precautions could be taken?

Safety Signage

Colours and Shapes

Safety signage comes in different **standard colours and shapes** to make them easier to follow.

Colour Code and Shape	Meaning	Explanation	Example
BLACK ON YELLOW TRIANGLE	*HAZARD*	• These signs **alert you to risk of injury** e.g. electric shock, burns, toxic fumes	
WHITE ON BLUE CIRCLE	*MANDATORY*	• These signs **instruct you to do something** e.g. wear a face mask	
RED LINE ON WHITE CIRLCE	*PROHIBITION*	• These signs **ban you from doing something** e.g. no smoking, no running	
WHITE ON RED RECTANGLE	*FIRE EQUIPMENT*	• These signs show you the **location and instructions for fire-fighting equipment**	
WHITE ON GREEN RECTANGLE	*SAFETY LOCATIONS*	• These signs show you the **locations of safety areas, exits or equipment**	

Common Safety Symbols

WEAR SAFETY GLASSES	WEAR EAR PROTECTION	WEAR FACE MASK	DANGER	RISK OF FIRE

RISK OF ELECTRIC SHOCK	SLIP HAZARD	TOXIC SUBSTANCE	CORROSIVE / ACID RISK	FIRE EXTINGUISHER

NO SMOKING	NO RUNNING	EMERGENCY STOP	EMERGENCY EXIT	FIRST AID KIT

General Workshop Rules

GENERAL CONDUCT

- **Report any accidents, breakages, spillages, sparks, smoke, fire** or **dangerous situations** immediately to your **teacher**
- **Do not enter** the workshop / machine area unless a teacher is present
- **No** running, messing, eating or drinking
- **Pay attention** to the teacher's instructions
- Do not approach, touch, or **distract someone** using a tool or machine
- **Store** bags, clothes, and your work and tools in the **designated area**
- **Tie back** any long hair, take off any **ties**, and do not wear **loose clothing** or **jewellery** when in an engineering workshop
- **Tidy up** as you work and before you leave a machine or the workshop
- Know where the **first aid kit** is located
- Know where your **fire assembly point** is

PERSONAL PROTECTION

- Wear **safety glasses** when using any **cutting** or **abrasive** tools, and when soldering
- Wear **ear protectors** when using loud machines
- Wear **safety gloves** when handling or when near anything **hot**
- Wear a **face mask** to protect against adhesive and solvent **fumes**

HANDLING MATERIAL AND TOOLS

- When handling **sheet metal**, use **gloves** and **eye protection**
- Do not leave rough pieces of metal **lying around**
- **Never wipe** work areas with your hands
- Do not leave **soldering irons** lying on the bench, always **replace** in the **holder**
- **Turn off** all electrical, gas, pneumatic and hydraulic equipment when not in use
- Never attempt to fix a mains electrical device

BEFORE USING ANY TOOL OR MACHINE

- Make sure it is the **right tool** for the job, make sure you know **how to use it**, and ensure you have **permission** to use it
- Ensure your workpiece is **secured** with the correct **work holding** method
- Never try to use a tool with **more than one person**
- Make sure you know exactly **how to turn off a machine** *before you turn it on*
- Make sure you know where the **emergency stop** button is, and make sure it is **not obstructed**

Activity 4 – My Safety Rules

Together with your teacher and class, **write out a set of safety rules** that you agree to follow in your engineering room:

Health and Safety Passport

Your personal **health and safety passport** a record of the **safety training** you receive on **hazardous equipment** in the engineering room, throughout your 3 year cycle. As your teacher introduces you to each new piece of equipment, complete a **new row** in the **table** below.

HEALTH AND SAFETY PASSPORT for _____ *(your name)*

Name of Equipment	I CONFIRM I have been shown HOW TO OPERATE this piece of equipment		I CONFIRM I have received SAFETY INFORMATION or completed a RISK ASSESSMENT on this piece of equipment	
	My Initials	*Date*	*My Initials*	*Date*

Unit 2 Revision

Revision Questions - Health & Safety

1. (a) Explain the term hazard.
    (b) Give one example of a hazard.

2. (a) Explain the term risk.
    (b) Give one example of a high-risk hazard in the engineering room.
    (c) Given one example of a low-risk hazard in the engineering room.

3. Identify the location of the first aid kit in your classroom.

4. Give the location of your fire assembly point.

5. Explain what you should do if you come across a spillage in the engineering room.

6. Identify four engineering processes for which you should wear eye protection.

7. Identify three engineering processes for which you should wear ear protection.

8. Identify one engineering process for which you should wear safety gloves.

9. Identify one engineering process for which you should wear a face mask.

10. Justify why materials and tools should be stored in a designated area.

11. Give three examples of the use of colour coding in safety signs, and explain what each of those three colour codes means.

12. Explain what each of these safety signs means:

(i)   (ii)   (iii)   (iv)   (v)

(vi)   (vii)   (viii)   (ix)   (x)

13. Explain why loose clothing and jewellery can be a hazard in the engineering workshop.

14. Explain why it is dangerous if you approach, touch, or distract someone who is operating a tool.

15. Explain: (a) what a health and safety passport is, and (b) why it is beneficial.

16. Explain why you should not try to fix or interfere with a mains electrical device.

17. What should you do if you come across a tool that has a loose handle?

Unit 3 – Key Ring

Objectives

PROJECT	Design and manufacture a single-piece **key ring** or similar from **acrylic**

- Learn basic **marking out, cutting**, **drilling** and **filing processes**
- Learn how to **interpret working drawings**, measure, draw and **mark out**
- Create your first **design drawings**. Learn to **plan** and **evaluate** your manufacturing
- Gain an introduction to **material properties** and **types of plastics**
- Understand more about **mechatronics**, **mechanisms** and **electronics** in a practical way

Content

PROCESSES AND PRINCIPLES	**Materials**	Acrylic, Introduction to Plastics
	Drawing	Drawing Notations, Dimensioning
	Marking Out	Ruler, Engineer's Square, Dot Punch, Ball Pein Hammer, Spring Dividers, Marking Out Techniques
	Cutting	Senior Hacksaw, Junior Hacksaw
	Drilling	Portable Drill, Pillar Drill, Bits, Drilling Acrylic
	Filing	Types of Files & Filing: Cross, Draw, Convex, Concave
DESIGN APPLICATION	Designing your own key ring. Choosing suitable materials	
	Interpreting working design drawings and manufacturing from them	
MECHATRONICS	Introduction to motion, mechanisms, electronics and mechatronic systems	
	Exploring power tools and equipment in the engineering room	

Learning Outcomes from this Unit

PROCESSES AND PRINCIPLES	DESIGN APPLICATION	MECHATRONICS
1.2, 1.4, 1.8, 1.9, 1.10, 1.11, 1.12, 1.13	2.8, 2.9	3.2, 3.3, 3.4, 3.5

Suggested Timeframes

START TIME	YEAR 1	September		DURATION	4-5 weeks

Working Drawings

Default Design

Elevation

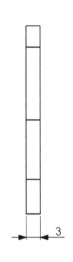

∅5

15

90°

R20

End Elevation

3

3D View

Plan

ITEM NO.	PART	DESCRIPTION	QTY.
1	KEY RING BODY	3mm Coloured Acrylic	1
2	METAL SPLIT RING	Diameter 24mm	1

Your Design Sketches - Carry out Storyboard Activities 1-5 before attempting this section

Your Design 1

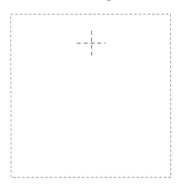

Your Design 2

Your Design 3

Your Design 4

TITLE	Unit 3 - Key Ring	SHEET 1 OF 1
DESCRIPTION	Default Design and Design Sketches	Brighter Minds

Project Storyboard

Drawing and Dimensioning Activities

See Drawing & Dimensioning Theory on Pages 32-36

Activity 1 - Dimensioning

Identify the following measurements by drawing labelled arrows pointing to the correct places on the ruler: (A) **40 mm**; (B) **12cm**; (C) **135mm**:

Activity 2 - Dimensioning

Measure the length of the lines below and **record** their lengths in the boxes:

Line: *Length (mm):*

_____

_____

___

Activity 3 - Dimensioning

Explain the meaning of these **symbols** on a working drawing:

90° _____

R _____

Ø _____

mm _____

Activity 4 – Dimensioning

From the working drawing for the **default design** key ring:

    (A) **Identify** the **diameter** of the key ring *(don't forget the units)*:

    (B) **Identify** the distance from the **centre of the hole** to the nearest **edge** of the key ring:

Design Activities

Activity 5 – Design

Explain why there is a **hole** in the key ring and why the hole is situated **close to the edge**:

_____

_____

DESIGN CONSTRAINTS FOR YOUR KEY RING

- Your key ring should **be** no **larger than 40mm x 40mm**
- The recommended **material** is **acrylic** (sometimes called Perspex)
- Your key ring should be able to **attach** to a metal **split ring** like that shown above

Design hint: Also think about how difficult it might be to mark out and cut out your shape...

Activity 6 – Design Sketches

Using a pencil, a ruler and a compass if required, **sketch your own key ring designs** in the boxes provided on the working drawings page. For each design, sketch the main **elevation** view only, and include **dimensions**. Your design should follow the **design constraints** listed above.

Activity 7 – Select a Design

Choose one of the designs to manufacture - one of your own designs or the default design - and **justify** your choice of design below:

My chosen design is (name or number): _____

I chose this design because: _____

_____

Activity 8 – Design Drawing

In the space below, **accurately draw to scale** *(i.e. actual size)* the **elevation** and **end elevation** of your **chosen design**. **Dimension** your drawing.

See Drawing & Dimensioning on Page 32

Elevation   *End Elevation*

Marking Out Activities

> **Marking Out** means **marking** the **lines to be cut** and the **holes to be drilled** on your **workpiece**

Activity 9 – Marking Out Planning

Identify the **marking-out equipment** you think you will need to **mark out** the key ring on your material:

See Marking Out Pages 36-39

Marking-out Equipment 1: _____

Marking-out Equipment 2: _____

Marking-out Equipment 3: _____

Activity 10 – Marking Out

Mark out your **chosen design** on your **workpiece** now

See Marking Out Pages 36-39

See Workholding, Drilling, Cutting, Filing, Pages 40-47

Manufacturing Activities

Activity 11 – Manufacturing Planning

Identify the **sequence** of engineering **processes**, and the **tools** and **equipment**, you think you will need to **manufacture** your key ring: *(Hint - will you make the hole first, or the shape?)*

_____

_____

_____

_____

Activity 12 – Manufacturing Safety

Identify **two safety precautions** you should take when manufacturing the key ring:

Safety Precaution 1: _____

_____

Safety Precaution 2: _____

_____

> *Fill in the Health and Safety Passport on page 20 for any power tools you may be using*

Activity 13 - Manufacturing

Manufacture your key ring now

See Workholding, Drilling, Cutting, Filing, Pages 40-47

Post-Manufacture Review Activities

Activity 14 – Manufacturing Evaluation

Explain the **tools** and **processes** you used to create the **hole** in the acrylic:

_____

_____

_____

_____

Activity 15 – Manufacturing Evaluation

Explain why and how **wood** is used when **drilling acrylic**:

_____

_____

_____

Activity 16 – Manufacturing Evaluation

Describe the **tools** and **processes** you used to **create the shape** of your key ring:

_____

_____

_____

_____

_____

Activity 17 – Manufacturing Evaluation

Explain the **filing techniques** you used to shape the key ring:

_____

_____

_____

_____

Activity 18 – Manufacturing Evaluation

Explain the steps required to produce a **high-quality finish** on an **acrylic cut edge**:

_____

_____

_____

_____

Activity 19 – Design Evaluation

Identify two reasons why **acrylic** is a good choice of **material** for a key ring:

Reason 1: _____

_____

_____

Reason 2: _____

_____

_____

Activity 20 – Design Evaluation

1. **Identify** an **alternative material** you think could be used to make the key ring:

Material: _____

2. Identify **one advantage** of this material for a key ring:

_____

_____

3. Identify **one disadvantage** of this material for a key ring:

_____

_____

Unit 3 Project Assessment

Student Self-Assessment

In this project, I gained the following **skills** and **knowledge**:

1. _____

2. _____

3. _____

I **evaluate** my project to have turned out well in the following areas:

_____

_____

If I were to carry out this project again, I would **modify** or **improve** the following aspects:

_____

_____

_____

On a scale of 1 to 10, I would give my project a **score** of...

Peer Assessment

Identify two manufacturing **processes** you think were carried out to a **high standard** on this project:

1. _____

_____

2. _____

_____

Identify any **skills** your peer could **improve** upon:

_____

_____

_____

_____

_____

Teacher Feedback

Comments on Project:

Not Graded	Partially Achieved	Achieved	Merit	Higher Merit	Distinction

Learning Topics for Unit ③

Processes and Principles

Materials and their Properties

Materials are the substances we make our engineered products from. The most common engineering materials are **metals** and **plastics**. Different materials have different **properties**.

> **Properties** describe how a material **behaves** under different conditions

For example, a material may be strong or soft, hard to cut, easy to melt, resistant to the weather, etc.

> We **choose** materials that have the **best properties** to match our needs

Common Material Properties

Property	Description	Examples
STRENGTH	A **strong** material needs a large amount of **force** to cause it to **deform** out of shape.	Steel, Concrete, Adhesives
BRITTLENESS	A **brittle** material **breaks easily** when impacted.	Glass, Ceramics
ELASTICITY	An **elastic** material can be deformed a lot and still **return to its original shape**.	Rubber
HARDNESS	A **hard** material is **difficult to scratch or indent**.	Diamond
TRANSPARENCY	A **transparent** material is **see-through**. The opposite of transparent is **opaque**.	Glass, Acrylic
INSULATION	An _electrical_ insulator does **not** allow **electricity** to flow. A _thermal_ insulator does **not** allow **heat** to flow through it.	Plastics, Ceramics
MELTING POINT	The **temperature** at which the material changes from **solid to liquid**.	Metals – high melting points Plastics – low melting points
WEIGHT	How **heavy** the material is. A simple but important property of a material.	Acrylic – light Steel – heavy

Introduction to Plastics

Acrylic is type of **plastic**. Plastics are **synthetic** (man-made) products, made from **crude oil**.

Properties of Plastics

PROPERTIES OF PLASTICS		
Light	Good Insulator	Non-toxic
Cheap	Waterproof	Most are recyclable
Weak	Does not corrode	Can be transparent

Types of Plastics

There are two main types of plastics: **thermoplastics** and **thermosetting** plastics.

> **Thermoplastics** can be **melted down and reshaped**.
> **Thermosetting** plastics can only be **shaped once**, when they are made (they cannot be re-melted).

THERMOPLASTICS	THERMOSETTING PLASTICS
• Easily **melted and reshaped**	• **Cannot** be melted and reshaped
• **Weaker** than thermosetting plastics	• **Stronger, harder, brittle** than thermoplastics
• **Lower** melting point	• **Higher** melting point. **Good insulators**
• Most thermoplastics are **recyclable**	• **Not recyclable**
Examples	*Examples*
Acrylic, Polythene, Nylon, PVC, Polystyrene	Bakelite, Melamine, Fibreglass Resin

We will be learning more about different plastics and their properties in the next unit.

Plastics Activities

Plastics Activity 1

Can you **name the raw material** that most plastics are made from?

_____

What does **non-toxic** mean?

_____

What is another word for **corrode**?

_____

Plastics Activity 2

List four keywords that you would associate with **acrylic** after manufacturing your keyring:

1. _____

2. _____

3. _____

4. _____

Plastics Activity 3

Identify two **advantages** of **thermoplastics**:

1. _____

2. _____

Identify two **advantages** of **thermosetting plastics**:

1. _____

2. _____

Plastics Activity 4

Tick which type of plastic you think these items are:	Thermo-plastic	Thermo-setting plastic
Plastic Bag		
Electrical Socket		
Toothbrush		
Food Container		
Boat Hull		
Plastic Chair		

Engineering Drawings

Orthographic Projection

An **orthographic drawing** is a **set of 'flat' 2D drawings** of the object, as seen from different angles.

Orthographic projections (views) are drawn at right angles to each other - e.g. from the **top**, **front** and **side**.

A top-down view is called a **plan**. Side-on views are called **elevations**.

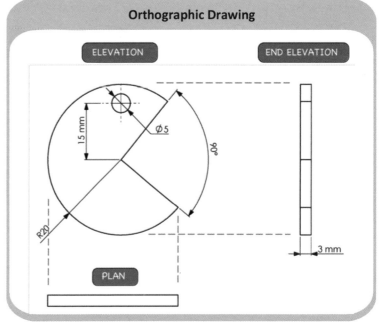

Orthographic Drawing

ELEVATION   END ELEVATION

PLAN

Drawing Activity 1

Place an object in front of you and draw a **plan view** of it below (*i.e. as seen from above*):

Drawing Activity 2

Sketch an **elevation view** of the same object below *(i.e. as seen from the side)*:

3D (Isometric) Drawings

A **3D drawing** tries to represent the 3D object as seen, i.e. to create the **illusion of depth** in the object.

An **isometric drawing** is a type of 3D drawing.

In an isometric drawing, **vertical lines** on the object are shown as vertical lines, but **horizontal lines** on the object are drawn at **30°** **to the horizontal**.

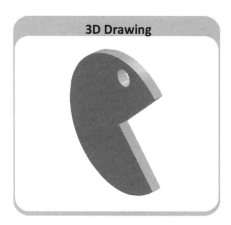

3D Drawing

Drawing Activity 3

Place a **rectangular object** (like a pencil case or small box) at an **angle** in front of you, and draw a **free-hand 3D line sketch** of it below as you see it:

Isometric 3D drawings are usually drawn on **isometric grid paper**, which has a faint grid of vertical and 30° horizontal lines on it.

Drawing Activity 4
Redraw the same rectangular object on the isometric grid below:

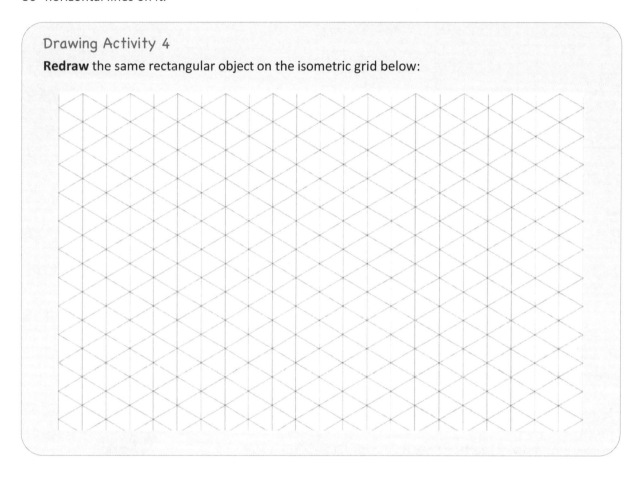

Dimensioning

Dimensioning is the way in which **dimensions** (i.e. the sizes of objects) are shown on an engineering drawing.

> A **dimension** is a **number** that specifies the **size** of a **line**, **radius**, **diameter** or **angle**.
> Dimensions are expressed in **millimetres (mm)** for lengths, and **degrees (°)** for angles.

*If units are not shown beside a linear dimension, the units can be assumed to be in **mm**.*

Dimensioning is used to indicate:

- the **shape of the part** and the **location of waste material** *(i.e. cutting instructions)*
- the **position** of <u>holes</u> on the part *(e.g. for drilling)*
- the location of <u>bend lines</u> *(for bending the workpiece into the desired shape)*

Dimensioning Methods

LINEAR DIMENSIONING
• A **linear dimension** is the **distance in a straight line**, expressed in **mm** or **cm**   • **Linear dimensioning** is how straight-line dimensions are specified on engineering drawings

LINEAR DIMENSIONING continued

(A) INCREMENTAL DIMENSIONING
Linear dimensions are shown relative to each other

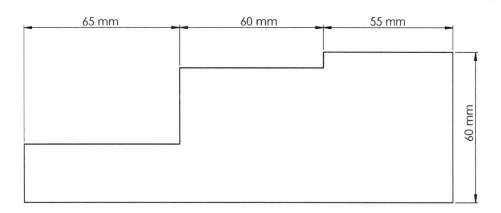

(B) PARALLEL DIMENSIONING
Linear dimensions are shown relative to a common reference point (a datum)

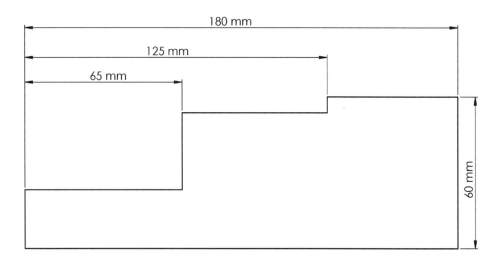

ANGULAR DIMENSIONING

- An **angular dimension** specifies the **size of an angle**, expressed in **degrees**
- **Angular dimensioning** is how **angles** are denoted on engineering drawings

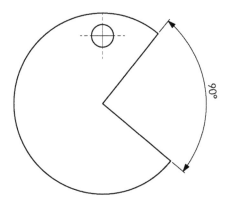
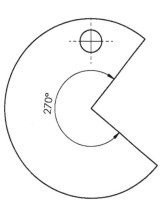

DIMENSIONING OF CIRCLES AND ARCS

DIAMETER Dimensioning	RADIUS Dimensioning
The **diameter** is the widest point across a circle *(passes through the centre point).*	The **radius** is the distance from the centre of the circle to the circumference.
Diameter dimensioning is used to specify **hole** and **cylinder sizes** - *e.g.* $\varnothing$ 5	**Radius dimensioning** is used to specify the **curvature of arcs** - *e.g. R20*

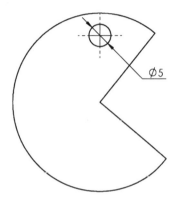

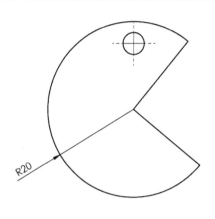

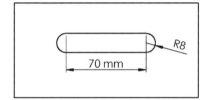

Marking Out

Marking Out means **marking the lines to be cut and the holes to be drilled on the workpiece**

Marking Out Tools

MARKING OUT TOOLS	
SHARPIE	A **marker** with a sharp point. Used to mark out on **plastics** (e.g. **acrylic**) without damaging the surface. Markings can be **wiped off** afterwards.
SCRIBER	Made from **metal** with a **very sharp point**. Used to mark out on **metals**, by scratching a thin line.

MARKING OUT TOOLS continued

ENGINEER'S RULE	Used to measure in **0.5mm**, **1mm** and **10mm** increments. Made from **metal** so the **edge doesn't get damaged** in an engineering workshop.
ENGINEER'S SQUARE	Used to **draw lines perpendicular** (i.e. at 90°) **to a straight edge**. Also used to **check whether an angle is 'square'** (i.e. 90°). The thick part is called the **stock**. The thin part is called the **blade**.
SPRING DIVIDERS	Used to **mark out circles, semicircles and arcs**. The **radius** of the arc can be set by twisting the **nut** on the side. Always store facing down for safety reasons.
CENTRE or DOT PUNCH	Creates a **small indent** in the metal surface when hit with a hammer, to mark out: *(1)* the **position of a hole** *(for drilling)* *(2)* the **centre of a circle** *(for spring-dividing)* *(3)* to mark out a **reference point** for further measurement and marking out.
BALL PEIN HAMMER	A hammer with **one flat** side and **one round** side. Used to hit a **centre / dot punch** (and chisels). Should be held near the end of the handle.

Marking Out Activity

Identify any **hazards** when using **marking-out tools**, and appropriate **safety precautions**:

Hazard(s)	Safety Precaution(s)

Marking Out Techniques

Marking Out on Plastic

Use a **'sharpie' marker** and an engineer's rule to mark out on plastic.

Marking Out on Metal

Use a **scriber** to scratch a thin line on metal.

Marking Out on PLASTIC

Marking Out on METAL

Marking Out a Perpendicular Line

Marking Out a Perpendicular Line

Use an **Engineer's Square** to mark out a line **perpendicular** to a **straight edge**.

Ensure the **stock** of the engineer's square is **pressed firmly** against the edge of the workpiece.

Checking for Squareness

The **Engineer's Square** is used to check whether two edges are at **90°** to each other.

Off-Square Corner

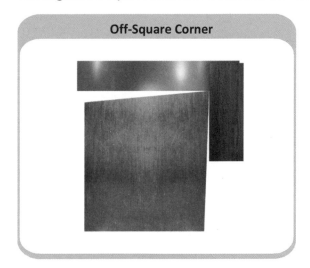

Square Corner

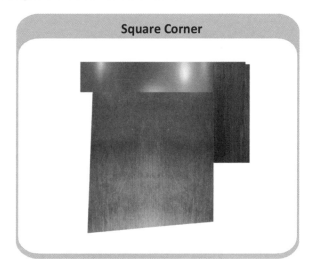

Establishing Datum Edges

- To mark out accurately in both horizontal and vertical directions, you need two reference edges that are at **right angles to each other**. These are called **datum edges**.

- **Make all measurements from the datum edges**

- This makes marking out more accurate because there is **no accumulation of measuring or marking out errors**

- Use an **engineer's square** to make sure your datum edges are 'square' – i.e. at right angles.

- If your workpiece does not have datum edges, then **make them first** before you mark out. Mark out a **line perpendicular to one straight edge** and **cut off the excess material.** You now have the reference datum edges to measure and mark out from.

Datum Edges

DATUM EDGE 1

90°

DATUM EDGE 2

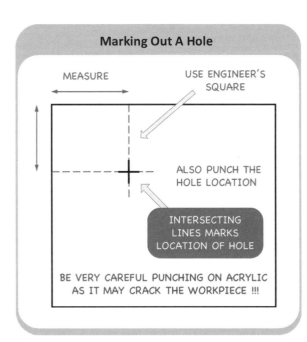

Marking Out A Hole

MEASURE

USE ENGINEER'S SQUARE

ALSO PUNCH THE HOLE LOCATION

INTERSECTING LINES MARKS LOCATION OF HOLE

BE VERY CAREFUL PUNCHING ON ACRYLIC AS IT MAY CRACK THE WORKPIECE !!!

Marking Out a Hole

- Using an **engineer's square** and a **ruler**, mark out **perpendicular horizontal** and **vertical lines** on the workpiece at the required distances

- Where the **lines intersect** marks the location of the hole

- Punch an **indentation** at the location of the hole using a **ball pein hammer** and a **dot punch**

- *Note - punching acrylic may crack it*

Finding the Centre of a Circle

1. Draw a **square** touching the circle
2. Draw the **diagonals** of the square
3. Where the **diagonals intersect** is the centre

Marking out a Circle or Arc

- **Mark out** the **centre point** of the circle (in the same way as marking out a hole)

- Set the **spring dividers** to the required **radius**

- Place one point of the spring dividers **in the punch indentation**, and **rotate the dividers** to scribe out the circle or arc

Marking Out a Circle

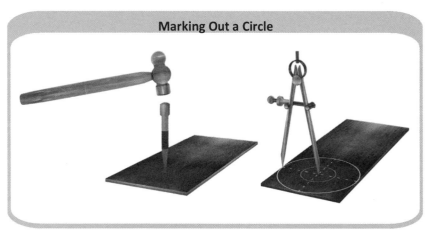

Workholding

For both **safety** and **accuracy**, it is <u>very important to **clamp your workpiece**</u> securely.

WORKHOLDING TOOLS		
BENCH VICE	A **bench vice** is fixed to a **workbench** Used to clamp workpieces for hand-held operations like **drilling, sawing** and **filing** A twistable **screw** closes the two plates onto the workpiece	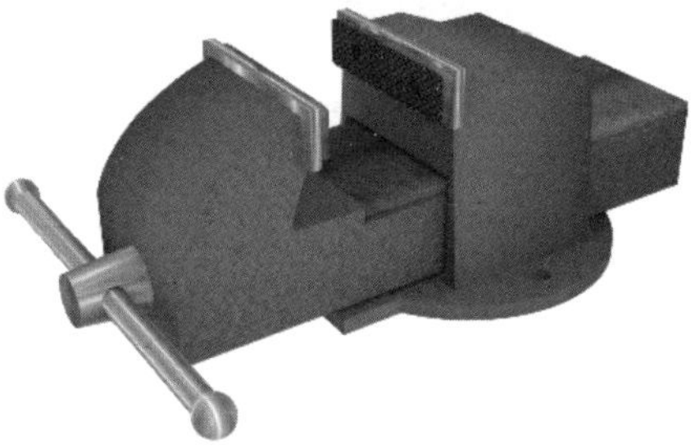
SOFT JAWS (Fibre Grips)	**Fibre grips** prevent the workpiece being scratched by the jaws of the vice Useful when working with **soft materials** like plastics	
MACHINE VICE	A **machine vice** is bolted to the **worktable** of a machine tool such as a pillar drill (see next section) Use **soft rubber jaws** on vices (or pieces of wood) to avoid scratching plastics like acrylic	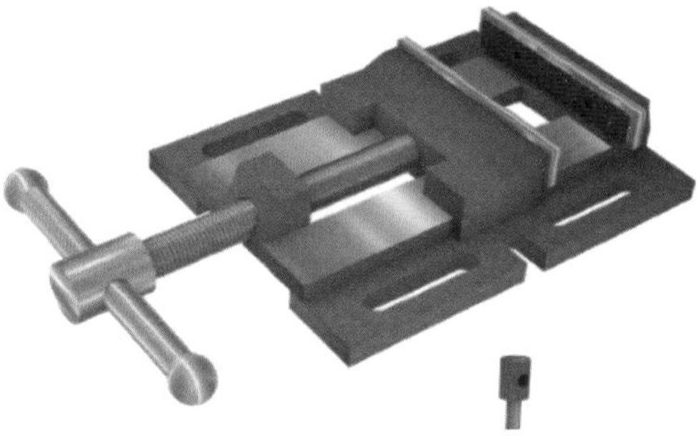

You will see more workholding tools and techniques in later units.

Workholding Activities

Give <u>two</u> possible **consequences of not clamping your workpiece** securely <u>before drilling</u>:
(Hints: think about the consequences for manufacturing and safety)

(1) _____

_____

(2) _____

_____

Cutting Tools

CUTTING TOOLS	
SENIOR HACKSAW	Used to cut **plastic or metal** workpieces Use **fine-toothed blade** for **plastic** Use with **two hands** **Teeth face away** from the handle, so it cuts on the **forward (push) stroke**
JUNIOR HACKSAW	Used to cut **small** plastic or metal **workpieces** or slots Used with **one hand** **Teeth face away** from handle

Cutting Techniques

Before Cutting

- **Clamp** the workpiece securely in a **bench vice**
- Ensure you have the **correct blade** in the hacksaw - use a finer-tooth blade to cut plastic
- Wear **safety glasses**

Senior Hacksaw Technique

- Grip the hacksaw with **two hands** as shown
- Keep the hacksaw **vertical**
- Cut **close to the vice**
- Cut with **slow steady strokes**
- Cut with **even downward pressure**
- Cut with **long strokes**, using the **full length of the blade**

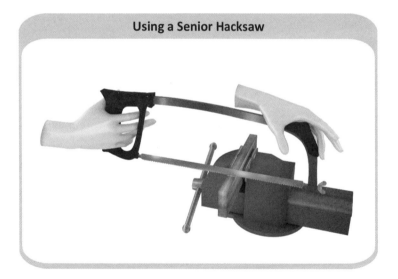

Using a Senior Hacksaw

Cutting Activities

1. Why is it better to use **long strokes** and cut with the **full length of the blade**?

_____

2. Identify two cutting **hazards** and their **safety precautions**:

Hazard / Injury Risk	Safety Precaution

Drilling

Drilling Tools

PORTABLE DRILL	**Hand-held** drill Workpieces are clamped in a **bench vice** or other clamp Very **convenient** **No electrical cable** on a **cordless** drill **More difficult to drill straight** and perpendicular to the workpiece, compared to a pillar drill *(see below)*

Pillar Drill

Pillar drills are bolted to the **floor** or to the work **bench**. Drilling is guided by the machine, so it is much **more accurate** than hand-held drills.

- Pillar drills provide **accurate drilling** because the drill bit is kept stable and **straight**, and **vibrations** are kept to a minimum

- The drill **bit** is held in the **chuck** (see next page)

- The workpiece is clamped in a **machine vice** or other clamp attached to the **worktable**

- The **worktable** can be moved up and down using a handle or wheel, which uses a **rack and pinion** mechanism

- The **feed lever** lowers the drill bit down over the workpiece

- A **depth gauge** or depth stop can be used to ensure the drill bit only extends the **required distance** into the workpiece

- The **chuck guard** is an acrylic shield that prevents swarf and chippings hitting the operator

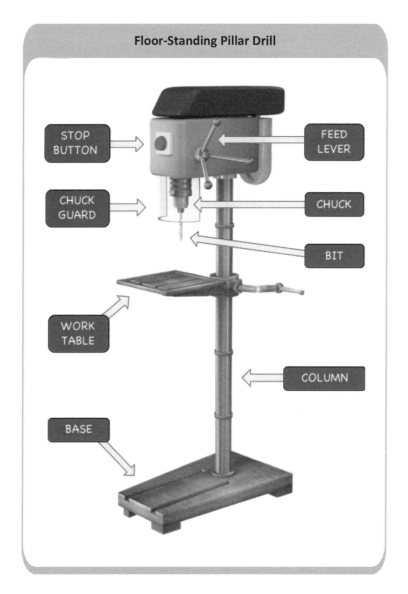

Floor-Standing Pillar Drill

STOP BUTTON · FEED LEVER · CHUCK GUARD · CHUCK · BIT · WORK TABLE · COLUMN · BASE

Drill Bits

A **drill bit** cuts with its **end surface** and transports the **chips** (waste material) up through the **flutes** to the outside of the workpiece.

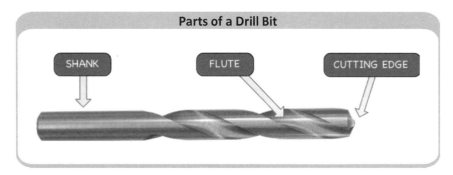

Parts of a Drill Bit

SHANK   FLUTE   CUTTING EDGE

The **shank** is held in the **chuck** (see below).

Drill bits come in many **different sizes**, measured by **diameter** (mm).

DRILL GAUGE	A **drill gauge** is a flat **steel** sheet with holes It is used to **check the diameter of the drill bit**, particularly if the diameter mark has worn off the shank of the bit	

Drill Chucks

The drill **chuck** holds the drill **bit**.

Chucks come in two main types:

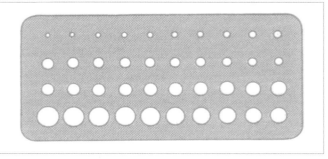

Chuck Key

Bit

Drill Chuck

DRILL CHUCK	Key Chuck	Keyless Chuck
	Tightened with a **chuck key**	Tightened **by hand**
	Stronger	Not as strong
	Safety hazard if key left in chuck	No safety hazard from key flying off

Drilling Safety

SAFETY PRECAUTIONS	• Ensure drill **bit is straight** and **tight in chuck** • Ensure **chuck key is removed** • Ensure **chuck guard** is in place • Ensure the workpiece is **securely clamped** • Wear **safety glasses** • Do not touch **sharp cut edges** • **Wear gloves** handing sheet metal	

Drilling Plastics

<table>
<tr>
<td rowspan="2">DRILLING PLASTICS</td>
<td>
<ul>
<li>Use a portable drill or a pillar / bench drill</li>
<li>Use a drill bit designed for plastic</li>
<li>Use a low speed to avoid melting the plastic</li>
<li>Clamp the plastic</li>
</ul>

</td>
</tr>
<tr>
<td>

DRILLING ACRYLIC

Acrylic breaks easily, so take the following precautions:

- Place a **protective piece of wood underneath the acrylic**. This prevents the acrylic **cracking** when the drill bit gets through to the other side.

- Drill a small-diameter **pilot hole** first. A **pilot hole** is easier to drill than a larger diameter hole, and it acts to **guide** and **centre** the larger drill bit. It makes it **easier to drill the larger hole** without breaking the acrylic.
</td>
</tr>
</table>

Activities

Drilling Safety

Identify two hazards (i.e. possible causes of injury) when **drilling**, and the **safety precautions** you could take to reduce the likelihood of those injuries:

Hazard / Injury Risk when drilling	Safety Precaution to reduce this risk
1	
2	

Safety Signage

Identify the meaning of these **safety signs**:

(a) _____   (b) _____

Surface Finishing

Hand Files

Files have a rough surface that **removes material** from a workpiece by **abrasion**.

Files come in **different shapes, sizes** and **grades** for different jobs.

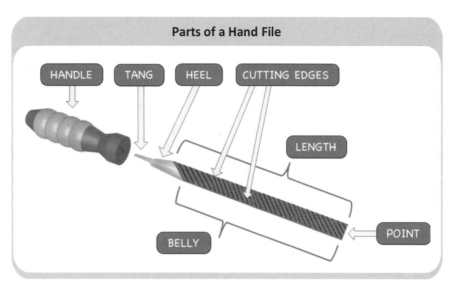

Parts of a Hand File

HANDLE TANG HEEL CUTTING EDGES

LENGTH

POINT

BELLY

File Cutting Surfaces

- The abrasive surfaces on a file are made from rows of sharp parallel **cutting lines** or 'teeth'.
- The cutting lines can be **coarse** (i.e. widely-spaced and deep) or **fine** (close together and shallow)
- The cutting pattern on a file can also be **double-cut** (criss-cross lines) or **single-cut** (one set of lines)
- **Rough files** have **coarse teeth** and are usually **double-cut**
- **Smooth files** have **fine teeth** and are usually **single-cut**

FILE GRADES		
DOUBLE-CUT / ROUGH FILE	**Two sets of cutting edges** in a **criss-cross** pattern Used to **remove large quantities** of material **Rough files** are usually double-cut	
SINGLE-CUT / SMOOTH FILE	**One set of parallel cutting edges** Removes **less material** but gives a **finer finish** Used after cutting or **rough-filing**	

File Shapes

FILE SHAPES		
FLAT FILE **SAFE EDGES**	A **flat file** has at least **two cutting surfaces** The **narrow sides** may also be cutting surfaces If a narrow side doesn't have a cutting surface it is called a **safe edge** A **safe edge** allow you to file into a corner without also filling the workpiece at right angles	

FILE SHAPES continued

TRIANGLE FILE	Used to file angles **less than 90°** Has three cutting sides and a **triangular cross-section** May **taper** towards the front
ROUND FILE **HALF-ROUND FILE**	**Circular** in cross-section Used to **smoothen** (deburr) **holes** and **slots** A **half-round** file has **one flat side** and **one convex cutting surface**
NEEDLE FILES	**Needle files** are small narrow files used for **small or delicate work**, and for creating **accurate angles** They come in a **variety of shapes** - flat, round, triangle etc

Filing Techniques

FILING TECHNIQUES

CROSS FILING	• Removes the most material • Hold the file in **both hands** • Hold the file **flat** against the surface to be filed • **Push the file forward** and **across the edge** to be filed, at a slight angle • Cut on the **forward** stroke • At end of the stroke, **lift the file** back to the starting position
DRAW FILING	• Used to **smoothen after cross-filing** • Hold the file in **both hands** • Place the file at **right angles** to the edge • Move the file **back and forth along the whole length of the edge**

FILING TECHNIQUES continued

CONVEX FILING	• Hold a **flat file** in both hands
	• Use **cross filing** to remove the most material:
	  ○ Move the file **across the edge** but also at a slight angle **around the curve** at the same time
	  ○ Keep the file **parallel** to the filed edge by twisting / angling the file to **match the curve**
	• Use **draw filing** for final smoothing:
	  ○ Hold the file across at **right angles** to the edge and move the file back and forth lengthways **around the curve** (not side-to-side across the edge)

CONCAVE FILING	• Use a **half-round file** • Hold the file in **both hands** • Hold the **curved side** of the file against the material • **Push the file forward** and **across the edge** while also moving the file **along the curve** • Keep the file **parallel** to the filed edge by twisting / angling the file to **match the curve**

Surface-Finishing Acrylic

When acrylic plastic is cut, it will have rough cut marks on its edges.

The cut edges need to be **filed**, **smoothened** and **polished** to create a **high-quality smooth finish**.

FILE	SMOOTHEN	POLISH
Draw file to remove any saw-cut or cross-file marks	Use **wet and dry emery paper** to remove draw file marks	Apply a **plastic polish** with a soft cloth

Filing Activity

Identify which types of files you would use to smoothen the edges of the following shapes:

To smooth this SHAPE	I would use the following TYPE(S) OF FILES
(a)	_____ _____
(b)	_____ _____
(c)	_____ _____
(d)	_____ _____
(e)	_____ _____
(f)	_____ _____

Mechatronics

Mechatronic systems incorporate **mechanisms**, **electronics**, **control systems** and **computer technology**. First we take a look at mechanisms.

Introduction to Mechanisms

In your projects, you will need to transfer **motion** from one place to another, or you may need to **change the type of motion**. Mechanisms help you do this. The most common types of mechanisms are **gears**, **cams**, **pulleys**, **levers** and **linkages**. You will meet these mechanisms throughout the units in this book.

What is a Mechanism?

> A **mechanism** is a device that **transforms** an **input motion** to an **output motion**.
> Mechanisms can change the **direction**, **size**, **speed** or **type** of motion.

LINEAR, ROTARY, RECIPROCATING, OSCILLATING → **INPUT MOTION** → **MECHANISM** → **OUTPUT MOTION** → LINEAR, ROTARY, RECIPROCATING, OSCILLATING

Mechanisms are found in all **machines** – anywhere there is motion.
To understand mechanisms, you first need to understand the different **types of motion**.

Types of Motion

Type of Motion	Meaning	Symbol	Example	
LINEAR MOTION	Movement in a straight line	→	A train moving along a straight track	
ROTARY MOTION	Movement around a circle, turning	↻	A wheel turning	
RECIPROCATING MOTION	Movement back-and-forth in a straight line	↔	A jigsaw blade moving up-and-down	
OSCILLATING MOTION	Swinging from side to side in an arc	⌣	A swing or a pendulum	

Activity - Types of Motion

When you used the **pillar drill**, you may have needed to **raise or lower the work table**.
Identify the **type of motion transformation** that is involved in raising the work table:

Type of Input Motion: *Type of Output Motion:*

Activity - Types of Motion

Can you identify **two other tools** or pieces of **equipment** in the engineering room that transform one type of motion to another type of motion, or transfer motion from one place to another?

Tool / Equipment	Type of Input Motion	Type of Output Motion
1. _____	_____	_____
2. _____	_____	_____

Introduction to Gears

Gears are **mechanisms** with **toothed wheels**. The teeth of the gears engage with each other to **transfer motion**. Gears usually **transform rotary motion** into **rotary motion** or **linear motion.**

Below is shown the **rack-and-pinion mechanism** that is used in the **pillar drill** to raise and lower the worktable. This transforms **rotary motion** to **linear motion**. We will see many more types of gears later.

Mechanism	Description	Example Applications	Image and Symbol
RACK AND PINION	Transforms **rotary motion** into **linear motion**, and vice versa. The **pinion** is the **round gear**. The **rack** is the **toothed bar**.	**Pillar Drill** Turning by pinion raises and lowers the worktable. **Sliding Doors / Gates** A motor turns the pinion to open and close the doors. **Car Steering** The steering wheel turns the **pinion**. The **rack** turns the wheels *(via a linkage - see later)*	Symbol:

Activity - Gears

Identify four **tools** or pieces of **equipment** in the engineering room that you think **contain gears**:

1. _____   2. _____

3. _____   4. _____

Introduction to Electronics

What is Electronics?

> '**Electronics**' are **control systems** powered by **electricity** that contain **electronic components**. Just like mechanisms, 'electronics' are **systems** that **transform inputs into outputs**.

Electronics can take a **wide variety of inputs** and turn them into a **wide variety of outputs**.

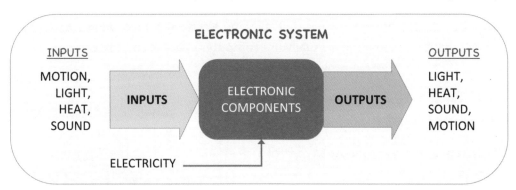

In everyday life, we use electronics all the time: to turn on lights, watch TV, make toast, and communicate via our phones. In school, we will build simple **electronic circuits to create light, sound and motion**. You will find out a lot more about electronics as you work through the units in the book.

Electronic Input Devices - Switches

Switches are one of the most common types of **inputs** into electronics systems.
The table below shows a few switches you have encountered already in the engineering room.

Type	Description	Applications	Image and Symbol
PUSH BUTTON SWITCH **PTB** (Push To Break) **SWITCH**	• A **push-button switch** contains an **internal spring**. The button only stays pushed in while you keep your finger on it • A **Push-To-Break** (PTB) **switch** *opens the circuit* (i.e. stops the current flowing) when it is pushed in	**Emergency Stop Button,** **Fridge light**	Push-button switch: Symbol *(push-to-break switch)*:

Type	Description	Applications	Image and Symbol
LIMIT SWITCH (Micro Switch)	• A **limit switch** contains a **spring metal lever** that is **operated by another object** or machine part • When an object presses on to the spring metal lever, it turns the switch on or off	**Safety switches** e.g. opening a **safety guard** releases a **limit switch** which turns off the machine tool **Limit Switches for Gates and Doors** e.g. when a sliding gate is opened to its fullest extent by a motor and a rack-and-pinion, the gate presses against a limit switch which stops the current going to the motor	Symbol *(normally-open version)*:

Introduction to Mechatronic Systems

What is Mechatronics?

Mechatronics refers to **control systems** that combine **electronics**, **mechanisms** and **mechanical systems**. Mechatronic systems also usually use **computer systems** and **software programming**.

• A **system** is a **set of parts that work together** to carry out a certain function

• A **control system** uses a set of **inputs** to **control** a set of **outputs**

• A control system is composed of **three stages**: **inputs**, **process** and **outputs** (see opposite)

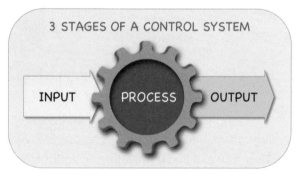

3 STAGES OF A CONTROL SYSTEM

INPUT — PROCESS — OUTPUT

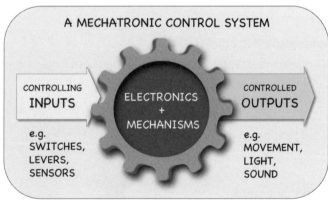

A MECHATRONIC CONTROL SYSTEM

CONTROLLING INPUTS — ELECTRONICS + MECHANISMS — CONTROLLED OUTPUTS

e.g. SWITCHES, LEVERS, SENSORS

e.g. MOVEMENT, LIGHT, SOUND

A **mechatronic system** uses **electronics** and **mechanisms,** and often **computers** too, to **control its outputs** based on its inputs.

Typical **inputs** to mechatronic systems are **switches**, levers and **sensors**.

Typical **outputs** from mechatronic systems are **movement**, **light**, and **sound**.

Examples of Mechatronic Control Systems

Cars, **robots** and **power tools** are good <u>examples of mechatronic systems</u>

A Pillar Drill seen as a Mechatronic System

A **pillar drill** is a mechatronic system – it has **inputs** in the form of switches and levers, and uses **electronics** and **mechanisms** to control its **outputs** (e.g. turning the chuck, raising/lowering the chuck).

The table below describes some of the main **control** subsystems in a **pillar drill**.
We describe these **control systems** in terms of their three stages: **inputs**, **process** and **outputs**.

Example Mechatronic Control Systems in a PILLAR DRILL			
	INPUT →	**PROCESS** →	**OUTPUT**
The **chuck** control system	• Operator **presses the on/off switch**	• Electric **current flows** into the **motor** • Motor **spindle turns** • Motor spindle turns a set of **gears** which connect to the **drill chuck**	• **Drill chuck turns**
The **worktable** control system	• Operator **turns the handle**	Uses a **rack-and-pinion** mechanism: • **Handle** turns the **pinion** • **Rack** is connected to **worktable**	• **Worktable rises**
The **safety guard** control system	• Operator **lifts the chuck guard**	• **Chuck guard** opens a **limit switch** • Electric **current** is interrupted to the motor	• **Drill chuck stops**

Activity – Recognition of Mechatronic Systems

Identify **three defining characteristics** / components of a **mechatronic system**:

1. _____

2. _____

3. _____

Activity – Impact of Mechatronics on Society

Research and identify one **benefit** and one **negative impact** of **robots** on society:

Benefit: _____

Negative Impact: _____

Unit ③ Revision

Unit 3 Revision Questions

1. (a) Identify the non-renewable resource used to manufacture plastics.
   (b) Explain the meaning of the word *synthetic.*

2. (a) Describe in your own words what the word *property* means in relation to materials.
   (b) List three common structural/mechanical properties of materials.

3. (a) List three key properties of thermoplastics.
   (b) Give two examples of thermoplastics.

4. Identify whether plastic is an insulator or a conductor and justify your answer.

5. Explain the difference between incremental dimensioning and parallel dimensioning.

6. Explain two main uses of an engineer's square.

7. Explain why a workpiece is dot punched before using spring dividers.

8. What is the purpose of a datum edge on a workpiece?

9. (a) Identify the direction that the cutting teeth face on a hacksaw.
   (b) Justify why the teeth face in this direction.

10. Invent 3 design constraints that could be given to someone designing a keyring.

11. Identify three safety precautions when using the pillar drill.

12. Identify the mechanism that raises and lowers the worktable on a pillar drill.

13. Explain and sketch the differences between a rough (double-cut) file and a smooth (single-cut) file.

14. What is the meaning of a blue safety sign?

15. Name and describe the differences between the two types of chucks you encountered in this unit.

16. Explain the purpose of a drill gauge.

17. Name the steps required to finish an edge on a piece of acrylic.

18. Name the four types of motion, and draw the symbol for each.

19. (a) Explain the motion transformation carried out by a rack-and-pinion mechanism.
    (b) Give two examples of the use of a rack-and-pinion mechanism.
    (c) Sketch the symbol for a rack-and-pinion mechanism.

20. Explain three filing techniques you used when manufacturing the key ring.
    Communicate using sketches to illustrate these techniques.

21. List five electronic devices you use in everyday life.

22. (a) Name two different types of switches that are incorporated into a pillar drill for safety reasons.
    (b) Sketch the symbol for each type of switch.

23. Name the three stages in a control system.

24. Give three defining characteristics of a mechatronic system.

Unit 4 – Timetable Bag Tag

Unit Objectives

PROJECT	Design and manufacture a single-piece folded acrylic **bag tag**

- Learn more about **plastics** and how to **bend acrylic** in a strip heater using the project
- Learn about **developments** - how to recognise, draw and manufacture them
- Learn further **marking-out** and **workholding** tools and processes
- Learn more about **mechanisms** and **electronics**
- Learn about the **micro:bit** and **create your first software programs** using guided tutorials

Content

PROCESSES AND PRINCIPLES	**Materials**	•	Types of thermoplastics and thermosetting plastics
	Drawing	•	Bend lines and Developments
	Marking Out	•	Odd-leg calipers, surface plate, angle plate, height gauge
	Workholding	•	Hand & workbench workholding: clamps, hand vice
	Forming	•	Using the strip heater to line bend plastics
DESIGN APPLICATION	• Modify existing designs. Designing within design constraints		
MECHATRONICS	**Mechanisms**	•	Screws, spur gears
	Electronics	•	Electrical terms. Further common electronic components: switches, bulbs, LEDs, buzzers, batteries, motors
	micro:bit	•	Introduction to the BBC micro:bit and programming

Learning Outcomes from this Unit

PROCESSES AND PRINCIPLES	DESIGN APPLICATION	MECHATRONICS
1.1, 1.2, 1.3, 1.4, 1.7, 1.8, 1.9, 1.10, 1.11, 1.12, 1.13	2.8, 2.9, 2.12	3.1, 3.3, 3.6, 3.8

Suggested Timeframes

START TIME	YEAR 1	October		DURATION	4-5 weeks

Working Drawings

Default Design

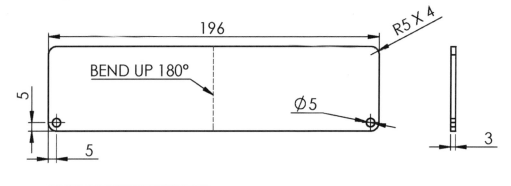

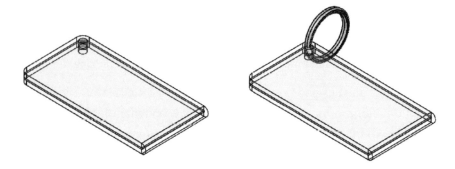

Bill of Materials

ITEM NO.	PART	DESCRIPTION	QTY.
1	BAG TAG	3mm Transparent Acrylic	1
2	METAL SPLIT RING	Diameter 24mm	1

Your Design Sketches (Follow the Project Storyboard activities before attempting these)

1. Your Design Sketch 1 (main elevation only)

TITLE	Unit 4 – Timetable Bag Tag	SHEET 1 OF 3
DESCRIPTION	Default Design and Student Design Sketches	Brighter Minds

Your Design Sketches   (Follow the Project Storyboard before attempting this section)

2. Your Design Sketch 2 (main elevation only)

3. Your Design Sketch 3 (main elevation only)

4. Your Design Sketch 4 (main elevation only)

TITLE	Unit 4 – Timetable Bag Tag	SHEET 2 OF 3
DESCRIPTION	Design Sketches	Brighter Minds

Your Design Sketches (Follow the Project Storyboard before attempting this section)

5. Re-draw Your Full Chosen Design Below to Scale (See Project Storyboard)

TITLE	Unit 4 – Timetable Bag Tag	SHEET 3 OF 3
DESCRIPTION	Final Design Drawing	**Brighter Minds**

Project Storyboard

Learning Goals of this Project

- Learn how to **bend acrylic** by making a **timetable bag tag** from transparent acrylic
- **Apply** your **design skills** to create different shapes
- Get used to working to **design constraints**, **collaborating** and **improving** designs
- Get further practice at **planning** and **executing** the **manufacturing process**, e.g.
  - thinking about the **best sequence** of manufacturing processes
  - thinking about the **tools** and **equipment** needed

*You can manufacture our **default design** or one of your **own designs***

Drawing and Design Activities

Activity 1 – Drawing Interpretation

See Page 67

Explain what the **dashed line** represents on the working drawing:

_____

DESIGN CONSTRAINTS FOR YOUR BAG TAG

- Your bag tag should be made from **3mm**-thick **acrylic**
- The **size** of your **completed** (folded) bag tag should not exceed **50mm x 99mm**
- Your design should contain a **bend line**, so that the acrylic can be **bent** over itself (your design drawing should be a **mirror-image** either side of your bend line)
- Your bag tag should contain a **hole** so that a metal **split ring** (like that shown in the picture above) can be looped into the hole
- Also think about the **manufacturability** of your design - how hard/easy it will be to make

---

Activity 2 – Design

in the spaces provided on the working drawings page, **sketch four different bag tag designs** of your own. For each of your designs, sketch the main **elevation** view and include **dimensions**. Your design must follow the **design constraints** given above.

Activity 3 – Design Review & Collaboration

Ask your **teacher** or **peer** (i.e. one of your fellow students) to **review** your design sketches and to assess how well they meet the design criteria. In the space below, **explain** any **modifications** you made to your design as a result of this review:

_____

_____

_____

Activity 4 – Select a Design

Choose one of the designs to **manufacture** – either the **default design** or one of your **own designs** – and **justify** your choice of design:

My chosen design is (name or number): _____

Why I chose this design: _____

_____

_____

_____

Marking Out Activities

Activity 5 – Planning Marking Out

Identify and list the **marking-out tools** you will need for this project: *(as used in Unit 3)*

_____

_____

_____

Activity 6 – Research Marking Out

Research and **explain** why an **odd-leg calipers** might be useful for this project:

See Page 70

_____

_____

Activity 7 – Optional Practice

Practice using the **odd-leg calipers** by scribing a line **50mm parallel** to the edge of a piece of **scrap plastic** or wood.

Activity 8 – Marking Out

Mark out your **chosen design** on your **acrylic workpiece** now.

See Marking Out on Page 71

Manufacturing Activities

Activity 9 – Planning Manufacturing

Investigate by looking through this unit, or by **exploring** the workshop, the **equipment** you will need to **bend the acrylic**. Name this equipment and **describe** how to use it:

See Page 74

Name of equipment: _____

How I will use it: _____

_____

_____

_____

Activity 10 – Safety

See Page 74

Identify **two safety precautions** you will need to follow when **bending acrylic**:

1. _____

2. _____

Activity 11 – Planning

Identify and list the remaining **tools** you think you will need to **manufacture** your bag tag:

_____

_____

_____

Activity 12 - Planning

List the **three** surface-finishing **filing techniques** that you will need to shape the bag tag:

Filing technique 1: _____

Filing technique 2: _____

Filing technique 3: _____

Activity 13 - Planning

Do you think you should **drill both holes** before bending the acrylic? _____

Justify your answer: _____

_____

_____

_____

Activity 14 - Manufacturing

Manufacture your bag tag now

See Workholding, Plastic Forming on Pages 72, 74

Post-Manufacturing Review Activities

Activity 14 – Manufacturing Evaluation

Explain why we used **transparent** acrylic instead of **opaque** acrylic to make the bag tag:

_____

_____

Activity 15 – Manufacturing Evaluation

Demonstrate using text and a sketch why a **dot punch** is useful before using **spring dividers**:

Description: *Sketch*:

_____

_____

_____

Activity 16 – Manufacturing Evaluation

Which manufacturing **process** did you find the most **difficult**? _____

What actions helped you **improve** the outcomes? _____

_____

Unit 4 Project Assessment

Student Self-Assessment

In this project, I gained the following additional **skills** and **knowledge**:

1. _____

2. _____

3. _____

I **evaluate** my project to have turned out well in the following areas:

_____

_____

If I were to carry out this project again, I would **modify** or **improve** the following areas:

_____

_____

_____

On a scale of 1 to 10, I would give my project a **score** of...

Peer Assessment

Identify two manufacturing **processes** you think were carried out to a **high standard** on this project:

1. _____

_____

2. _____

_____

Identify any **skills** your peer could **improve** upon:

_____

_____

_____

_____

Teacher Feedback

Teacher comments on student's project:

Not Graded	Partially Achieved	Achieved	Merit	Higher Merit	Distinction

Learning Topics for Unit 4

Processes and Principles

Materials - Plastics

Recap - **refresh your knowledge** of plastics from previous units by completing the questions below:

Revision Questions - Plastics

1. What **raw material** are most plastics made from? _____

2. List some key **differences** between **thermoplastics** and **thermosetting plastics**:

   _____

   _____

   _____

3. Explain the meaning of **opaque**: _____

4. Explain why **electrical insulation** is an important property of **plastics**:

   _____

5. Identify two common **products** that use plastic as an **electrical insulator**:

   (a) _____ (b) _____

Properties of Thermoplastics and Thermosetting Plastics

THERMOPLASTICS	THERMOSETTING PLASTICS
• Easily **melted and reshaped** • **Weaker** than thermosetting plastics • **Lower** melting point • Most thermoplastics are **recyclable**	• **Cannot** be melted and reshaped • **Stronger**, **harder**, **more brittle** than thermoplastics • **Higher** melting point • **Better electrical insulators** than thermoplastics • **Not recyclable**

Common Thermoplastics

Thermoplastic	Properties	Applications	
POLYTHENE (polyethylene) (PE)	• Can be made **clear** and **thin** • **Not strong** • **Hygienic**, non-toxic • **Biocompatib**le • Low melting point • Does not vacuum form well	• **Bottles** • **Food packaging** • Lunchboxes • Shopping bags • Cling film	
POLYPROPYLENE (PP)	• Light • **Tough, stiffer than polythene** • Resistant to wear • Cheap • Biocompatible • Difficult to glue	• **Chairs** • Bottle tops • Food boxes • Clothes hangers	
ACRYLIC ('Perspex')	• Very **transparent** • **Smooth, high-quality finish** • **Hard** (can crack) • Low cost • Shapes in a **vacuum former** • Bends on a **strip heater**	• Glass substitute • **Car lights** • Safety glasses • **Shop signs** • Fridge trays	
NYLON	• **Strong, hard to break** • **Hard-wearing** • **Slippy, low-friction** • Can be machined	• **Gears**, bearings • **Ropes**, fishing lines • **Tent frames** • **Fabric** for clothes	
ABS and **HIPS** (High-Impact Polystyrene)	• **Impact-resistant**, tough • **Non-toxic**, safe • **High gloss finish** • Easy to vacuum-form	• **Toys** • Electronic **casings**	

Thermoplastic	Properties	Applications	
PVC (Polyvinyl Chloride) **uPVC** (Unplasticised PVC)	• **Strong, dense, heavier** • Resistant to **chemicals** • Can be made **rigid** (uPVC) or **flexible** (PVC) • Cheap • Low melting point	• Drain **pipes** • Bank cards • **Wire insulation** • **Window frames** • Vinyl records	
EXPANDED POLYSTYRENE (EPS) (styrofoam, aeroboard)	• **Very light** (90% air bubbles) • **Absorbs impacts** • **Heat insulation** • Shape with a wire cutter • Doesn't degrade or recycle	• **Packaging** • **Cavity wall insulation** (beads) • Liners for cycling helmets	

Common Thermosetting Plastics (Thermosets)

Thermoset	Properties	Applications	
BAKELITE (PHENOL FORMALDEHYDE) **MELAMINE**	• **Hard, stiff, hard-wearing** • **Heat** and **flame resistant** • **Electrical insulator** • **Absorbs impacts** without chipping or cracking • **Chemical resistant**	• **Handles** for cooking pots • **Electrical plugs**, sockets, switches • **Snooker balls** • **Printed circuit boards** • Kitchen worktops	
POLYURETHANE FOAM	• Expanded with **bubbles** • Can be stiff or flexible • Good **thermal insulation**	• **Building** foam and **attic insulation** • Furniture stuffing	

Activity – Environmental Impact of Plastics

THINK	**Think** about the positive and negative impacts of plastics on society
PAIR	**Discuss** your thoughts with your neighbour
SHARE	**Share** your findings with the class

Issues with Disposing of and Recycling Plastics

LONG LIFE	• Plastics **do not biodegrade**, they can take hundreds of years • However, bacteria are being discovered that can break down plastics
THERMOSETS	• Unlike thermoplastics, **thermoset** plastics **cannot be melted down and recycled**
LANDFILL	• Disposing of plastics in landfill can **pollute groundwater** and harm **wildlife**
INCINERATION (burning)	• Incineration of plastics **reduces the amount of plastic waste** in landfill • Incineration of plastics can **generate useful heat and electricity** • Incineration produces **toxic gases**, but most of the harmful effects can be treated

Engineering Drawings

Bend Lines

Bend lines are indicated on an engineering drawing using a **dashed line**.
The **required angle** and **direction** for the bend will also be indicated on the drawing.

Example:

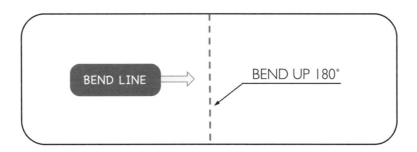

Developments

A development is an **unfolded flat representation of a 3D object**.
By folding a development along its **bend lines**, you can create a 3D object.

*Create a development yourself by **opening out a cardboard box** and noticing its shape when it is flat.*

The diagram below gives an example of an engineering development drawing, along with its 3D view equivalent. *(Note in the 3D view the right-hand 'tab' is folded behind the main body so you can't see it)*

Engineering Drawing – Example of a Development

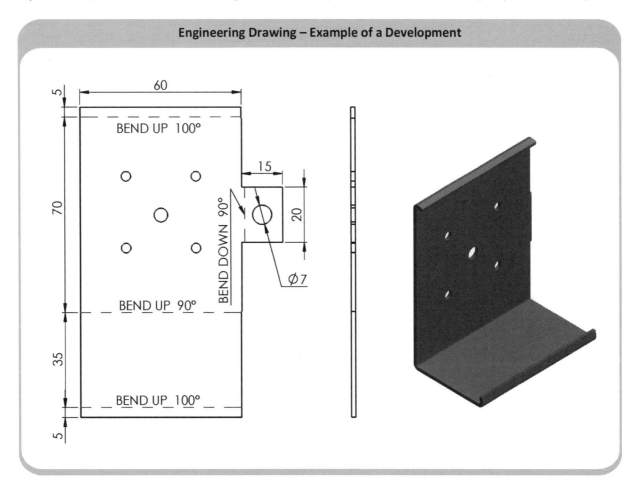

Development Activity

Sketch the **development** of the acrylic photo frame shown below, indicating the bend lines.

Your sketch of the development

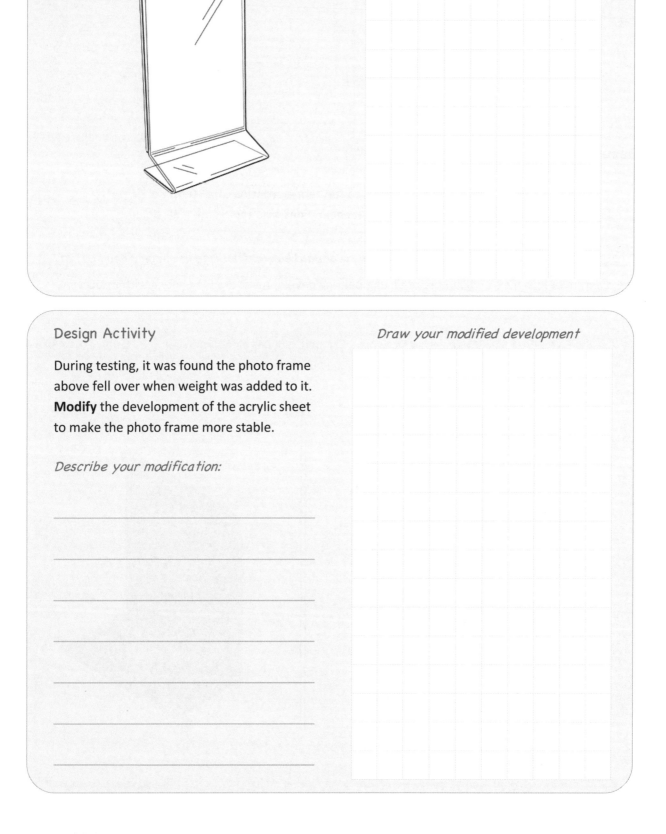

Design Activity

During testing, it was found the photo frame above fell over when weight was added to it. **Modify** the development of the acrylic sheet to make the photo frame more stable.

Describe your modification:

_____

_____

_____

_____

_____

_____

_____

Draw your modified development

Drawing Activity – Development

Sketch the development of the bracket below.

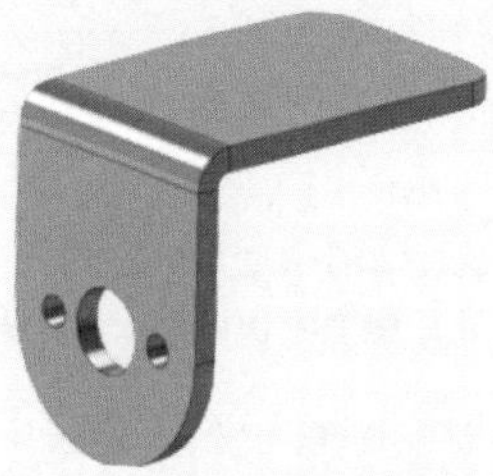

Sketch

Marking Out

Recap - **refresh your knowledge** of marking out from previous units by completing the questions below:

Revision Questions – Marking Out

1. **Explain** how you would check the **squareness** of a piece of material (edges at 90°):

   _____

2. **Explain**, using both text and a sketch, what a **datum edge** is, and why is it useful:

   Description: *Sketch:*

   _____

   _____

   _____

   _____

   _____

Marking Out Tools

ADDITIONAL MARKING OUT TOOLS	

ODD-LEG CALIPERS	• An **odd-leg calipers** is used to **scribe a line parallel to an edge**
	
	• The **long leg** is placed against the **edge**
	
	• The **short leg** contains a **scriber** which is placed on the material, as far from the edge as possible
	
	• The length of the scriber can be **adjusted with a screw**
	
	• The end of the **long leg** can be **curved** or can contain a **notch**
	
	• To **scribe a line parallel to an edge**:
	
	    ○ move the calipers along the edge
	    ○ keep the long leg touching the edge
	    ○ keep the scriber on the material, keeping the calipers perpendicular to the edge

SURFACE PLATE	• A **surface plate** provides an **accurate flat surface** for **measurement** and for **marking out** • A surface plate be used to **check the flatness** of object surfaces • A surface plate also has accurate **right-angle corners**
ANGLE PLATE	• An **angle plate** is placed on a surface plate to provide an **accurate 90° right angle** for **marking out**
(VERNIER) HEIGHT GAUGE	• Used to **measure** or **mark out heights** • A **knife edge** made of hardened steel can be used to **scribe** a line on metal • Has a **fixed main scale** rule and a **sliding Vernier scale** • Has a **heavy flat base** • Can be placed on a **surface plate** for more accurate marking out

Marking Out Techniques
Marking Out Bend Lines

> Mark out a **bend line** on a workpiece as a **dashed line**.
> This distinguishes a bend line from a cut line which is marked out as a solid line.

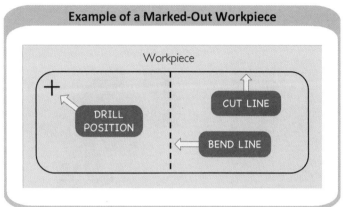

Example of a Marked-Out Workpiece

Workpiece

DRILL POSITION

CUT LINE

BEND LINE

To mark out your timetable **bag tag**, you will need an **engineer's square**, **ruler**, **sharpie** marker or **scriber**, plus a **spring dividers** and a **dot punch** to mark out any curves (arcs).

Workholding

Recap - **refresh your knowledge** of workholding from previous units by trying the questions below:

Revision Questions – Workholding

1. **Give two reasons** why it is important to clamp your workpieces securely:

(i) _____

(ii) _____

2. **Name** the **two types of vices** you encountered in Unit 3 Key Ring:

Vice Type 1: _____ *Vice Type 2:* _____

3. **Explain** the **differences** between the above two named types of vices:

_____

_____

Hand and Workbench Workholding

MORE WORKHOLDING TOOLS	
HAND VICE	• Like a spring-loaded set of **tongs** • The **screw** brings the jaws together and apart • Used to **hold small items** for drilling, sawing, filing etc. 
IRWIN CLAMP	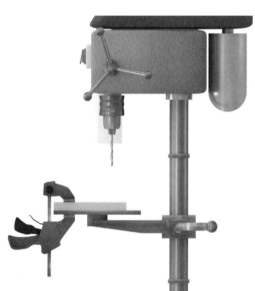 • Can be operated with **one hand** • **Squeeze** the **large black handle** multiple times to **tighten** the jaws of the clamp towards each other • **Pull** the **small black trigger** to **release** the clamp, allowing you to slide the jaws freely in or out • Can be used to **clamp sheet metal or acrylic** to your **bench** for drilling • Often used to clamp pieces of **wood** together while **gluing** *Irwin Clamp used with Pillar Drill*
G-CRAMP or **G-CLAMP** or **C-CLAMP**	 • The **screw** tightens on the workpiece(s) held between the jaws • Often used to hold pieces together while **gluing** or **drilling** 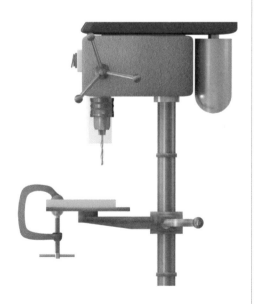 *G-Cramp used with Pillar Drill*

Cutting

Recap - **refresh your knowledge** of cutting from previous units by completing the questions below.

Revision Question – Cutting

Explain, with the aid of a sketch, the **direction** that the **cutting teeth** face on a **hacksaw**:

Direction of Teeth: *Sketch:*

_____

More Cutting Tools

| COPING SAW | • Has a **high frame** and **thin blade**
• Suitable for **cutting curves**
• The **teeth** face **backwards** towards the handle
• Cuts on the **pull** stroke
• Use a **fine-tooth blade** for plastics | 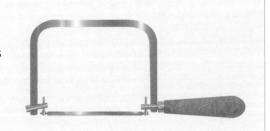 |

Surface Finishing

Recap - **refresh your knowledge** of surface finishing from previous units by trying the questions below.

Revision Questions – Surface Finishing

1. **Communicate** the **processes** and equipment required to **create a smooth edge on acrylic**:

_____

_____

2. **Explain** the **cross-filing technique** and identity the **type of file** you would use for it:

Type of File used for Cross Filing: _____

Cross-Filing Technique: _____

3. **Explain** the **draw filing technique** and identity the **type of file** you would use for it:

Type of File used for Draw Filing: _____

Draw Filing Technique: _____

Plastics Forming

> **Forming** means changing the shape of a workpiece **without removing material**
> **Shaping** involves **removing material** from the workpiece e.g. by cutting, drilling, filing

Line Bending using a Strip Heater

A **strip heater** is used to soften a **thermoplastic sheet** along a **line**. The sheet can then be **bent** along this line, often using a **former** (see below) to set the bend angle. When the plastic sheet **cools**, it stays in the new bent shape.

PLASTICS SUITABLE FOR STRIP HEATER	
STRIP HEATER PLASTICS	• Thin (3-5mm) sheets of **Acrylic**, **ABS** and **HIPS** are suitable for use with a **strip heater**

SAFETY PRECAUTIONS WHEN FORMING PLASTICS

- Wear **protective gloves**. <u>Do not touch hot plastic</u> with your hand
- Wear a **face mask** to protect against any **fumes**
- **Do not overheat plastic**, as it will produce **toxic fumes** and could go on **fire**

STEPS FOR USING A STRIP HEATER

SETTING UP

- Ensure the **bend line** has been **marked out** on the plastic sheet and is clearly **visible**
- Place the thermoplastic sheet onto the **supporting bars** of the strip heater
- **Line up** the **bend line** over the **heating element**
- **Turn on** the heater

SOFTENING

- **Wait** until the plastic **softens** and can be bent with a little pressure - this takes about 2 minutes for 3mm acrylic or 3 minutes for 5mm acrylic
- **Switch off** the heater and **remove** the sheet

BENDING

- When bending **acrylic**, do not apply too much pressure or it may **crack**
- The sheet can be bent around a **rod**, using an **engineer's square**, or using a **former** (see next page)
- An **engineer's protractor** can be used to check the angle of the bend (see next page)

Additional Plastic Forming Equipment

ADDITIONAL PLASTICS FORMING TOOLS	
FORMER	• A **former defines the bend angle** and holds the sheet while it **cools down** • After the bend line has been heated and softens, **press the sheet** gently **into the former** • **Formers** are often made from **wood** • Use safety **gloves** • In the type of former shown opposite (bottom), the distance between the strips of wood (and the length of the workpiece) determines the bend angle 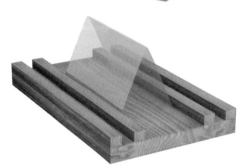
ENGINEERING PROTRACTOR	• An **engineering protractor** is used to accurately **measure** or **mark out angles** on your drawing or workpiece • It can be used to **check the bend angle** when bending plastic or metal 

Activity - Research

Research the person who invented the first **electric heating element**. Include three important facts about this **inventor** or invention.

Inventor: _____

Fact 1: _____

Fact 2: _____

Fact 3: _____

Manufacturing with Acrylic – Summary of Steps

MANUFACTURING WITH ACRYLIC – SUMMARY OF STEPS	
Step 1 **MARKING OUT**	• **Mark out** the **cut lines**, **drill positions** and **bend lines** on the acrylic sheet • Use a **sharpie** marker or **scriber**, steel ruler, **engineer's square**, **spring dividers** and **dot punch**
Step 2 **CUTTING**	• **Clamp** the acrylic sheet in a **bench vice**, between two pieces of **waste wood** • Cut off the waste material with a **senior hacksaw** (good for straight lines), **junior hacksaw** or **coping saw** (good for curved lines) • *A **band saw** can also be used to cut acrylic – see later units*
Step 3 **FILING**	• Clamp the material in a **bench vice** • **Cross file** the cut edges to remove large amounts of material • **Draw file** the edges to smoothen further

Step 4
DRILLING
	• Choose your **drilling** and **clamping** methods, usually either:
	  ○ A **pillar drill** and a **machine vice**, **G-cramp** or **Irwin Clamp**
	  ○ A **cordless drill** and a **bench vice**, **G-cramp** or **Irwin Clamp**
	• Place a **waste piece of wood underneath** the acrylic to **prevent it cracking**
	• If a large diameter hole is required, drill a small **pilot hole** first (see later units)

Step 5 **FINISHING**	• Ensure the edges are **draw filed** • Use **wet and dry paper** and WD40 oil to remove any remaining marks • Apply a **plastic polish** with a soft cloth

FILE
Draw file to remove any saw-cut or cross-file marks

SMOOTHEN
Use **wet and dry emery paper** to remove draw file marks

POLISH
Apply a **plastic polish** with a soft cloth

	MANUFACTURING WITH ACRYLIC – SUMMARY OF STEPS	
Step 6 **BENDING**	• **Ensure bend line is visible** on the workpiece • Place the workpiece on the **strip heater** supporting bars, **lining up the bend line** with the **heating element** • Wait a few minutes until the plastic **softens** at the bend line • Bend the line around a **rod** or use a **former**	

Mechatronics

Mechanisms

Recap - refresh your knowledge of **motion** and **mechanisms** by completing the below.

Revision Questions – Motion and Mechanisms

1. **Identify** the **four types of motion** that you studied in the keyring unit.
   Sketch the relevant **symbol** beside each one:

Name of Type of Motion	Symbol

2. Identify the type of **motion transformation** that takes place in a **bench vice**:

Type of Input Motion	Type of Output Motion

3. Identify two **applications** for a **rack and pinion** mechanism:

Application 1	Application 2

More Mechanisms

Mechanism	Description	Applications
SCREW MECHANISM	• **Converts rotary** motion to **linear** motion	• G-Clamp • Bench Vice • Car Jack • Bolt and Nut
SPUR GEARS	• **Changes** the **speed** and **direction** of **rotary** motion • The **speed** of rotation changes according to the **number of teeth** in each gear - see below	• Simple **machinery** • **Clocks** and **watches** *Symbol:*

Driver and Driven Gears

In any system of connected gears, one gear is the **driver gear**, and one gear is the **driven gear**.

This **driver gear** is the **input gear** – it provides the turning force that drives all other connected gears.

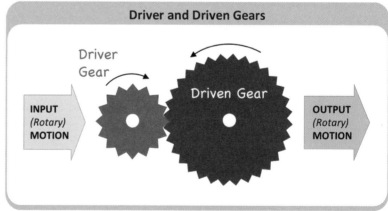

Driver and Driven Gears

The final **output gear** is called the **driven gear**.

The **driver gear** is often connected to an electric **motor**, and the **driven gear** is often connected to an **axle** to drive a set of connected wheels.

Activity – Gear Speeds

1. In the system of gears shown directly above, **which gear will turn faster** – the **driver gear** or the **driven gear**?

_____

2. **Justify** your answer to question 1 :

_____

_____

Gear Speeds

Gears are used to change the **direction** and **speed** of **rotary motion**.

> **Speed** of rotary motion is measured in **RPM** – revolutions or rotations per minute

Calculating Gear Speeds

> Output speed of the **driven gear** = Input speed of the **driver gear** x $\dfrac{\text{Teeth on Driver Gear}}{\text{Teeth on Driven Gear}}$

Worked Example – Calculating Gear Speeds

Question:
In the gear system shown opposite, what is the speed of
the **driven gear**, if the speed of the **driver gear** is **100 RPM**?

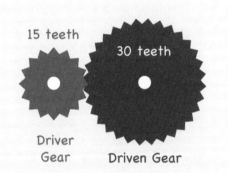

15 teeth
30 teeth
Driver Gear
Driven Gear

Answer:
Using the formula:
Driven gear speed = 100 RPM x 15/30 = **50 RPM**

Using reasoning:
The output speed must be half the input speed because the driver gear has to rotate twice
(using 2 x 15 teeth) in order to rotate the driven gear around once (30 teeth)

Activities – Calculate Gear Speeds
Calculate the **speed** of the **driven gears** below. **Demonstrate** how you calculated the figures.

GEAR SPEED QUESTION 1	GEAR SPEED QUESTION 2

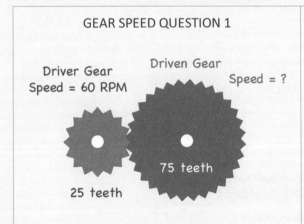

Driver Gear
Speed = 60 RPM

Driven Gear
Speed = ?

75 teeth

25 teeth

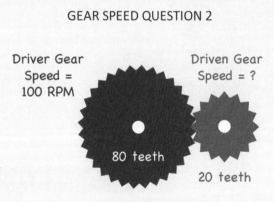

Driver Gear
Speed = 100 RPM

Driven Gear
Speed = ?

80 teeth

20 teeth

Driven Gear Speed Calculation:

Driven Gear Speed Calculation:

Electronics

Recap - **refresh your knowledge** of electronics by trying the questions below.

> ### Revision Questions – Electronics
>
> 1. **Identify** and draw the **symbol** for the **type of switch** associated with an **emergency stop**:
>
>   *Name of Switch*   *Symbol*:
>
>   _____
>
> 2. **Explain** how a **limit switch** (micro switch) could be used in the operation of a **pillar drill**:
>
>   _____
>
>   _____

Important Electrical Terms

Term	Description	Units
ELECTRICITY	• **Electricity** is **energy** caused by the movement of **electrons** - the tiny charged particles found in the atoms of all materials	
CURRENT	• Electric **current** is a measure of the **number of electrons flowing** from one place to another in a given time • Current is measured using an **Ammeter** • *Electric current can be compared to a river flowing down a hill*	**Amps / milliamps** (A/mA)
VOLTAGE	• **Voltage** exists between **two points**. It is a **driving force** that causes electric current to flow between those two points • Voltage is measured by a **Voltmeter** • *Voltage can be compared to the height of the hill that causes the water (current) to flow downhill*	**Volts** (V)

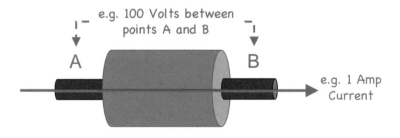

VOLTAGE IS <u>ACROSS</u> A COMPONENT

e.g. 100 Volts between points A and B

A   B

e.g. 1 Amp Current

CURRENT FLOWS <u>THROUGH</u> A COMPONENT

Types of Electrical Supply

Type	Description	Images
AC	• In **Alternating Current** (AC) electricity, the voltage and current continually **reverse direction** many times a second • **Mains electricity** which comes into our homes, is **220 Volts AC** • Mains electricity is dangerous and can kill • High-voltage AC is powerful enough to drive large motors and loads • High-voltage AC can be transported over long distances	
DC	• In **Direct Current** (DC) electricity, the voltage remains constant and the **current flows in one direction only** • Low-voltage DC is used in all our **electronic devices** • Low voltage DC is safe to touch	

Sources of DC Electricity

Source	Description	Images
POWER SUPPLY	• A **power supply converts high-voltage AC** to **low-voltage DC** • An example is the 'charger' for your phone	
BATTERY	• **Batteries** supply a few volts DC • This is enough to power electronic devices such as phones and laptops	9V

More Electrical Inputs – Switches

Device	Description	Images and Symbols
SPST TOGGLE SWITCH	• A **SPST toggle switch** is a **simple on/off switch** operated by a **lever** • **SPST** means **single-pole, single-throw** - this means it just has **two connections** • One position of the switch **closes** the circuit (i.e. allows current through) and the other position **opens** (or **breaks**) the circuit	
PTM SWITCH	• A **Push-To-Make** (PTM) switch *closes the circuit* (i.e. creates an electrical connection between the two terminals), when it is **pushed in**	

More Electrical Outputs

Device	Description	Images and Symbols
BULB	<ul><li>A **bulb emits light and heat** when current passes through it</li><li>Made from **tungsten wire** in a **vacuum**</li><li>**Energy wasteful** – a lot of the input electrical energy **is lost as output heat** energy instead of being converted into output light energy</li><li>**Not long-lasting** compared to LEDs, they **burn out** because of the heat generated</li><li>**Fragile** - can break easily</li></ul>	
LED	<ul><li>**Light-Emitting Diode**</li><li>**Very energy-efficient**</li><li>Only needs a **low DC voltage**, and uses very **little current** (mA)</li><li>**Polarised** (i.e. only works one way round)</li><li>Much more **resistant to shocks and vibrations** than a bulb</li><li>Made from **semiconductor** materials</li></ul>	
BUZZERS, BELLS and SIRENS	<ul><li>A **buzzer** emits a sound when activated by a voltage</li><li>A **bell** is a type of buzzer that emits a ringing sound</li><li>Buzzers and bells are often used in devices such as hand-held electronic games</li><li>A **siren** is a loud device, typically used in house alarms</li></ul>	Buzzer: Siren: Bell:
MOTOR	<ul><li>An electric **motor** converts input **electrical energy** into output **mechanical energy** (movement / rotation)</li><li>Motors can be powered by **AC or DC current**</li><li>A **DC motor** is shown opposite</li><li>The **rotation** of a DC motor can be **reversed** by reversing the direction of the **current** through it</li></ul>	

We will see these electronic components again in later units.

Mechatronic Control Systems

Recap - refresh your knowledge of **control systems** and **mechatronics** by trying the questions below.

Revision Questions – Mechatronic Control Systems

1. Identify **three different types of technology** usually present in a mechatronic system:

2. Name the **three different stages** that a **control system** can be broken down into:

Stage 1	Stage 2	Stage 3

Introduction to the BBC micro:bit

If you don't have a physical micro:bit, you can still program it online and see it all working!
The micro:bit a super **easy way to learn programming**, and how to **control mechatronic devices**.

- The BBC **micro:bit** is a **pocket-sized computer**

- You can use the micro:bit to make interesting **projects** and learn about **programming** and **control systems**

- The micro:bit can be used on its own, or as the **control stage** of a larger mechatronic system

- Later in the book, you will be able to use a micro:bit to **control** the **projects** you make in those later units

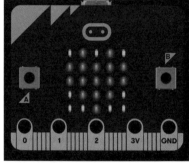
Front of the micro:bit

USEFUL THINGS YOU CAN DO WITH A **micro:bit**

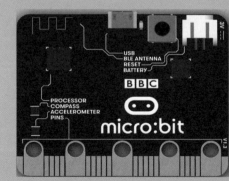
Back of the micro:bit

- Turn on and off **LED** lights
- Make **sound**
- Control **motors** *(via an expansion board)*
- Detect **movement**
- Detect **light**
- Detect **temperature**
- Detect compass **direction**
- **Communicate** with other micro:bits

Our Recommended Approach to Learning the micro:bit

- First we explain the **basic inputs and outputs** and concepts of **micro:bit programming** *(see overleaf)*
- Then we recommend you carry out a number of online **tutorials** on the micro:bit website *(see later)*
- This is the easiest guided way to create your first program. After that, we will guide you further

Inputs and Outputs of the micro:bit

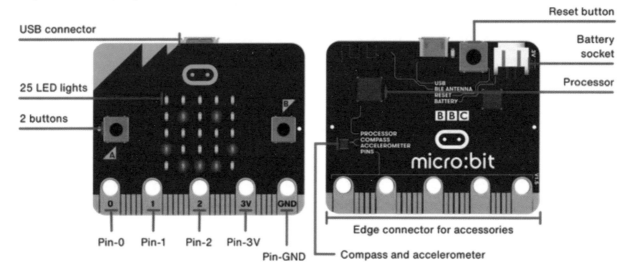

The micro:bit has many inputs and outputs. Here are the most important ones we will use:

Input/Output	Description
USB CONNECTOR	• Connects your micro:bit to a **computer** via a **USB cable** • This allows you to **download** your programs to your micro:bit • The USB cable also **powers** the micro:bit if you do not have batteries connected
BATTERY SOCKET	• Here you can attach a **battery pack** with **two AAA batteries** to power your micro:bit *(if your micro:bit is not already powered through the USB cable)* • This is useful if you build the micro:bit board in to one of your **projects**
LEDs	• There are **25 red LEDs** on the front panel, arranged in a **5 x 5 grid** • Your micro:bit program can control these LEDs to display different patterns, letters or numbers • These LEDs can also be used as **light sensors** (to detect light and make something else happen, such as switching off a light)
PINS	• The **25 pins** on the micro:bit can be connected to **external input or output devices** such as LEDs, switches or speakers to add more life to your projects, and to control your engineering projects • The **large pins 0, 1, 2, 3V** and **GND** are most commonly used • We will look at **pins** in more detail later at the end of **Unit 6**
BUTTONS A and **B**	• You can **program** the micro:bit to **respond to the buttons** when they are pressed • For example, you could use the buttons to change the pattern displayed on the LEDs, or to create a sound, or to communicate with another micro:bit

Introductory Videos

 You can find out more about the micro:bit **features** by going to **microbit.org** and playing the videos at 'Getting Started' -> 'User Guide' -> 'Features in Depth'.

These videos are also available on the **micro:bit Educational Foundation** channel on **YouTube**.

Programming the micro:bit

You **create** and **test** all your **micro:bit programs** at the **makecode.microbit.org** website

If you want to download your program to your physical micro:bit, there are **three basic steps**:

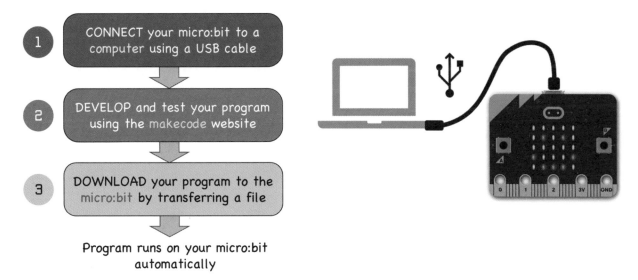

1 CONNECT your micro:bit to a computer using a USB cable

2 DEVELOP and test your program using the makecode website

3 DOWNLOAD your program to the micro:bit by transferring a file

Program runs on your micro:bit automatically

Create your program using the micro:bit "makecode" Editor

- Open a **web browser** on your computer
- Type in **makecode.microbit.org** in the address bar

Create all your microbit programs at makecode.microbit.org

*Save this web page as a **favourite** or **bookmark** on your browser to make it easier to return to*

micro:bit Projects

When you go to makecode.microbit.org you will see a screen similar to that shown below.

(Note: screens are correct at time of writing, however microbit.org may redesign their site - but the concepts should be the same)

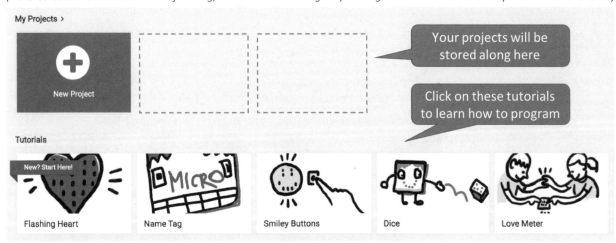

My Projects >

New Project

Your projects will be stored along here

Click on these tutorials to learn how to program

Tutorials

New? Start Here!

Flashing Heart   Name Tag   Smiley Buttons   Dice   Love Meter

- The **"My Projects"** area is where you will create and save all your projects
- If you select **"New Project",** you will see the **makecode editor** screen shown on the next page

micro:bit Tutorials

- Below 'My Projects' you will see **Tutorials**. We recommend you complete a number of these tutorials as part of this unit (see later for details). This is a great way to learn how to program the micro:bit

The makecode Editor Screen

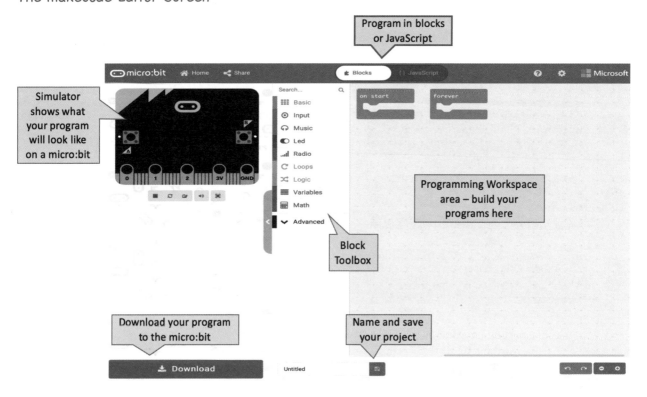

Program in blocks or JavaScript

Simulator shows what your program will look like on a micro:bit

Programming Workspace area – build your programs here

Block Toolbox

Download your program to the micro:bit

Name and save your project

Main Parts of the makecode Editor

Area	Position	Description
SIMULATOR	*Top Left*	• The simulator is a **virtual micro:bit** that displays what your program will do - as soon as you create your program online • It allows you to fully **test your program** and get it working, before you download it to your micro:bit device
TOOLBOX	*Middle*	• The **toolbox** contains lots of **code blocks**, arranged into categories • You **drag code blocks** from the **toolbox** into the **programming workspace** to create your program
PROGRAMMING WORKSPACE	*Right*	• The programming workspace is where you **assemble** your program, by slotting code blocks together • The workspace comes with **two special starter code blocks**:

The '**On Start**' code block	The '**Forever**' code block
on start	forever
Any code block you drag inside this 'On Start' block will **run only once** - when the program first runs	Any code block you drag inside this 'Forever' block will **run** and **loop** around **continuously**

Area	Position	Description
DOWNLOAD BUTTON	*Bottom Left*	• Click this button to **download** your program to your Downloads folder

Summary of micro:bit Programming

Create your program by:

(1) **dragging** code blocks from the **toolbox** into the **programming workspace**

(2) **test** by watching what happens on the on-screen **simulator**

(3) **download** your working program to your **micro:bit** device

DRAG	TEST	DOWNLOAD
Drag code **blocks** from the **Toolbox** to the **Programming Workspace**	Watch the **Simulator**	Click on the **Download** button, then **copy** the hex file to the **MICROBIT drive**

Before we go on to create some micro:bit programs, we first explain how to download your program to your micro:bit.

Downloading your Program to your micro:bit

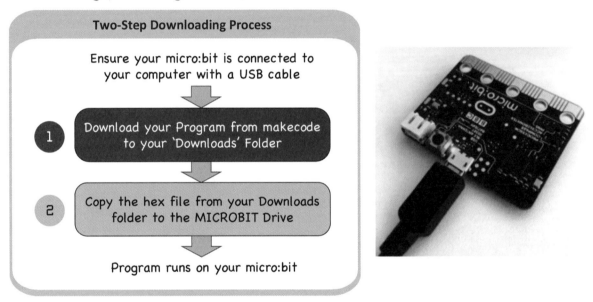

Two-Step Downloading Process

Ensure your micro:bit is connected to your computer with a USB cable

⬇

1 Download your Program from makecode to your 'Downloads' Folder

⬇

2 Copy the hex file from your Downloads folder to the MICROBIT Drive

⬇

Program runs on your micro:bit

Detailed Download Instructions

- After you have tested / simulated your program in the makecode editor, click on the Download button in the lower left corner of the makecode screen

- Your browser will now **save your program** as a '.hex' file to your browser's default download location (usually your 'C:\Downloads' folder)

- **Connect your micro:bit** to the computer using a USB cable

- The micro:bit will appear on your computer file system as an **external drive** called 'MICROBIT' (the same way that a USB memory stick appears on your computer)

- **Drag** the downloaded "xxxx.hex" file from your Downloads folder to the MICROBIT drive

- While the program file is transferring, the yellow LED on the back of the micro:bit **flashes**

- When the yellow LED stops flashing, the **program runs on the micro:bit**

micro:bit Tutorials – Exploring the Input Buttons and Output LEDs

- We recommend you **carry out the tutorials shown below** on the **makecode.microbit.org** website. These tutorials are available under the 'My Projects' area

- These tutorials a great way to learn micro:bit programming because:

    o they **show you exactly what to do** for each step – you just copy the actions
    o you can create a **working project** really **quickly**
    o you can see a lot of different **code blocks** and what they do
    o you can make program **without a micro:bit** because you can test on the **simulator**

For the first two tutorials we reproduce the steps below, but the online tutorials will tell you all the steps in more detail. In the activities below, **record** how far you progressed with each tutorial.

---

micro:bit Tutorial 1 – Flashing Heart

Using the "show leds" code block

(1) Go to **makecode.microbit.org**, click on the **Flashing Heart Tutorial**, and follow the steps presented on screen. **Alternatively** click on **New Project** and follow the steps outlined below:

(2) Place the show leds block in the forever block.

(3) Draw a heart design by clicking on the LEDs.

(4) Place another show leds block under the first one. Leave this one blank.

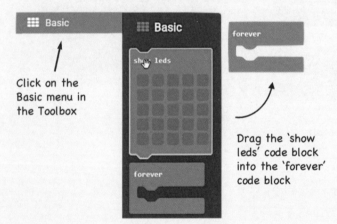

Click on the Basic menu in the Toolbox

Drag the 'show leds' code block into the 'forever' code block

Click on the LED dots to light them up

(5) Look at the virtual micro:bit in the simulator. The heart design will be flashing.

(6) If you have a micro:bit, click Download , transfer the code file to your micro:bit as described earlier, and watch the heart flash!

(7) **Tick** your progress with this tutorial:

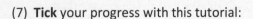

Too Difficult: Partially Completed: Completed:

micro:bit Tutorial 2 – Smiley Face, Frowny Face

Using the "show leds" and "on button pressed" blocks

(1) On **makecode.microbit.org**, click on the **Smiley Buttons Tutorial** and follow the steps shown on screen. **Alternatively** click on **New Project** and follow the steps outlined below:

(2) Place an on button pressed block in the workspace to run code when button **A** is pressed.

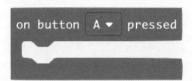

(3) Place a show leds block inside the on button pressed block.

(4) Click on the LEDs to create a smiley face.

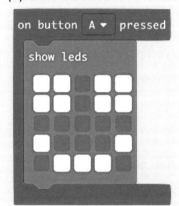

(5) Press the **A** button in the simulator to see the smiley face on the virtual micro:bit

(6) Place another on button pressed block and another show leds block to display a frowny face when button **B** is pressed.

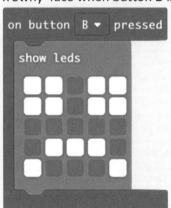

(7) Add a secret mode that happens when buttons **A** and **B** are pressed together. For this, add multiple show leds blocks to create an animation.

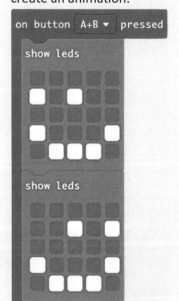

(8) Click Download and transfer the code file to your micro:bit.

Click on buttons A and B in different combinations to see what happens.

(9) **Tick** your progress with this tutorial:

Too Difficult: Partially Completed: Completed:

micro:bit Activity 3 – Smiley Blocks

Create an LED animation by (1) displaying a smiley face
on the LEDs, then (2) display an image with no LEDs lit.

Not a website tutorial – use the code blocks you know already

This will make it look like the smiley face is flashing as the display switches between images.

Tick your progress with this tutorial:

Too Difficult: Partially Completed: Completed:

micro:bit Tutorial 4 - Name Tag

Display your name on the micro:bit LEDs.

Using the "show string" block

Follow the tutorial called "**Name Tag**" on the makecode.microbit.org website.

Tick your progress with this tutorial:

Too Difficult: Partially Completed: Completed:

micro:bit Tutorial 5 - Coin Flipper

(1) **Create a coin flipping program** to simulate a real coin

Using the "show icon" block

toss. Images are used to represent heads or tails. **Follow the 'Coin Flipper' online tutorial**.

Tick your progress with this tutorial:

Too Difficult: Partially Completed: Completed:

(2) In your own words **explain** how this program works:

_____

_____

_____

_____

Extension Programming Tutorials for Home or School

micro:bit Extension Activities

To continue your programming development, try the following **tutorials** on the micro:bit website:

	Too Difficult:	Partially Completed:	Completed:
1. **Love Meter**			
2. **Dice**			
3. **Rock Paper Scissors**			

Unit 4 Revision

Unit 4 Revision Questions

1. Explain the word thermoplastic.

2. Name three types of thermoplastic and give one application of each.

3. Explain what is meant by a thermosetting plastic.

4. Identify four options when plastics reach their end of life, in order of favourability.

5. Explain what a development is in relation to engineering drawings.

6. Explain what an odd-leg callipers is used for.

7. Name and describe four filing techniques

8. Name three types of hand and workbench workholding clamps.

9. Name the equipment required to bend acrylic in the workshop.

10. Rewrite the words below in an order that would represent an appropriate sequence of six process steps required to manufacture an acrylic product:
    bending   filing   drilling   cutting   painting   marking-out   finishing

11. (a) Explain the motion transfer that takes place in a screw mechanism.
    (b) Give two applications of a screw mechanism.

12. Explain the difference between the driver gear and the driven gear.
    Use a sketch to support your answer.

13. If a driver gear with 10 teeth rotates at 100RPM, how fast is a driven gear with 20 teeth rotating?

14. Draw the symbol that represents meshing spur gears.

15. (a) Explain the term electrical current.
    (b) Identify the equipment used to measure current.

16. Draw the electrical symbol for a 9V battery.

17. (a) Draw the electrical symbol for a motor.
    (b) Give two everyday applications of an electric motor.

18. What is the purpose of the micro:bit simulator on the makecode dashboard?

19. How many LEDs are built into the micro:bit?

20. Sketch the micro:bit board and label the key parts of the board.

21. Identify the type of connector required to connect the micro:bit to your computer.

Unit 5 – Phone or Tablet Stand

Unit Objectives

PROJECT	Design and manufacture a single-piece **metal stand** for a phone or tablet

- Learn working with **metals**, types of **non-ferrous metals**, how to **cut** and **finish metals**
- Learn how to **measure accurately** using calipers and micrometer
- Enhance your **drawing**, **design** and **research** skills
- Learn about **levers**, and create your own micro:bit **software programs** from scratch

Content

PROCESSES AND PRINCIPLES	Materials	• Properties of metals, non-ferrous metals, semiconductors
	Drawing	• Further sketching practice
	Marking Out	• Outside Calipers, Vernier Calipers, Micrometer
	Cutting	• Metal Notcher, Guillotine
	Drilling	• Pilot Holes
	Filing	• Safe Edges, Pinning
DESIGN APPLICATION		• Selection of appropriate materials • Generating own designs, evaluating and modifying existing designs
MECHATRONICS		• **Lever** mechanisms • **micro:bit**: Programming with the LEDs and buttons. Programming with the temperature and accelerometer sensors.

Learning Outcomes from this Unit

PROCESSES AND PRINCIPLES	DESIGN APPLICATION	MECHATRONICS
1.1, 1.2, 1.3, 1.4, 1.5, 1.6, 1.7, 1.8, 1.9, 1.10, 1.11, 1.12 & 1.13	2.3, 2.5, 2.6, 2.7, 2.8, 2.9	3.5, 3.6

Suggested Timeframes

START TIME	YEAR 1	November		DURATION	4 weeks

Working Drawings

Default Design:

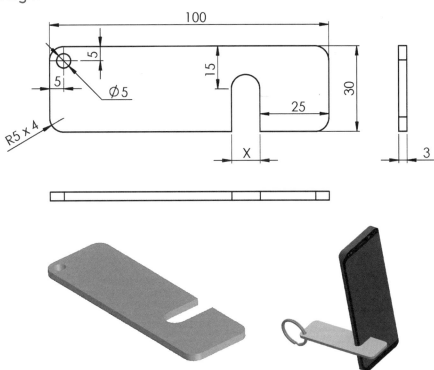

Bill of Materials

ITEM NO.	PART	DESCRIPTION	QTY.
1	PHONE STAND	3mm Aluminium	1
2	METAL SPLIT RING	Diameter 24mm	1

Your Concept Sketches: (Read the Project Storyboard Activities before attempting these)

TITLE	Unit 5 – Phone / Tablet Stand	SHEET 1 OF 3
DESCRIPTION	Default Design and Design Sketches	Brighter Minds

Your Concept Sketches and Design Drawings: (Read the Project Storyboard first)

TITLE	Unit 5 – Phone / Tablet Stand	SHEET 2 OF 3
DESCRIPTION	Your Design Drawings	Brighter Minds

Your Design Drawings and Final Design Drawing (Follow Project Storyboard Activities)

TITLE	Unit 5 – Phone / Tablet Stand	SHEET 3 OF 3
DESCRIPTION	Your Design Drawings	Brighter Minds

Project Storyboard

Learning Goals of this Project

- **Apply your design skills** to develop a **stand** for your phone or tablet
- Further develop your **freehand sketching** skills, and enhance your **engineering drawing** skills
- Learn how to take **accurate measurements** using appropriate measuring tools
- Learn **how to work with metals** – cutting, filing, finishing

*You may choose to manufacture the (modified) **default design** or develop one of your **own designs**.*

Your Design Brief / Constraints

- Your stand should be made from a **single piece** of **aluminium, copper or brass**
- The material should between **2mm** and **4mm** thick
- Your stand needs to **support** a phone or tablet at a small angle **without falling over**
- There are no specific shape or size constraints, however:
  - o   do not waste school resources
  - o   think about how the stand is going to **support the weight** (centre-of-gravity) of the phone or tablet
  - o   think about whether your stand could accommodate **different sizes** of phones / tablets
  - o   think about how **portable** the stand might be when not in use
- You design may contain **bends** (creating a *development* drawing). If you choose to include bends, **see Unit 6** for how to bend metal. | *See Bending Metal on Page 132*

Our Default Design

Our design for a phone / tablet stand is shown on the **working drawings** page.
This design uses a **slot** to hold the phone. This results in a stand that is small, light and portable.
The **width of the slot** is **crucial** to whether the stand works for particular devices.

Design Activities – Evaluating the Default Design

Design Activity 1 – Dimensions

1. On the default design working drawing, one dimension is labelled **'X'**. Explain **why** you think **this dimension is not provided**:

_____

2. **Measure the depth of your phone** or tablet accurately (*see the measurement section later in this unit*) | *See Vernier Calipers, Micrometer on Pages 108-109*

3. **Write the measured dimension** on the **default design drawing** in pencil in place of 'X'.

Design Activity 2 - Evaluating the Default Design

1. Why do you think the **default design** includes a **hole**?

_____

2. If you were using the **default design** for your own phone or tablet, do you think the **overall length and width** of the stand is correct? If not, **what length and width** would you use?

_____

Design Activities - Choosing Materials

Design Activity 3 - Choosing Materials

1. **Apply** your understanding of materials and **explain** why you think **metal** may be a better choice rather than **acrylic** to make your phone or tablet stand:

_____

_____

2. Why do you think a **non-ferrous metal** like aluminium, copper or brass is suggested?

_____

_____

3. Write the **name of your chosen material** below:

_____

See Non-Ferrous Metals
on Pages 104-105

4. **Justify** your choice of material:

_____

_____

Design Activities - Sketching and Choosing a Design

A **concept sketch** is a **free-hand drawing** used as a quick and simple way of **exploring initial design ideas**. Concept sketches don't have to be accurate, use straight lines or provide dimensions.

Design Activity 4 – Freehand Concept Sketches

Using only a **pencil**, draw a number of different free-hand **concept sketches** of your own designs for a phone/tablet stand - in the 'Your Concept Designs' sections in the working drawings pages. When designing, think about the following:

- Think about what your stand needs to do, what size phone/tablet it needs to hold
- Remember you can only use a **single piece of material** - no joints (but bends are allowed)
- You could draw what comes in to your head, one design may lead to another
- You could do some **research** on the internet into phone and tablet stands
- You could **prototype** some design ideas using **stiff cardboard** in order to test them out

Design Activity 5 – Design Drawings

Take **two** or three of your favourite / the most-promising freehand concept designs, and draw them with a **pencil**, **ruler**, **compass**, **set square** and **protractor** in the 'Your Design Drawings' section of the working drawings. If possible, draw your designs **to scale**. Include **dimensions**.

Design Activity 6 – Selecting a Design

1. **Select** one of your own designs, or the default design, as your **chosen design** and redraw it **accurately to scale** in the 'Your Final Design Drawing' section of the working drawings pages.

2. **Justify** below why you choose this particular design to manufacture:

_____

_____

_____

Marking Out Activities

Activity 7 – Planning for Marking-Out

Choose and list the **marking-out tools** that you will need to mark out your design:

_____   _____

_____   _____

_____   _____

Activity 8 – Marking Out

Mark out your chosen design on the material now

Manufacturing Activities

Activity 9 – Planning Your Manufacturing – Creating a Slot

Demonstrate using text and sketches how you would **remove the material to create the slot** in the default design:

Explanation: _____

_____

_____

Sketches:

Activity 10 – Planning Your Manufacturing – Finishing / Smoothness

1. **Any rough or sharp edges left on your stand may scratch your phone.**
Describe the **processes** you will use to **remove all sharp edges** and create a **highly smooth finish** (especially around the **slot** if using):

See Finishing Metals, Page 112

_____

_____

2. Outline any **other technique** that might reduce the risk of the stand scratching your phone:

_____

Activity 11 – Planning Your Manufacturing – Order of Processes

In the default design, the **hole**, and the corner **arc** around it, share the same centre point.
Explain why it might be better to **cut out the arc before drilling the hole**:

_____

_____

Activity 12 – Planning Your Manufacturing - Safety

Identify a **safety precaution** you should take when **handling sheet metal**:

_____

Activity 13 - Manufacturing

Manufacture your phone / tablet stand now

See additional Metal Cutting Tools on Page 110

If required, see Metal Bending tools on Page 132

Post-Manufacture Evaluation

Activity 14 – Safety Assessment

Identify any **hazards** you were exposed to while manufacturing your phone / tablet stand. Identify two **safety precautions** you took to minimise your **risk**.

Safety hazards: _____

_____

Precautions taken: _____

_____

Research Activities

Activity 15 – Materials Research - Production of Metals

Research the following topics and write your answers below:

(1) Explain what **ore** is: _____

_____

(2) Explain what a **mine** is: _____

_____

(3) Name two current or former **mines in Ireland**, and the **metals** mined there:

(a) Mine: _____   Metal: _____

(b) Mine: _____   Metal: _____

(4) At the industrial refinery plant based **in Aughinish**, County Clare:

(a) What type of **ore** is taken in? _____

(b) What **output material** is produced? _____

(c) What **metal** is the this output used to produce? _____

Activity 16 – Technology Research - Mobile Phones

Research images on the internet that show the evolution of **mobile phones** from the first commercially available in 1983 to today. Research further to answer the following:

1. Who invented the first **telephone**? Include 3 important facts about this **inventor**.

   Inventor: _____

   Facts: _____

   _____

2. Do you consider a modern mobile phone to be **mechatronic** device? **Justify** your answer.

   _____

   _____

3. **Compare** and contrast **early** mobile phones with **current** mobile phones.

   (Hints: shape, size, weight, aesthetics, functionality, cost, battery life, environmental impact)

   _____

   _____

   _____

   _____

   _____

   _____

4. **Evaluate** the positive and negative **impacts** that mobile phones have had on **society**:

   Positive: _____

   _____

   _____

   Negative: _____

   _____

Project Assessment

Student Self-Assessment

In this project, I gained the following new **skills** and **knowledge**:

1. _____

2. _____

3. _____

I **evaluate** my project to have turned out well in the following areas:

_____

_____

If I were to manufacture this project again, I would **modify** or **improve** the following aspects:

_____

_____

_____

On a scale of 1 to 10, I would give my project a **score** of...

Peer Assessment

Identify two manufacturing **processes** you think were carried out to a **high standard** on this project:

1. _____

_____

2. _____

_____

Identify any manufacturing or design **skills** your peer could **improve** upon:

_____

_____

_____

_____

_____

Teacher Feedback on Student Project

Teacher comments on student's project:

| Not Graded | Partially Achieved | Achieved | Merit | Higher Merit | Distinction |

Learning Topics for Unit 5

Processes and Principles

Materials

More Material Properties

The properties listed below relate to all materials, but can be especially relevant to **metals**.

Property	Description	Examples
PLASTICITY	• **Plasticity** means how much a material can be permanently deformed before it breaks • Plasticity is different from **elasticity**. With plasticity the material does **not** return to its original shape, with elasticity it does • Plasticity is where **plastics** got their name from – when you heat thermoplastics, they deform hugely without breaking and form a new shape • Plasticity is also applied to **metals**. There are two types of plasticity that are usually applied to metals:	
	DUCTILITY — A **ductile** material **will stretch a lot** under a tensile (pulling) force.	*Copper, Aluminium*
	MALLEABILITY — A **malleable** material **will flatten easily** under a **compressive (squashing) force.**	*Gold, Silver*
ELECTRICAL CONDUCTIVITY	**Electrical conductivity means how easily electricity flows through the material.** Materials that do not conduct electricity well are called **electrical insulators.** • **Metals** are good electrical **conductors** • **Plastics** and **ceramics** are good electrical **insulators**	*Conductors = metals* *Insulators = plastics, ceramics*

Property	Description	Examples
THERMAL CONDUCTIVITY	**Thermal conductivity** means **how easily heat flows through the material.** Materials that do not conduct electricity well are called **thermal insulators.** • **Metals** are good thermal **conductors** • **Plastics** and **ceramics** are good thermal **insulators**	*Conductors = metal* *Insulators = plastics, ceramics*
CORROSION RESISTANCE	**Corrosion resistance** means how well a material can withstand **damage** caused by **oxidising** (rusting), or other **chemical reactions** of the **surface of the material** with the environment.	*Corrosion-resistant = Stainless steel* *Damaged by corrosion = Iron and steel*

*Other properties relevant to metals that we met in Unit 3 are: **strength, brittleness, hardness, elasticity**.*

Metals

WHAT ARE METALS?

- Metals are **hard**, **strong**, **shiny** materials
- Metals are extracted from **rocks** and minerals through **mining**
- Metals are **good conductors** of heat and electricity
- Metals can be **shaped** by heat and force
- Metals are **recyclable** (e.g. by melting them down)
- The term 'metal' is often loosely used to mean/include **alloys** as well *(see below)*

Classification of Metals

Metals can be divided into **three categories**:

1. Ferrous Metals - ferrous metals **contain iron**

2. Non-Ferrous Metals   - non-ferrous metals **do not contain iron**

3. **Alloys** - alloys are **mixtures of metals and other elements**, created to improve their properties

This unit looks at **non-ferrous metals** and alloys. Unit 8 looks at **ferrous metals** and alloys (i.e. iron and steel) and how they are produced.

General Properties of Non-Ferrous Metals and Alloys

NON-FERROUS METALS	NON-FERROUS ALLOYS
• **Do not contain iron** • **Do not corrode** (or corrode very slowly) • Are **non-magnetic** • Relatively **low melting** points • **More expensive** than ferrous metals • e.g. **Aluminium, copper, gold, silver, lead, zinc, tin**	• Made by **melting** a non-ferrous metal with another non-ferrous metal or element • Alloys can have **better properties** than pure metals – they may be **harder**, **stronger**, or more **resistant to corrosion** • Examples: **Brass, Bronze, Solder**

Non-Ferrous Metals

Metal	Properties	Applications	Image
ALUMINIUM	• Light • Non-toxic • Resistant to corrosion • Good conductor of heat	• **Aircraft** bodies • Food and drink **cans** • Cooking: **aluminium foil**, **pots** • Window and door frames	
COPPER	• Conducts electricity & heat • Ductile • Non-corrosive in water	• Electrical **wires** • Water **pipes**, plumbing • **Cookware**	
ZINC	• Resistant to corrosion	• **Roof panels**: zinc-coated steel prevents corrosion	
LEAD	• Soft, malleable • Dense, heavy • Low melting point • Resistant to corrosion • Toxic	• **Roof flashings** (easily moulded by hand) • **Shielding** against X-rays • **Car batteries** • Weight for ship **keels**	
TIN	• Soft, low melting point • Non-corroding • Non-toxic	• Coats **steel** to make **tinplate**, for food and drink cans • Alloys with **lead** to form **solder**	
TUNGSTEN	• Very high melting point • Hard, dense	• **Alloys for cutting tools**: tungsten carbide, high-speed steel • **Light bulb filaments**	
TITANIUM	• Extremely light, strong • Very corrosion resistant • Bio-compatible • Expensive	• **Aircraft parts**, jet engines • **Medical implants** - artificial bones, staples, stents • **Prosthetic limbs**	
CHROMIUM	• Very shiny • Does not corrode	• Alloys with steel to form **stainless steel** • Coats steel to form **chrome**	
SILVER, GOLD	• Do not corrode, shiny • Good conductors of electricity	• **Jewellery**, ornaments • High-quality **electrical connections**	

Non-Ferrous Alloys

Copper-Based Alloys

Alloy	Composition	Description	Applications	Image
BRASS	**Copper** **Zinc**	• **Resistant to corrosion** • **Ductile** and easy to work • **Decorative**	• Electrical fittings • Plumbing fittings • Hinges, screws • Musical instruments	
BRONZE	**Copper** **Tin**	• **Stronger** and **harder** than brass • Resistant to corrosion	• Statues • Propellers • Valves	

Other Non-Ferrous Alloys

Alloy	Composition	Description	Applications	Image
SOFT SOLDER	**Tin** (60%) **Lead** (40%)	• **Low melting point** • Good **electrical conductivity**	• Making **electrical connections** *(See Unit 6)*	
LEAD-FREE SOLDER	**Tin** (95%) **Silver** (4%) **Copper** (1%)	• Low melting point • Good electrical conductivity • **No toxic lead**	• Has replaced soft solder • Wave soldering in electronics factories	

Recycling of Metals and Alloys

- **Metals** can be **recycled easily**, by melting them down. This is a major **environmental benefit**
- A large proportion of all **steel** is made from **recycled iron and steel** *(see Unit 8)*
- **Gold**, **silver**, **copper**, **brass, zinc** and **lead** are expensive so they are generally recycled

Semiconductors

- **Semiconductors** are a set of pure materials **(elements)** that **conduct electricity poorly**
  (Elements are substances that cannot be broken down chemically into simpler substances)
- The have properties that **fall between conductors** *(e.g. metals)* **and insulators** *(e.g. plastics).*
- **Silicon** is the most commonly available, and most commonly used semiconductor material
- Semiconductors are very important materials because they are used to make **electronic components**, such as **transistors** - *see Unit 11* - which are in turn used to make **computers, smartphones** and **electronic devices** - *see Unit 12*

Engineering Drawings

Drawing Revision / Practice Activities

Drawing Activity 1

Name the three **views** associated with an orthographic projection:

1. _____   2. _____

3. _____

Drawing Activity 2

Sketch an **elevation** of the book stand looking in the direction of arrow X.

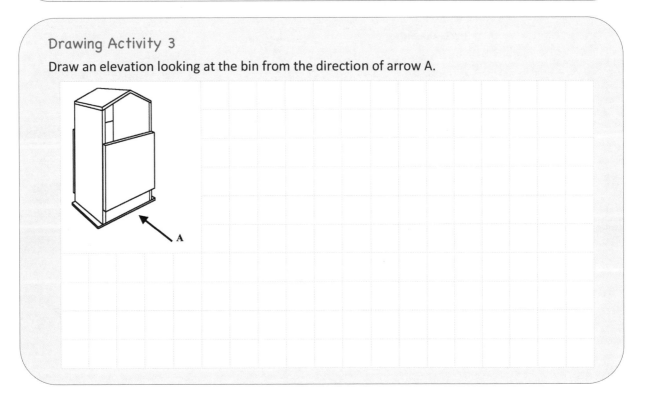

Drawing Activity 3

Draw an elevation looking at the bin from the direction of arrow A.

Drawing Activity 4

Draw a plan (top) view of the object shown.

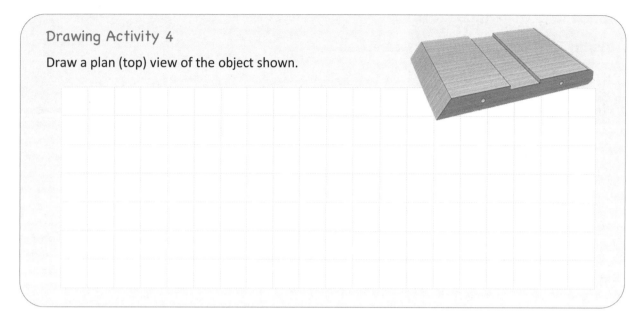

Measuring Equipment

OUTSIDE CALIPERS	• Used to **measure the outside diameter** of a bar or cylinder • Move the legs move in and out by adjusting the **nut.** • The **spring** keeps the calipers open / pressed against the nut • When the curve is at the correct width, place the legs against a **ruler** to read off the measurement    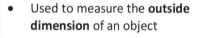
MICROMETER	• Used to measure the **outside dimension** of an object • The **spindle** is tightened onto the workpiece by twisting the **ratchet** which **prevents over-tightening** • The **lock** stops movement while taking the measurement • **Main scale** is on the **sleeve** • **Vernier scale** is on the **thimble** 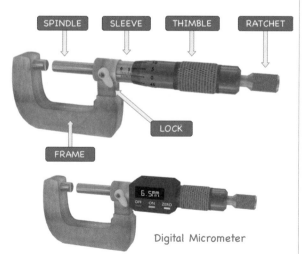 Digital Micrometer 

Main Scale (Sleeve) — Vernier Scale (Thimble)

VERNIER CALIPERS

- A **Vernier Calipers** can be used to measure:

  (1) the **inside diameter of a hole** - open the **internal jaws** until they hit the internal edges

  (2) the **outside diameter of a bar** - close the **external jaws** of the around the object

  (3) **The depth of a hole** - insert the **depth rod** into the hole until it hits the bottom

- The Vernier calipers has a **main scale**, and a **secondary Vernier scale** for greater accuracy (see below)

- Alternatively, there is an **electronic version** with a **digital readout** (see below)

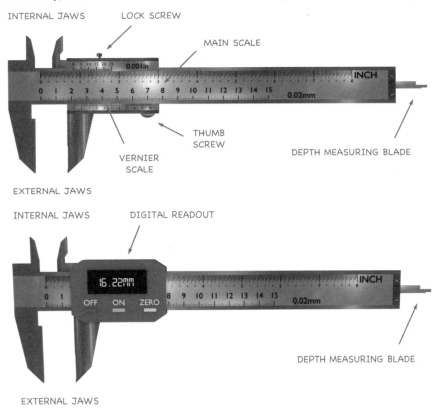

How to Read a Vernier Calipers

1. Read the **largest whole cm** mark to the left of the Vernier scale zero; in this case 2cm / **20mm**

2. Read the largest **whole mm mark** to the left of the Vernier scale zero; in this case **3mm**

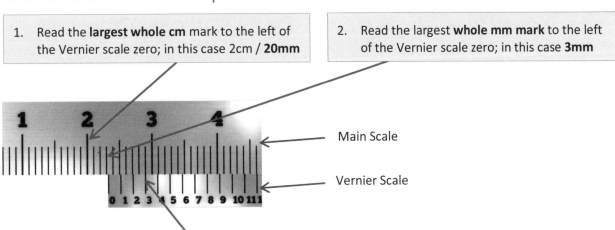

Main Scale

Vernier Scale

3. Read the point where the **Vernier scale matches up with the mm line on the main scale**. This gives the number of tenths of a millimetre; in this case **0.3 mm**

4. **Add** the readings together.

   20mm + 3mm + 0.3mm = **23.3mm**

Metal Cutting Tools

GUILLOTINE	• Strong, **sharp blade** • **Quick** way of cutting sheet metal up to **4.8mm thick** • Operated by a **lever** (long handle) • Generally **mounted to a bench**	

NOTCHER	• Similar to a Guillotine, but used to **cut slots** in a wide variety of metals
	
	• It **does not distort the metal** being cut
	
	• The thickest metal capacity of a notcher is usually:
	  ▪ <u>Non-Ferrous metals</u>: up to **3.2mm**
	  ▪ <u>Mild steel</u>: up to **1.6mm**
	  ▪ <u>Stainless steel</u>: up to **1.4mm**

Hacksaw Blades

Hacksaw blades have a certain number of **teeth per inch / TPI** (1 inch Is 25.4 mm). Fine-tooth blades have a high TPI. Coarse blades have low TPI. In the classroom, blades are usually 24TPI.

> **TPI** stands for the number of **Teeth Per Inch** in a cutting blade

Teeth Per Inch	Suitable for:
14 TPI	Aluminium and other soft metals
18 TPI	General workshop cutting
24 TPI	Steel plate up to 5/6 mm, Plastic, Acrylic
32 TPI	Metal and plastic hollow sections and tubing, Acrylic

Drilling

Recap - refresh your knowledge of drilling by completing the activity below.

Revision Activity – Drilling

Name **two types of chuck** available in the workshop. **Give** one advantage of each.

Type 1 _____ Advantage: _____

Type 2 _____ Advantage: _____

Activity – Research

Who invented the first electric **drill**? Include 3 important facts about the **inventor**(s)

Inventor: _____

Three facts: _____

_____

_____

Drill Hole Types

THROUGH HOLE	• A **through hole** goes all the way through a material - from one side to the other (*A **blind** hole doesn't come out on the other side*) • A **clearance hole** means the hole is larger than the object that fits into the hole 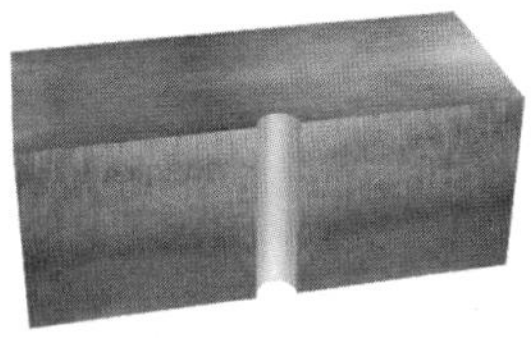
PILOT HOLE	• A **pilot hole** is a **small hole** drilled **before drilling a larger hole** • The pilot hole **guides** the larger drill bit and keeps it **centred** to ensure a symmetrical hole 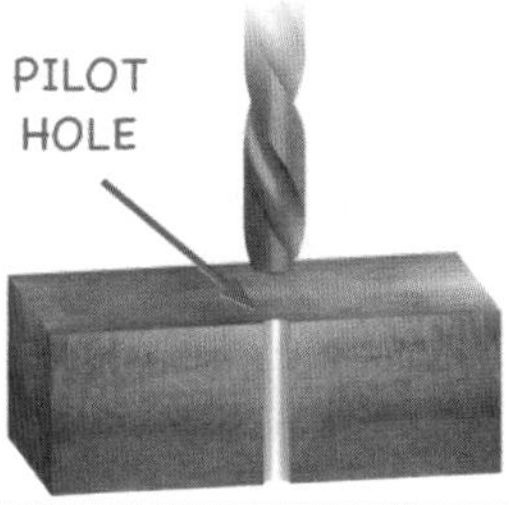

Surface Finishing

Recap - refresh your knowledge of filling by completing the activity below.

Revision Activity – Filing

1. **Explain** briefly what a **needle file** is used for: *(refer to Unit 3 if required)*

_____

2. **Communicate** using notes and sketches below, the difference between a **single-cut file** and a **double-cut file**:

Hand Files

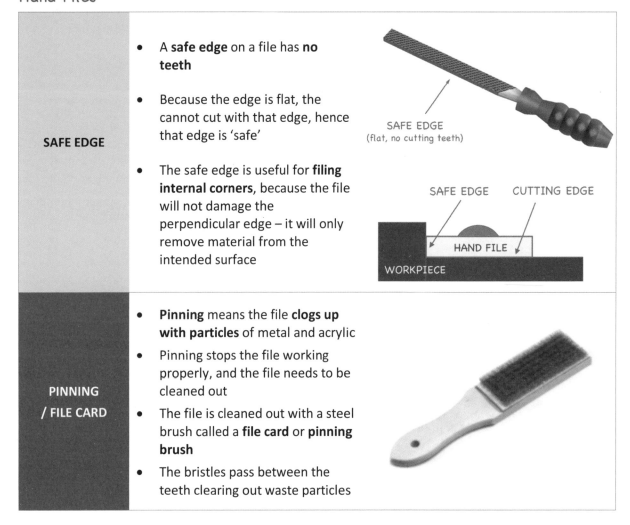

SAFE EDGE	• A **safe edge** on a file has **no teeth** • Because the edge is flat, the cannot cut with that edge, hence that edge is 'safe' • The safe edge is useful for **filing internal corners**, because the file will not damage the perpendicular edge – it will only remove material from the intended surface
PINNING / FILE CARD	• **Pinning** means the file **clogs up with particles** of metal and acrylic • Pinning stops the file working properly, and the file needs to be cleaned out • The file is cleaned out with a steel brush called a **file card** or **pinning brush** • The bristles pass between the teeth clearing out waste particles

Finishing of Aluminium, Copper and Brass

Edge Finishing

Follow these steps to obtain a smooth finish on the edge of aluminium, copper and brass:

FILE	SMOOTHEN	POLISH
Draw file to remove saw-cut and cross-file marks	Use **fine-grade steel wool** to remove draw file marks	Use **WD40** oil with **steel wool**

Surface Finishing

Polishing the **surface** of **aluminium or any non-ferrous metals surface** improves the quality and shine, and can remove tarnish, discolouration and oxidation.

For aluminium, copper and brass, use a metal polish called **Peek**
- Apply Peek sparingly with a clean wet or dry cloth
- Immediately polish to a shine

Mechatronics

Mechanisms

Recap - refresh your knowledge of mechanisms by completing the questions below:

> Revision Questions – Motion and Mechanisms
>
> 1. Name the type of **motion** followed by a **drill bit** when in use: _____
>
> 2. Name the **mechanism** used in a **bench vice**: _____
>
> 3. What **mechanism** would you use to **change the direction or speed of rotary motion**?
>
> _____

Levers

> A **lever** is a **rigid bar** that **pivots** around a fixed point called a **fulcrum**

- Levers are used to **magnify force**
- This occurs when one side of the bar is longer than the other
- A lever is a type of **linkage**.
  We will see more types of linkages later

The following are the important terms with levers:

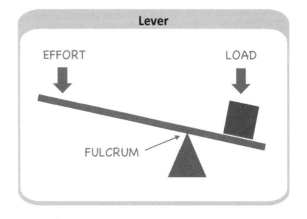

Term	Meaning
EFFORT	- the input force applied to the lever
FULCRUM	- the point that the lever pivots about
LOAD	- the weight that is moved as a result

Classes of Lever

For a lever to work, the fulcrum doesn't always have to be in the middle, and the effort doesn't always have to be at the end. This gives rise to **three classes of levers** shown below.

You can remember these classes by **which element is in the middle** – fulcrum, load or effort.

Class	Picture	Which Element is in the Middle?	Examples
CLASS 1	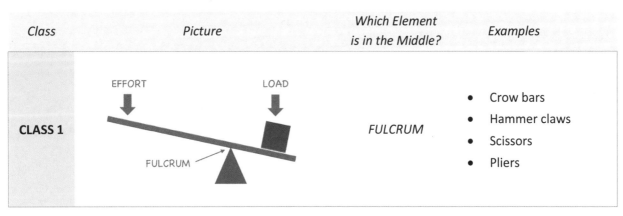	FULCRUM	• Crow bars • Hammer claws • Scissors • Pliers

Class	Picture	Which Element is in the Middle?	Examples
CLASS 2	LOAD FULCRUM EFFORT	*LOAD*	• Wheelbarrow • Paper stapler • Nut crackers • Nail clippers
CLASS 3	LOAD FULCRUM EFFORT	*EFFORT*	• Fishing rod • Shovel • Tweezers • Human arm

Lever Activity 1

Identify the **lever class** of a **guillotine**:

Lever Class: _____

Sketch a simplified side-profile of a guillotine below, and label the **load**, **effort** and **fulcrum**:

Lever Activity 2

(1) Identify the **lever classes** of the tools below.
(2) Indicate using arrows and letters where the **effort**, **fulcrum** and **load** are on each tool:

Class: _____

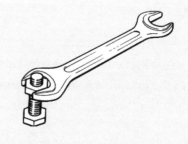

Class: _____

Class: _____

micro:bit Programming

In this section we explore **more things you can do** with the micro:bit.

Note - we are not following online tutorials anymore – **you will need to create programs from scratch**.

Return to your micro:bit Projects Area

- Go to **makecode.microbit.org** on your web browser   *(type in, or select your saved bookmark)*
- Click on '**New Project**', and this will bring you into the **makecode editor**

Recap - refresh your knowledge of micro:bit programming by completing the activity below.

Micro:bit Revision Activity

The picture below shows the **makecode editor** screen, where the micro:bit is **programmed**. **Name** the **three areas** indicated below and explain what they are used for.

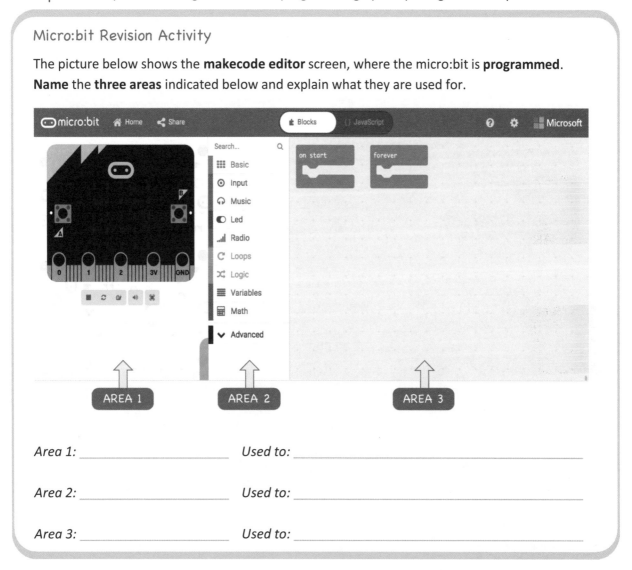

Area 1: _____   Used to: _____

Area 2: _____   Used to: _____

Area 3: _____   Used to: _____

micro:bit Sensors

In the previous unit, we created programs using the micro:bit input **buttons** and output **LEDs**.

In this unit, we will use the micro:bit input **sensors** in our programs, and discover new **code blocks**.

A **sensor** is an **input device** that detects **changes in the environment**
and translates those changes into an **electrical signal**

A common **example** of a sensor is a **microphone** (which detects changes in air pressure), or a **camera** (which detects changes in light intensity and colour).

The **micro:bit** has a number of **in-built sensors**. In this unit, you will explore the **temperature sensor** and the **accelerometer**. The accelerometer detects when the micro:bit moves!

Useful Code Blocks

These code blocks listed below will help you with the programming activities on the next page.

Explore code blocks in your makecode Editor as follows:

- Find the **code block** in the **Toolbox** and drag it into the **Programming Workspace** (usually into a *forever* code block)
- Note the special way that the code blocks are designed to **fit in to each other**
- Change the **parameters** on the code block (i.e. the text or numbers or selections)
- Observe what happens on the micro:bit **simulator**

Code Block	Description
on shake ▾	Found in the **Input** section of the toolbox. Uses the built-in **accelerometer sensor**. • When the micro:bit is **shaken**, any code blocks that are placed inside this code block will be executed • The 'shake' parameter can be changed to select different types of triggering movements, e.g. **tilting** the micro:bit
show string "Hello!" show number 0	Found in the **Basic** section of the **toolbox**: • "**show string**" scrolls the entered **text** across the micro:bit LEDs • "**show number**" scrolls the entered number across the LEDs Example use: if you wanted to display a number when the micro:bit was shaken, you would place the "**show number**" block **inside** the "**on shake**" block
temperature (°C)	Found in the **Input** section of the toolbox: • Returns the **current temperature** in degrees Celsius • To **display** the temperature, place the "**temperature**" block **inside** a "**show number**" block
set score 0 change score by 1	Found in the **Game** section of the toolbox: • "**set score**" sets the current score to the entered number • "**change score**" changes the score by the selected number

rotation (°) pitch ▾	Found in the **Input** section of the toolbox:
	
	• Returns the degrees the micro:bit is tilted from horizontal
	    ○ "**pitch**" refers to the tilt between top and bottom edges
	    ○ "**roll**" refers to the tilt between left and right edges

Programming Activities

Carry out the programming activities below, using the code blocks on the previous page to help you. Test on the micro:bit makecode website first, then download to your micro:bit if you have one. Track your progress in the table at the bottom.

Programming Activity 1 – Name and Age
Create a program to **display** your **name** and your **age** in the LEDs.

Programming Activity 2 – Name and Age on Buttons
Modify the program above so that pressing **button A** displays your **name**, and pressing **button B** displays your **age**.

Programming Activity 3 – Hello from a Shake!
Create a program to display "**Hello**" followed by your **name** when the micro:bit is **shaken**

Programming Activity 4 – Temperature and Emoji
   a) Create a program to display the room **temperature** when **button A** is pressed
   b) Update the program to display an **emoji** shape when **button B** is pressed.

Programming Activity 5 – What's the Score?
Create a program to display an **initial score** of 0, **increase** the score by 1 whenever **button A** is pressed, **decrease** by 1 when **button B** is pressed, and **reset** to 0 if **A and B** are pressed together.

Programming Activity 6 – What's my Angle?
Display the **degree of rotation** when you **tilt** the micro:bit. Test it out.

Track your programming progress by ticking in the appropriate boxes below:

No	Activity	Too Difficult	Partially Completed	Completed
1	Name and Age			
2	Name and Age on Buttons			
3	Hello from a Shake			
4	Temperature and Emoji			
5	What's the Score?			
6	What's my Angle?			

Unit ⑤ Revision

1. Explain the difference between a conductor and an insulator.

2. Name two materials that are good conductors and two of materials that are good insulators.

3. Describe the term corrosion resistance in relation to metals.

4. Explain what is meant by a non-ferrous metal.

5. Name three non-ferrous metals and give one application for each one.

6. Identify one key application for the non-ferrous metal zinc.

7. Explain the term alloy.

8. Name two copper-based alloys and give one application for each.

9. Name the metals required to make solder.

10. Name one location where mining occurs in Ireland.

11. Explain the three type of measurements that can be carried out using a Vernier Calipers.

12. Describe the differences between the manufacturing equipment guillotine and a notcher.

13. Explain the term TPI in relation to hacksaw blades.

14. Explain the purpose of a pilot hole. Draw a sketch of this type of hole.

15. Describe using sketches the purpose of a safe edge on a file.

16. Describe the term pinning in relation to files.

17. Explain how to get a smooth finish on an aluminium edge.

18. What is Peek used for?

19. Explain what a lever is, and what levers are typically used for.

20. Complete the table below:

Class of Lever	Which element is in the middle: the fulcrum, load or effort?
1	
2	
3	

21. (i) Explain the term semiconductor.
    (ii) Name one type of semiconductor material.
    (iii) Name one component made from a semiconductor material.

Unit 6 – LED Photo Frame

Unit Objectives

PROJECT	Design and manufacture a **photo frame** that can hold and **illuminate** a photo

- Learn to create a **multi-part**, **multi-material** project that includes **electronics**
- Learn **mechanical and adhesive joining** processes and how to **cut and bend metal**
- Learn about **resistors**, **LED circuits**, and **circuit assembly** processes like **soldering**
- Learn how to use **control external LEDs** using a **micro:bit**
- Provide opportunities to **research modern technological developments** and **mechatronics**

Content

PROCESSES AND PRINCIPLES	Cutting	• Tin snips
	Drilling	• Countersinking and counterboring, pilot holes
	Bending	• Folding bars, Bending machine
	Joining	• Mechanical Fasteners: nut, bolts, washers • Fastening Tools: wrenches, pliers, vice grips • Adhesive Joining
DESIGN APPLICATION		• Designing a project with multiple parts and different materials • Integrating electronics with mechanical parts
MECHATRONICS	Electronics	• Resistors, LEDs, Series & Parallel Circuits • Breadboards, Soldering
	micro:bit	• Programming the Input and Output Pins

Learning Outcomes from this Unit

PROCESSES AND PRINCIPLES	DESIGN APPLICATION	MECHATRONICS
1.1, 1.2, 1.3, 1.4, 1.5, 1.7, 1.8, 1.9, 1.10, 1.11, 1.12, 1.13	2.3, 2.8, 2.9, 2.11, 2.12	3.4, 3.5, 3.6

Suggested Timeframes

START TIME	YEAR 1	January		DURATION	6 weeks

Working Drawings

Default Design

Frame

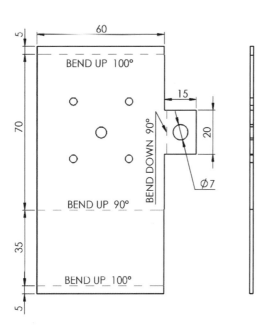

Backplate

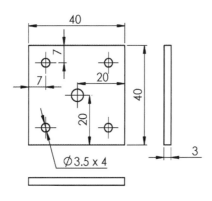

LED Holder

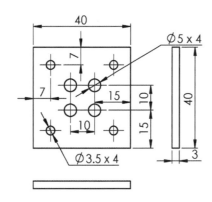
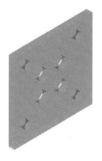

TITLE	Unit 6 – Photo Frame	SHEET 1 OF 4
DESCRIPTION	Default Design	Brighter Minds

Default Design continued

Exploded View

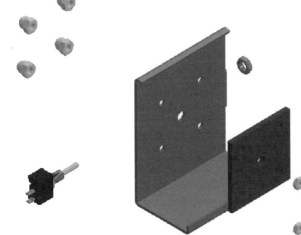

ITEM	PART	DESCRIPTION	QTY.
1	MAIN FRAME	1.5mm COPPER	1
2	BACK PLATE	3mm ACRYLIC	1
3	LED HOLDER	3mm ACRYLIC	1
4	BOLTS	M3 X 30 PAN HEAD	4
5	NUTS	M3 Hex Nut	8
6	CAP NUTS	M3 Cap Nut	4
7	TOGGLE SWITCH	SPST with Screw Fitting	1
8	LEDS	5mm LEDS with BUSHINGS	4
9	RESISTOR	330 OHM	1
10	9V BATTERY	WITH SNAP CONNECTOR	1
11	BATTERY HOLDER	To Be Designed By Student	1

Circuit Diagram

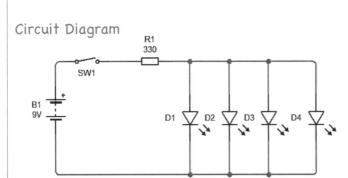

Assembled View

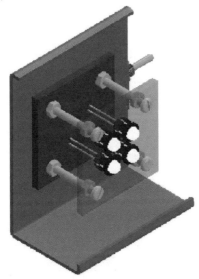

The paper photo is mounted in front of the LEDs, bent slightly and held at the top and bottom edges by the copper flanges

TITLE	Unit 6 – Photo Frame	SHEET 2 OF 4
DESCRIPTION	Default Design	Brighter Minds

Your Concept Sketches (Follow the Project Storyboard Activities before attempting these)

TITLE	Unit 6 – Photo Frame	SHEET 3 OF 4
DESCRIPTION	Concept Design Sketches	Brighter Minds

Your Final Frame Design (Follow the Project Storyboard activities)

TITLE	Unit 6 – Photo Frame	SHEET 4 OF 4
DESCRIPTION	Final Frame Design Drawing	Brighter Minds

Project Storyboard

Project Description

- Your project is a **photo frame** which contains **LEDs** that **light up** your photo from behind
- This photo frame project works best if you print your image on **back-lit paper**
- The default design photo frame consists of **three parts**:

    (1) An acrylic **LED holder**, which holds 4 LEDs

    (2) An acrylic **backplate**, which attaches to the frame and support the LED holder

    (3) The **main frame** – you may create your own design, or use our default design

- The three parts are **joined** with nuts and bolts as shown in the drawings
- The LEDs are powered by a **9V battery** and current is limited by a 330Ω (ohm) **resistor**

DESIGN OPPORTUNITIES IN THIS PROJECT   *Follow the design activities provided in this unit*

- You need to design a way to **hold the 9V battery**
- You may **design your own frame**, keeping the default LED holder and backplate
- You could choose a **different material** for your frame
- You could use a **micro:bit** to power the LEDs   - *See programming section at end of this unit*
- You could use a **USB connector** to power the LEDs from your computer *(details not provided)*

DESIGN CONSTRAINTS / REQUIREMENTS FOR YOUR FRAME DESIGN

- Your frame should be capable of **holding a photo** in front of the LED holder part
- Keep the same size and spacing of the **5 holes** that are shown on the default design frame
- The material for your frame should be **between 1.5mm and 2mm thick**
- You could base your design on a **theme**, e.g. music, sports, or a specific event or person
- Your design should include the supply of power / storage of **battery**

Project Analysis and Design Activities

Activity 1 – Understanding Circuit Diagrams

1. What does **L.E.D.** stand for?

_____

2. **Sketch** the symbol for an LED:

3. **Why** do you think **LEDs** were chosen for this project rather than **bulbs**?   See p.140

_____

4. What is the **name** / acronym of the **type of switch** that has **two connections** and can be used to **turn on and off** electrical current?

See p.81

5. **Sketch** the symbol for this switch:

_____

Activity 2 – Understanding Circuit Diagrams

1. **Tick** the relevant box to indicate which way the **LEDs are connected** in the **circuit diagram** in the working drawings:

In Series ☐   In Parallel ☐

See page 141

2. **Explain** what the **dashed lines** mean on the working drawing of the **main photo frame**:

_____

Activity 3 – Requirements Analysis

1. The **size of your photo** is a key factor in the design of your photo frame.
Research and write the **dimensions** of the photo you wish to hold in the frame below:

Photo dimensions: _____

2. In preparation for design sketches later, **research** and **explore** different ways that a frame could be used to **hold a paper photo**.

Activity 3 – Design Planning

Decide and tick which option you will be using to **power the LEDs** on your photo frame:

(1) Using a **9V battery** and **switch** ☐   <u>OR</u>   (2) Using **2 AA batteries** and a **micro:bit** ☐

Activity 4a – Design Battery Holder

If you are powering the LEDs with a 9V battery, **explore** two different ways of **attaching the 9V battery** to the main photo frame. **Demonstrate** how the 9V battery will be attached to the frame in your <u>design sketches</u> (see next page).

- The **dimensions** of the 9V battery are: H 48 mm × L 25 mm × W 15 mm

- *Hint 1:* you could think about an (non-permanent) **adhesive** solution

- *Hint 2:* you could think about a **housing**-style solution at the back of the frame, where you already have some existing holes & bolts that might be re-usable

Activity 4b – Design micro:bit Holder

If you are using a **micro:bit** to control the LEDs, **explore** how you will **attach the micro:bit** (and its 2 AA batteries) to the main photo frame. **Demonstrate** how the micro:bit will be attached to the frame in your <u>design sketches</u> (see next page).

- The **dimensions** of the micro:bit board are W 52mm x H 43mm

- *Hint 1:* you could think about using the **large holes** on the micro:bit board

- *Hint 2:* you could think about using two pieces of **acrylic** to allow the micro:bit board to slide in and out

Activity 5 - Concept Designs

On the 'Concept Sketches' page in the working drawings, using free-hand, sketch three different concept design ideas for your photo frame. Practice your design ideas on separate paper if you wish first, before transferring to the book.

- Remember the dimensions of your photo, and how it might be held in a frame
- Remember that the LEDs need to shine through the photo paper
- Don't forget the 5 holes that are needed to attach the LED holder and backplate parts
- Remember to incorporate a holder for battery and switch, or a micro:bit board

Activity 6 - Prototyping

1. Choose your favourite concept design for the main photo frame component and make a cardboard prototype of it.

2. Evaluate your cardboard prototype as to how well it can (a) hold the photo and (b) incorporate the other parts needed. Ask your teacher or peers to review it.
Were any modifications needed? If so, list them below, and re-design your frame.

Modifications needed: _____

_____

Activity 7 - Final Design

1. In the 'Final Frame Design' area of the working drawings, accurately draw the final design for the frame part of your photo frame, including a way to hold the battery / batteries.

- You may reproduce the default design or choose your own design.
- Include all dimensions and bend lines and label parts as required
- Include drawings for any separate parts required for the battery or micro:bit holder

2. Justify why you chose this design to manufacture: _____

_____

Activity 8 - Materials

Research the suitability of copper as a material for the photo frame. List your 3 key findings:

(a) _____

(b) _____

(c) _____

Activity 9 – Choosing a Material

Choose a **material** for **your photo frame**. Give **two reasons** for your choice:

Material: _____

Reason 1: _____

Reason 2: _____

Manufacturing Activities

Activity 10 – Planning the Manufacture of Parts 1 and 2

1. The **holes** for the LEDs on the acrylic are marked Ø8. What does **Ø8** mean?

_____

2. What **type of hole** should you drill first in order **not to crack the acrylic**?

_____

3. Describe other **actions** you can take to **prevent acrylic cracking** when being **drilled**:

_____

3. Name a piece(s) of **equipment** you could use to **bend acrylic** if needed:

_____

Activity 11 – Manufacture Parts 1 and 2

Mark out and **manufacture** the **acrylic LED holder** and **backplate** parts now

(Teacher Note: If progress is slow due to low numbers of drills, CAM files are available online for laser cutter)

Activity 12 – Planning the Manufacture of Part 3

The **5 holes** on the main **frame** part are **not dimensioned** on the default design drawing. The holes on the main frame could be difficult to mark out or drill accurately **until the backplate is made**. Explain why you think this is - why the 5 holes on the main frame were not dimensioned:

_____

_____

Activity 13 – Planning the Manufacture of Part 3

Explain how you can use the **backplate** to **mark out** the positions of the holes on the **main frame**, so that the holes are centred on the main frame:

_____

_____

Activity 14 – Manufacture Part 3

Mark out and **manufacture** the **main frame** part(s) now (including battery / micro:bit holder)

Metal Cutting pages 110, 130

Metal Bending, page 132

Activity 15 – Mechanically Assemble the Parts

Assemble your photo frame:

See Joining, pages 132-137

- Assemble the **LEDs** into the **LED holder plate** using the plastic LED sleeves

- Assemble the **LED holder plate**, **backplate** and **main frame** using the **bolts** and **nuts**

Activity 16 – Planning the Electrical Assembly

Assembling Circuits p.142-144

1. What **joining technique** will you use to make the **electrical connections**?

_____

2. Identify the **alloy** used to make **permanent electrical connections**. Give one key **property** of this alloy.

Alloy: _____

Property: _____

3. Which **leg** of the **LED** needs to be connected to the **negative side of the battery**?

_____

Activity 17 – Assemble the Electronics and Test

Assemble your **electrical circuit** and **test** the operation of your photo frame.

See Soldering on Page 144.
Micro:bit Programming p.149

If using a micro:bit, create and download your program to the micro:bit.

Project Assessment

Student Self-Assessment

In this project, I gained the following new **skills** and **knowledge**:

1. _____

2. _____

3. _____

I **evaluate** my project to have **turned out well** in the following areas:

_____

_____

If I were to carry out this project again, I would **modify** or **improve** the following aspects:

_____

_____

_____

_____

On a scale of 1 to 10, I would give my project a **score** of...

Peer Assessment

Identify **manufacturing processes** that were carried out to a **high standard**:

_____

_____

_____

Identify **manufacturing skills** or **design skills** your peer could **improve** upon:

_____

_____

_____

Teacher Feedback on Project

Teacher comments on student's project:

Not Graded	Partially Achieved	Achieved	Merit	Higher Merit	Distinction

Learning Topics for Unit ⑥

Processes and Principles

Cutting

Sheet Metal Cutting

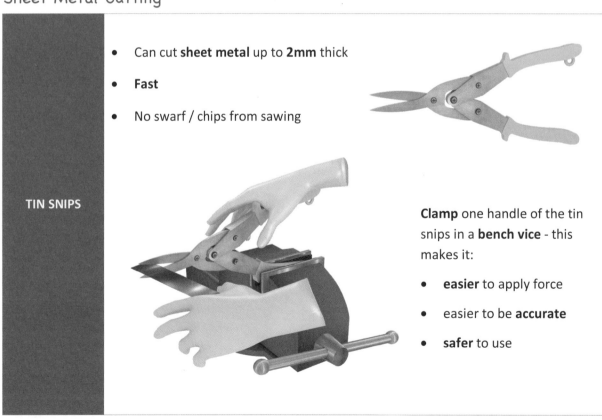

TIN SNIPS

- Can cut **sheet metal** up to **2mm** thick
- **Fast**
- No swarf / chips from sawing

Clamp one handle of the tin snips in a **bench vice** - this makes it:

- **easier** to apply force
- easier to be **accurate**
- **safer** to use

Drilling

More Drill Bits and Hole Types

Countersinking and **counterboring** are used to **hide / embed** the heads of screws and bolts in the material, creating a **flush** surface with no fasteners jutting out.

COUNTER SINKING	• **Counter-sinking** means using a **countersink bit** to drill a **CONICAL shape** at the top of a previously-drilled hole • This creates a **countersunk hole** • This allow conical **countersunk screws** or **conical bolt heads** to sit into the cone shape • This keeps the screw/bolt heads **flush** with the material surface • Mainly used for **decorative** purposes
COUNTER BORING	• **Counter-boring** means using a **counterbore bit** to drill a larger-diameter **STRAIGHT hole** at the top of a previously-drilled hole • This allows **round-head** or **cheese-head screws / bolts** to sit into the material, flush with the surface
STEP DRILL BIT	• The width of a **step drill bit** increases in steps • This allows you to drill many **different hole sizes** with just **one bit** • Works well on **thin materials**

Bending Sheet Metal

BENDING MACHINE (BOX & PAN FOLDER)	• **Manual** metal bending machine • Can bend sheet metal **accurately** • Can bend metal **up to 2.5mm thick** • Can bend **up to 120°** 
FOLDING BARS	• The folding bars are made from a **single piece** of mild steel - so the bars **spring together** and hold themselves on the workpiece • Place the sheet metal **between the bars** • Align the top of the bar with the **bend line** • **Clamp** the bars in a **bench vice** • Bend the metal over the bars / bend line using a **ball pein hammer** and a **piece of wood** - to prevent marking the metal surface 

Joining

Temporary and Permanent Joints

TEMPORARY JOINTS	PERMANENT JOINTS
• **Can be dismantled** with a little effort • Used to join parts that may need to be **disassembled** for maintenance or replacement • Can withstand **moderate** pressure and vibrations	• Cannot be dismantled without **damaging** the joint • Used for parts that are expected to **stay assembled** • Can **withstand high pressure** and vibrations
EXAMPLES OF TEMPORARY JOINTS	**EXAMPLES OF PERMANENT JOINTS**
• Screws • Nut and Bolts	• Adhesives • Rivets, Pop Rivets • Soldering and Welding

Joining Methods

MECHANICAL JOINING	Temporary. Some types can be Permanent	• Uses **mechanical fasteners** to pull and hold parts together • Mechanical fasteners are things like **screws**, **nuts**, **bolts**
ADHESIVE JOINING	Permanent	• **Chemically bonds** the materials together using **adhesive**
SOFT SOLDERING	Permanent	• Bonds **metals** together using a layer of **molten filler alloy** called **solder**

Mechanical Joining – Screws, Nuts and Bolts

SELF - TAPPING SCREWS	**Self-tapping screws cut their own thread** in the material. They usually require a starting **pilot hole**. They can be used to join **thin metal or plastic sheets**.	*Self-tapping screw*
BOLTS and MACHINE SCREWS	**Machine screws** are threaded cylindrical rods. They are used in two ways: 1. They are passed through **pre-drilled clearance hole**s in the parts to be joined and fastened to a **nut** on the other side. In this use, they are often called **bolts**. 2. They screw into a matching **internal thread in the part** to be joined. Machine screws come in variety of **sizes**, **thread types** and **head shapes**: square, slotted, countersunk, round, cheese head, Philips head, and hexagonal socket. *Bolts are generally named like **M4 x 30*** *where M4 is the external diameter of the thread in mm, and 30 is the length of the bolt in mm.*	*Hex nut and bolt* *Round head, slot drive* *Hexagonal socket screw* *CSK Bolt – Flat / Philips head, posidrive*
GRUB SCREW	A **grub screw** has **no head** (just threaded shank)	Useful for small discreet screws
NUT	A **nut** threads on to a matching bolt or machine screw to tighten on the parts between the nut and a bolt head. A **hex nut** has a **hexagonal** (6-sided) shape.	*Hex nut*
CAP NUT / DOME HEAD	A **cap nut** is used to to cover an external thread. It ensures that the thread does not get damaged. It is more aesthetically pleasing than a hex nut.	*Cap nut*
WING NUT	A **wing nut** is a nut with a pair of wings that allow it to be **easily tightened and loosened by hand**.	Wing nut

Components to Prevent Loosening of Nuts, Create Better Seals

LOCK NUT	• Tighten a **second nut** onto the first nut • This creates **extra friction** that is harder to overcome	LOCK NUT FIRST NUT
SELF-LOCKING LOCK NUT	• A **self-locking nut** has **nylon insert** or sleeve • The screw **cuts into** the nylon insert • The nylon insert provides **greater friction** and **reduces the impact of vibrations**	NYLON INSERT
WASHERS	A **washer** is a small flat metal, rubber, or plastic **ring** placed between a nut or screw head and the material being joined. A washer: • **spreads the load** over a wider area • can act as **seal** to prevent liquid or gas coming through the joint • prevents the nut or screw head **scratching the surface** of the material • **keep additional pressure on the nut** after tightening, to help prevent it becoming loose	*Plain washer* *Split / Spring washer* *Rubber seal washer*

Fastening Tools

These tools are used to **tighten mechanical fasteners** such as screws, nuts and bolts.

SCREWDRIVER	A **screwdriver** is used to tighten and loosen screws and bolts. They come in a variety of head shapes - flat, philips, posidrive, hex etc - to fit the corresponding type of screw / bolt. *Philips head* *Flat head*	
ALLEN KEYS	**Allen Keys** are used to tighten / loosen Allen hexagonal head bolts They come in a wide range of sizes	
PLIERS	**Pliers** are used to hold objects firmly in place for various tasks, such as: • holding a nut while its bolt is being tightened • bending sheet metal Pliers can also be used to snip wires to size	

More Fastening Tools

LONG-NOSE PLIERS	**Long-nose pliers** have long jaws which can reach into tight spaces that other pliers cannot.
COMBINATION SPANNER (or WRENCH)	**Combination spanners** usually have an **open wrench** at one end and a **ring spanner** at the other end, as shown. Used to tighten and loosen nuts or bolts that have **hexagonal** heads.
SOCKET WRENCH	A **socket wrench** fits over the nut completely. You can buy socket sets where you can fit different socket sizes on to the same shank.
ADJUSTABLE SPANNER (or WRENCH)	An **adjustable spanner** is an open-end spanner with **jaws** that can be moved closer together or further apart by turning the **worm wheel.**
VICE GRIPS	A **vice grip** is a type of **locking pliers**. The nut on the straight handle can be adjusted to open the jaws for gripping larger diameters object.

Activity – Fastening Tools as Mechanisms

Revision Activity – Lever Mechanisms

(a) Pick one of the **fastening tools** listed above that you think is an example of a **lever**:

Name of Tool: _____

(b) Draw a small free-hand **sketch** of your selected tool, and label the **fulcrum**, **load** and **effort**:

Sketch:

(c) Circle which **class of lever** this tool belongs to:

Class 1   *Class 2*   *Class 3*

Adhesive Joining

Adhesives create a **chemical bond** between surfaces. Adhesives are a type of **permanent joining**.

ADVANTAGES of ADHESIVES	DISADVANTAGES of ADHESIVES
• Can **bond different types of materials**	• Some adhesives need **time to set** (cure)
• **Strong. Spreads the load** over a wide area	• You need to **prepare surfaces**
• Can **seal a joint** against air and liquids	• Very **difficult to disassemble**
• **Visually attractive** – no ugly fasteners or joints	• Bond can weaken at **high temperatures**

Safety Precautions with Adhesives

SAFETY HAZARDS / RISKS	SAFETY PRECAUTIONS
• Risk of damage to **skin** and **eye damage**	• Wear **safety goggles, fume mask** and **gloves**
• **Breathing** or respiratory issues from fumes	• Work in a **well-ventilated area**

Some Common Types of Adhesives

Type	Application	Description	
TWO-PART EPOXY GLUES	**Metals** and **Plastics** (thermoset & thermoplastic)	**High-strength** adhesive, comprising two parts: **Resin** and **Hardener.** When the parts mix, they react chemically and start to cure • **Takes some time to cure** • Can handle **extreme conditions**	
SUPERGLUE (cyano-acrylates)	**Most materials** But **NOT** acrylic	• Bonds almost anything • **Low strength** • Good for **small tight-fitting parts** • Turns **acrylic** white • **Dangerous** because so fast setting	
HOT GLUE GUN	**Thermoplastics**	The hot glue gun applies **hot thermoplastic** to the joint area, which melts and bonds to the workpiece plastic. Different types of **plastic rods** can be inserted in the gun • **Quick to apply & to set** • **Low strength**	
LIQUID SOLVENT CEMENT / ACRYLIC CEMENT	**Thermoplastics** like **Acrylic** and ABS	• Surfaces must be **very flat** or matching • Solvent is drawn between the surfaces by capillary action • Looks like water • Dissolves and **fuses** the pieces together • Creates a **welded** plastic **clear** joint	

REQUIREMENTS FOR A GOOD ADHESIVE JOINT	
✓ **Design the joint shape** to be structurally strong in all directions	✓ Surface must be **clean**, and free from oil, grease, water and dust
✓ **Maximize the surface area contact** between the parts	
✓ Choose the **correct adhesive** for the materials	✓ Use a **degreaser**
✓ Use a fine **sandpaper** to give surfaces a slightly **rough finish**	✓ Allow enough **time to cure**

Comparison of Mechanical and Adhesive Joining

	ADVANTAGES	DISADVANTAGES
MECHANICAL JOINING Screws, Nuts, Bolts	• Can be **disassembled** • **Cheap**, easy	• Can become **loose** • Holes must be **drilled**
ADHESIVE JOINING Glues	• Can join **different materials** • **invisible joints** • **Doesn't deform** the parts • Can **seal** a joint	• Needs **surface preparation**, takes **time to cure** • Can't be **disassembled** • Poor at **high temperature**

Mechatronics

Electronics

Recap - refresh your knowledge of **electronics** from previous units by completing the questions below:

Revision Questions - Electronics

1. Name and sketch the symbol for an electronic **device** that converts its input electrical energy into output energy of a different form- such as light, sound or kinetic (movement):

   Device Name: _____   *Symbol:*

2. List three electronic **input devices** and sketch their electronic **symbol**s:

   Device Name: _____   *Symbol:*

   Device Name: _____   *Symbol:*

   Device Name: _____   *Symbol:*

3. **Explain** the following electrical **terms**:

   (i) *Current*: _____

   (ii) *Voltage:* _____

   (iii) *AC:* _____

More Electrical Terms

CIRCUIT	A **circuit** is a **loop** of components that allows **current to flow** A circuit typically contains: • a source of **voltage** - such as a **battery** - to drive the current around • **input** and **output devices** that do useful things **THE 3 STAGES OF A CIRCUIT** **INPUT Stage** — The **input** part of a circuit: • **takes in** information from the **environment**, for example: ○ a **switch** operated by a person or machine ○ a **sensor** component that responds to light or heat • **sends** an electrical **input signal** to the **process** stage **PROCESS Stage** — The **process** part of a circuit: • **amplifies** or **changes the input signal** ○ often uses **transistors** or a **chip** (Integrated Circuit (IC)) • **sends** a **processed electrical signal** to the **output** stage **OUTPUT Stage** — The **output** part of a circuit: • **converts** the processed electrical signal to another form of output energy such as **light**, **heat**, **sound** or **motion** • e.g. the output stage could be a **motor** or **LED** or **speaker**
RESISTANCE	• Electrical **resistance** measures how **difficult** it is for electric current to flow through a material • The **higher** the resistance, the **less current** will flow through the material • Resistance is measured in **Ohms (Ω)** • Resistance in electronic circuits is mainly provided by **resistors** *(see later)* • Resistors are used to control and **limit the current** in a circuit
POWER	• **Power** is the **amount of electrical energy transferred per second** • It is calculated by **multiplying voltage by current** (P = V x I). The units are **Watts**
POLARISED COMPONENT	• A **polarised component** must be connected the **right way around** to work • A polarised component has a **positive** leg and **negative** leg (connection) **EXAMPLES** • **Batteries** – have a positive and a negative connection • **LEDs** - the **long leg** is **positive** and the **short leg** is **negative**
NON-POLARISED COMPONENT	• **Non-polarised** components can be connected **either way round** - they **do not** have positive or negative sides **EXAMPLES** • Wires, Bulbs, Resistors, Speakers

Resistors

> **Resistors** are electronic process components **that reduce the amount of current flowing in a circuit**. The electrical resistance of resistors is measured in **Ohms (Ω)**

WHY ARE RESISTORS USEFUL?

- **Resistors protect electronic components from being damaged by too much current**
  - Electronic components only require a **small amount of current** to function
  - Too much current will **burn them out**

- For example, If you connect a **9V battery** to an **LED** without using a **resistor** in-between, the LED will **burn out** and will not work anymore

- Resistors **set the current to the correct level** required by the component

Types of Resistors

Resistors come in two types: **fixed** and **variable**.

- **Variable resistors** have a screw or knob on them that can be turned to set the resistance
- **Fixed resistors** come in fixed resistance values – see below

<table>
<tr><td>

FIXED RESISTOR

</td><td>

The resistance of a **fixed resistor** can be calculated using the **coloured bands** on the body (referencing the colour table on the right):

- The **1st colour band** tells us the **1st digit** of the resistor value

- The **2nd colour band** tells us the **2nd digit** of the resistor value

- The **3rd colour band** tells us the **number of zeros** that follow

- The **4th colour band** tells us the **tolerance** of the resistance value:

  - A **gold band** tells us the resistance value has a **5% tolerance**, i.e. it is accurate to ±5%

  - A **silver band** tells us the resistance value has a **10% tolerance**, i.e. it is accurate to ±10%

</td><td>

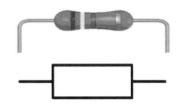

Resistor Band Colour Values:

Black	0
Brown	1
Red	2
Orange	3
Yellow	4
Green	5
Blue	6
Violet	7
Grey	8
White	9

</td></tr>
</table>

Worked Example 1 - Reading Resistor Values

1st band = **brown** → the 1st digit of the resistor value is **1**

2nd band = **black** → the 2nd digit of the resistor value is **0**

3rd band = **red** → the number of zeros that follow is **2**

→ The value of this resistor is **1000Ω**, or **1kΩ**

Worked Example 2 - Reading Resistor Values

1ˢᵗ band = **yellow** → the 1ˢᵗ digit of the resistor value is **4**

2ⁿᵈ band = **violet** → the 2ⁿᵈ digit of the resistor value is **7**

3ʳᵈ band = **brown** → the number of zeros that follow is **1**

→ The value of this resistor is **470Ω**

Electronics Activity 1 – Reading Resistor Values

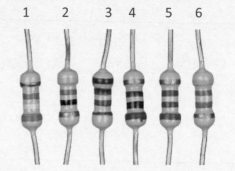

1 2 3 4 5 6

- Calculate the **values of the resistors** pictured (or 6 resistors your teacher gives you)

- Complete the table below

- Remember the gold or silver band is the 4ᵗʰ band

Resistor	3 Colours = Digits 1, 2 and Numbers of Zeros	Calculated Resistance
1	1ˢᵗ = Orange = 3, 2ⁿᵈ = White = 9, 3ʳᵈ = Orange = 3	
2		
3		
4		
5		
6		

More Output Devices - LEDs

LED

- **Light-Emitting Diode**
- Very **energy-efficient**
- Can work with a **low DC voltage**
- Needs very **little current**
- **Polarised** component - must be connected the right way round:
  - **Long Leg** = Positive
  - **Short Leg** = Negative
    (it's also closest to the flat edge)
- **Advantages**: cheap, long-lasting, energy-efficient, brighter than a bulb of the same voltage, choice of colours and sizes

Symbol:

Flat Edge

Short Leg

−

+

Applications:

- Car headlights
- Traffic Lights
- House Lighting
- Camera Flash
- Torches
- Device on/off indicators

Series and Parallel Circuits

Components can be connected in **series** (one after the other) or in **parallel** (one beside the other). Both circuits shown below contain a 9V battery, an SPST switch and three bulbs – except one is wired in series, and the other is wired in parallel. Let's explore the differences.

SERIES CIRCUIT	PARALLEL CIRCUIT
• Current flows from the battery through the switch and **through each bulb in sequence -** out of one bulb and into the next • If one bulb blows, **all bulbs go out** because the current cannot flow through the blown bulb • The battery voltage is **divided between the 3 bulbs**, each bulb only gets 3V and so **glows more dimly** than if it got 9V • If you add more bulbs, the bulbs will get less voltage and less current, and glow dimmer	• Current flows from the battery through the switch and **through each of the bulbs separately** • Each bulb gets the full 9V and maximum current from the battery, so each bulb glows with **maximum brightness** • You can add more bulbs and each bulb will glow with the same brightness • If one bulb fails, the rest **will still work** • A disadvantage of the parallel circuit is that is uses 3 times the current of the series circuit, and so the **battery will run out faster**
Applications: Lamps, fridges, old-style / cheap Christmas Tree Lights (if one bulb blows, they all go out)	Applications: Classroom lights, car lights, modern Christmas Tree Lights (if one bulb blows, the others stay lighting)

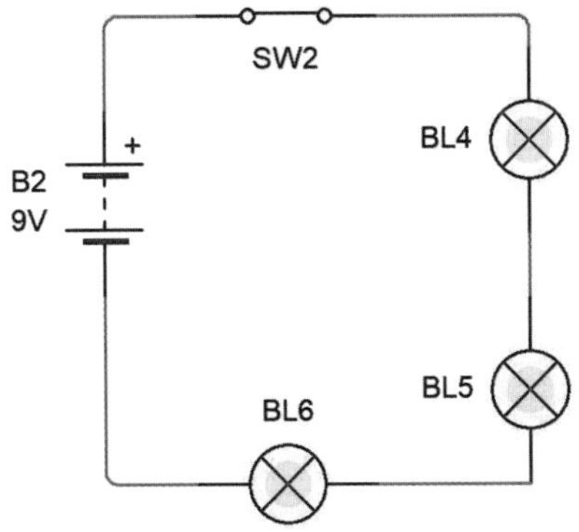

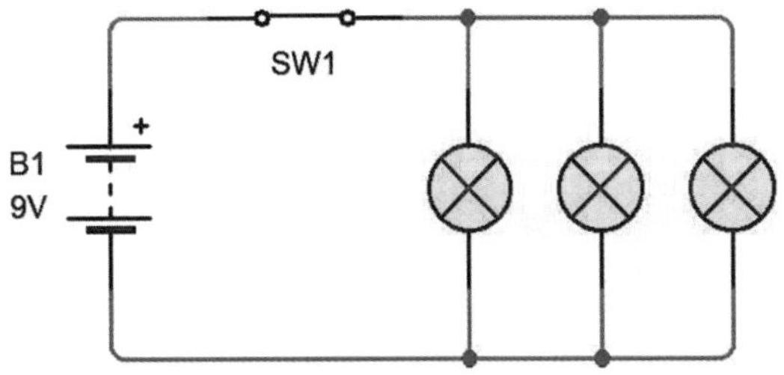

Electronics Activity 2 – Understanding Circuits

In the space below, or on circuit software (or both), draw the **parallel circuit** above, except **replace each bulb with an LED and a resistor**. *Don't forget that LEDs have polarity.*

Circuit Sketch:

Electronics Activity 3 – Understanding Circuits

In the space below, or on circuit software (or both), draw the **series circuit** above – except **replace the SPST switch with a PTM switch.**

Circuit Sketch:

Explain how this circuit works differently as a result of changing the switch:

_____

_____

Electronics Activity 4 – Understanding Circuits

Give **two reasons** why **car headlights** are wired **in parallel** instead of in series:

_____

_____

Circuit Assembly using a Breadboard

The best way to quickly connect and test out a circuit – before making any permanent connections – is to use a **breadboard**. A breadboard is a small plastic board with tiny holes in it. You simply push your wires and legs into the holes, and the breadboard connects them for you.

BREADBOARD	<ul><li>Breadboards are used to make **temporary** circuits</li><li>The legs of the electronic components or wires are **pushed into holes** in the breadboard</li><li>Inside the breadboard, the rows and columns of holes are **connected internally** in special patterns (see next section) and make electrical connections between the holes</li><li>**No soldering needed**</li><li>Breadboards are **reusable** (just pull out the components to make another circuit)</li></ul> 

HOW A BREADBOARD IS WIRED

Top View

How the holes are connected internally

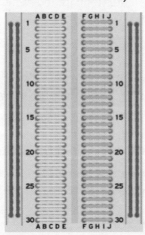

- The long lines of holes on the outside edges of the breadboard (coloured **red** and **black** here) are used to connect to the positive and negative **power** lines

- Connect the **positive** power supply to the **red** line and the **negative** power supply to the **black** line

- To connect **two components** together, push the wires or legs you want to connect into the **same row** (coloured **yellow** and **green** here)

ASSEMBLING A BREADBOAD CIRCUIT - EXAMPLE

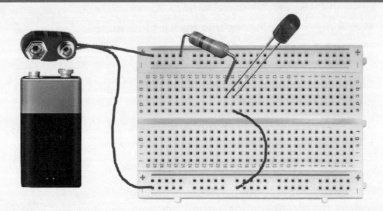

- The **red** wire from the **positive** terminal of the battery is pushed into the **top row**

- The **black** wire from the **negative** terminal of the battery is pushed into the **bottom row**

- The top leg of the **resistor** is also pushed into the top row. Because the holes are connected internally, this means the top leg of the resistor is now connected to the positive supply (9V)

- The bottom leg of the **resistor** is pushed into the same column as the **positive (long) leg** of the **LED** - this means those components are now connected together

- The **negative (short) leg** of the **LED** is pushed into the same column as the **wire** connecting to the bottom row / negative power supply

- This means a **circuit has been created** and the LED will light

Note: the resistor shown in the picture is only for illustration purposes. For example, the resistor value required to light and protect a standard 5mm LED from a 9V battery would be 330, 390 or 470 ohms.

| **PRINTED CIRCUIT BOARD (PCB)** | <ul><li>**PCB**s are widely used in industry to create circuits - they are **custom-made** for each specific circuit</li><li>Conductive **copper tracks** are etched onto an insulated plastic or fibreglass board</li><li>Components are pushed through **holes** in the board and **soldered** on to the copper *(see soldering on next page)*</li></ul> |  |

Circuit Assembly using Soldering

> **Soldering** creates **excellent permanent electrical connections**. A **metal joint** is created by melting **solder** around the metal components to be joined, which cools and sets quickly.

Soldering Tools

CORED SOLDER	• We met **solder** back in Unit 5 – it is an **alloy** of tin and lead. It is **soft** and has a very **low melting point** (for a metal) • **Cored solder** is composed of an **outer tube of solder**, with an **inner core of flux** - a soft waxy substance • **Flux** spreads over the joint and helps the solder to **flow** • The **flux** also **prevents the metals oxidising** when they get hot (which will prevent a good electrical connection)
SOLDERING IRON	• A **soldering iron** is a hand-held tool that supplies heat through a small **iron tip** • The tip of the soldering iron heats the connection area and **melts the solder** onto the joint • **Always place the soldering iron back into its stand** – never leave it lying around!
DE-SOLDERING PUMP	• A **de-soldering pump** is a **vacuum pump** that is used to **suck up melted solder** • A de-soldering pump is used with a soldering iron to 'undo' a poorly-soldered or unwanted connection
WIRE STRIPPERS	• A **wire strippers** is hand-held tools designed to **remove the plastic coating** around wire • It can also **snip the wire** to the desired lengths

Soldering Process

- Ensure the tip of the soldering iron is **clean**
- **Tin** the tip of hot soldering iron using a small bit of solder and rub the tip into a damp sponge
- **Heat the junction** of the two metals to be joined with the hot soldering iron tip
- **Apply the solder** to the heated metals, not to the soldering iron
- The **solder melts and flows** around the junction
- **Remove** the soldering iron and **wait** for the solder to cool and set
- **Snip off** any long wires

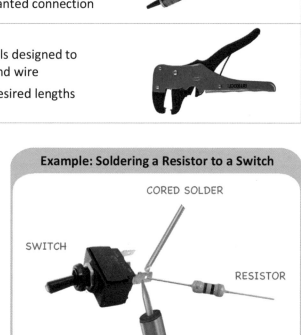

Example: Soldering a Resistor to a Switch

CORED SOLDER

SWITCH

RESISTOR

SOLDERING IRON

Safety Precautions when Soldering

- Always **return** the soldering iron to its **stand**
- Take care not to burn the soldering iron **cable**
- Work in a ventilated room, wear a **face mask**
- **Do not power on** the circuit being soldered

Mechatronics

Research Activities

Research Activity 1 – Analysis of a Mechatronic Device

Choose an **existing mechatronic device**. **Research** and describe this device under the following headings:

Name of device: _____

Sketch the device:

Who is this device intended for? _____

Describe how this device functions as a mechatronic system:

_____

_____

_____

Describe particular aspects of the design that you like, and why:

_____

_____

Describe particular aspects of the design you think could be improved:

_____

_____

Research Activity 2 – Inventors

Research who invented the **world wide web** and identify **three key facts** about this inventor:

Name: _____

Fact 1: _____

Fact 2: _____

Fact 3: _____

Research Activity 3 - Modern Technological Development

Choose an **emerging** (i.e. relatively new) **technology,** and discuss its operation, pros and cons, how it may **impact on individuals, society** and the **environment**. As an alternative option, examine the **technological issues and solutions** encountered during the 2020 **coronavirus** outbreak, touching on how the technologies work, their importance, economic cost, solutions found to combat scarcity, and impact on society and environment.

micro:bit – Connecting Input and Output Devices

> The edge **pins are** used to **connect external devices** such as **LEDs** and **motors** to the **micro:bit**.
> In our projects, we only connect to the **large pins**.

PINS

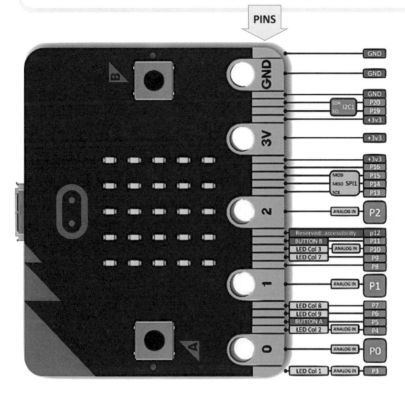

Connecting to the Large Pins

The **large pins** are labelled **0**, **1**, **2**, **3V** and **GND**. They have large **holes** in them and are easy to connect to using **crocodile clip** or **banana clip** cables.

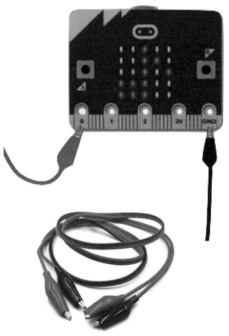

The Large Pins

Pin	Description
0	• Connect low-power **output devices** like **LEDs** to **pins 0, 1** or **2**
1	• You can also connect **input devices** (like **sensors**) to **pins 0, 1** or **2**
2	
3V	• Used to supply or receive **fixed 3 Volt Power** only to/from external devices
GND	• Used as the **ground** or **negative** connection for **all external pin connections** to the micro:bit

Example – connecting an LED to Pin 0

The **negative** leg of the LED is connected to **GND**. The **positive** leg of the LED is connected to **Pin 0** via a **resistor**.

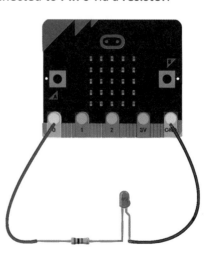

Connecting to the Small Pins

If you want to connect to the **small pins**, you'll need to use a micro:bit **edge connector** or **breakout board**. You can push the connector onto the edge of the micro:bit, and solder or push-connect your wires to the connector pins.

Connecting a DC Motor to the micro:bit

On its own, the micro:bit **cannot supply enough current** to drive a DC motor. You need to use a **motor drive expansion board**. The micro:bit board plugs into the motor drive expansion board, and you connect the DC motor(s) to the expansion board. You will see the motor drive expansion board again in **Unit 10 Motorised Vehicle**.

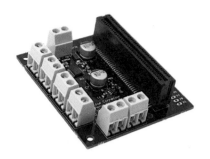

Understanding Analog and Digital

When working with the electronics and the micro:bit, it is important to know the difference between **digital** and **analog**.

ANALOG	• An **analog** signal can take **any value** between its minimum and its maximum • All the **natural world** is **analog** – i.e. movement, sound, light, temperature, time • In **electronics**, if zero volts is our minimum and 3 volts is our maximum (as with the micro:bit), then a micro:bit **analog signal** can take any value **between 0 and 3 volts**

DIGITAL	• A **digital** signal can have only **one of two values**: '**0**' or '**1**' (**on** or **off**)
	• In electronic circuits:
	  • the '**0**' (off) state is represented by **zero volts**
	  • the '**1**' (on) state is represented by the **maximum voltage** of the device (which in our micro:bit case is 3 Volts)
	• A single 1 or 0 (called a bit) is useful, but not much. However, we can use a sequence of 1s and 0s to **represent any number** and so create **data** (information)
	• This is why **computers** are **digital, flexible and powerful:**
	  • they work with **numbers** which are represented by 1s and 0s
	  • they can be **programmed** to do almost any task

Digital and Analog Inputs and Outputs (I/O) on the micro:bit

So how does a digital computer, which only works with 1s and 0s, interact with the real (analog) world? This is done using **sensors**, **analog-to-digital converters** (ADC) and **digital-to-analog converters** (DACs). These convert analog signals to digital and back again. This concept is shown in the diagram below.

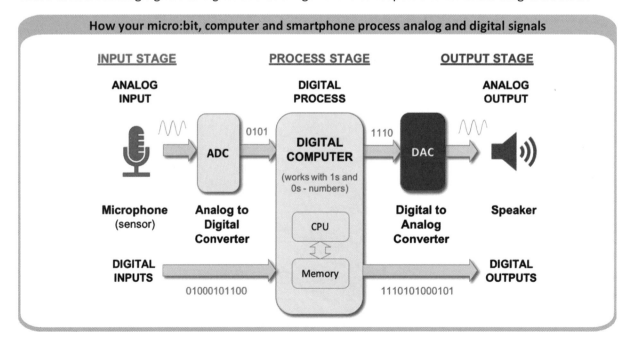

Programming the micro:bit Digital Output Pins

In this unit we use the micro:bit's **digital** output pins – i.e. the outputs that can only be 0 or 1 (0V or 3V). We use a **digital write pin** code block to set the output pin to 1 or 0 to turn an **external LED** on an off.

Return to the micro:bit makecode editor

- Go to **makecode.microbit.org**
- Click on '**New Project**' to bring you into the **makecode editor**
- Find the **digital write pin** code block in the **Advanced -> Pins** section of the toolbox

Tip: There is **Search** box at the top of the Toolbox area.
Start typing text and the toolbox will display matching code blocks

Useful Code Blocks	Description
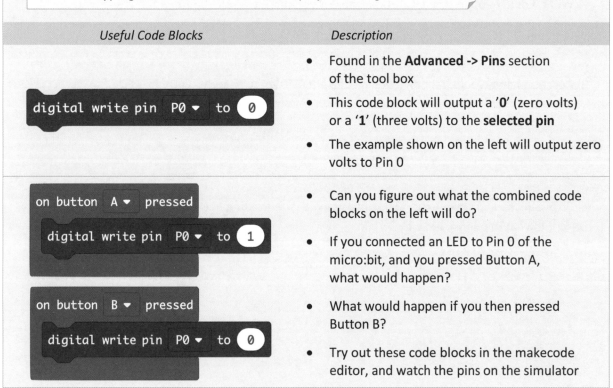	• Found in the **Advanced -> Pins** section of the tool box
	• This code block will output a '**0**' (zero volts) or a '**1**' (three volts) to the **selected pin**
	• The example shown on the left will output zero volts to Pin 0
	• Can you figure out what the combined code blocks on the left will do?
	• If you connected an LED to Pin 0 of the micro:bit, and you pressed Button A, what would happen?
	• What would happen if you then pressed Button B?
	• Try out these code blocks in the makecode editor, and watch the pins on the simulator

Programming Activities – Controlling an External LED from the micro:bit

micro:bit Activity 1 – Lighting an External LED

- Create a makecode **program** to light an external **LED** when **button A** is pressed, and to turn off the same LED when **button B** is pressed
- **Test** this program in the makecode editor using the **simulator**
- Make the basic micro:bit LED circuit on page 147. Note – it is safer to turn off the micro:bit before making any **connections** to its **pins** (unplug the battery pack connector or USB cable)
- Use **crocodile clip cables** to connect your components and micro:bit pins

  Note 1: You could also use a breadboard to join part of your circuit
  Note 2: kitronik.co.uk has a handy calculator to calculate the resistor value needed to drive a LED

- Connect the USB cable, **download** your program to the micro:bit, and test

Too Difficult: Partially Completed: Completed:

Note on powering LEDs from the micro:bit: *Because a micro:bit operates on 3V and it internally limits the current to its output pins, a micro:bit may successfully power a LED without a resistor. However, it is not good practice to do this. An LED should always be accompanied by a resistor to limit the current.*

micro:bit Activity 2 – Understanding your micro:bit External Circuits

Complete the following:

1. Are your **LED** and your **resistor** connected in **series** or in **parallel**?

_____

2. What would happen to the LED brightness if you **increased the value** of the resistor?

_____

3. Describe what would happen if you placed a **PTM switch** in series with the LED:

_____

_____

4. Physically connect **two extra LEDs in series** with the existing LED in your micro:bit circuit. Describe what happens, and why:

_____

_____

_____

5. Do you think it would be **possible to light all four LEDs** needed for the **photo frame** using the micro:bit? **Investigate** the options for lighting four LEDs using the large pins on the micro:bit:

Description: _____

_____

_____

Sketch:

Unit 6 Revision

Unit 6 Revision Questions

1. Describe what an exploded view is in the context of engineering drawings.
2. Name a tool that can be used to cut sheet metal without sawing.
3. Name two pieces of equipment that can be used to bend sheet metal.
4. Describe and sketch a countersunk hole.
5. Describe and sketch a counterbored hole.
6. Explain the advantage of using a step drill bit.
7. Give two examples of temporary joining methods
8. Give two examples of permanent joining methods.
9. Give two examples of mechanical joining.
10. Name and sketch four different types of bolts.
11. Name and sketch three different types of nuts.
12. List two advantages and two disadvantages of mechanical joining.
13. List two advantages and two disadvantages of adhesive joining.
14. Describe three safety precautions associated with adhesives.
15. What is liquid solvent cement used for?
16. Explain the term electrical resistance.
17. Explain the terms polarised and non-polarised in relation to electronic components.
18. Calculate the resistance of the following resistors: (colour bands listed in order 1,2,3)
    (a) red, red, red
    (b) brown , black, orange
    (c) yellow, violet, black
19. Describe with sketches two ways of determining the negative leg of an LED.
20. Give two advantages of an LED over an incandescent bulb.
21. What is the key defining characteristic of an electrical circuit?
22. Name two input electronic components.
23. Name two output electronic components.
24. Give three differences between a parallel circuit and a series circuit.
25. Name a piece of equipment that can be used to assemble temporary circuits.
26. Name a process that can be used to create permanent electrical connections.
27. Describe what tinning is.
28. Describe the steps required to solder two electronic components together.
29. Give two safety precautions to be observed when soldering.
30. Explain what each of the pins 0, 1, 2, 3V and GND are used for on a micro:bit.
31. Describe in detail the difference between an analog signal and a digital signal.
32. Name two components that can be connected directly to a micro:bit output pins.
33. Explain whether a DC motor can be connected directly to a micro:bit.

Unit 7 – Jitterbug

Unit Objectives

PROJECT	Design and manufacture a **vibrating animal** using a **motor** and **cam**

- Learn how to use **DC motors and mechanisms** in a project to create **movement**
- Learn about the **design process**, **design factors** and practice **lots of design activities**
- Learn about **project management** and **Gantt Charts**
- Continue to enhance knowledge of **mechanisms**, **electronics** and **programming**

Content

PROCESSES AND PRINCIPLES	**Materials**	• Woods, Composites, Ceramics and Smart Materials
	Joining	• Pop Riveting
	Design	• Design Factors and the Design Process • Computer-Aided-Design (CAD) • Prototyping
	Project Management	• Project Phases, Work Breakdown, Gantt Charts
DESIGN APPLICATION		• Apply design factors to create new designs and evaluate existing designs • Apply project management techniques to a real project
MECHATRONICS	**Mechanisms**	• Cams and Followers
	Electronics	• Motors, Battery Boxes and Holders, Variable Resistors
	micro:bit	• Programming with Light Sensors, Music, Radio Control

Learning Outcomes from this Unit

PROCESSES AND PRINCIPLES	DESIGN APPLICATION	MECHATRONICS
1.1, 1.2, 1.3, 1.4, 1.7, 1.8, 1.9, 1.10, 1.11, 1.12, 1.13	2.1, 2.2, 2.3, 2.4, 2.5, 2.6, 2.7, 2.8, 2.9, 2.10, 2.11, 2.12	3.1, 3.2, 3.3, 3.4, 3.6, 3.7, 3.8, 3.9, 3.10 & 3.11

Suggested Timeframes

START TIME	YEAR 1	Late Feb / Early March		DURATION	6-8 weeks

Working Drawings

Default Design

Top

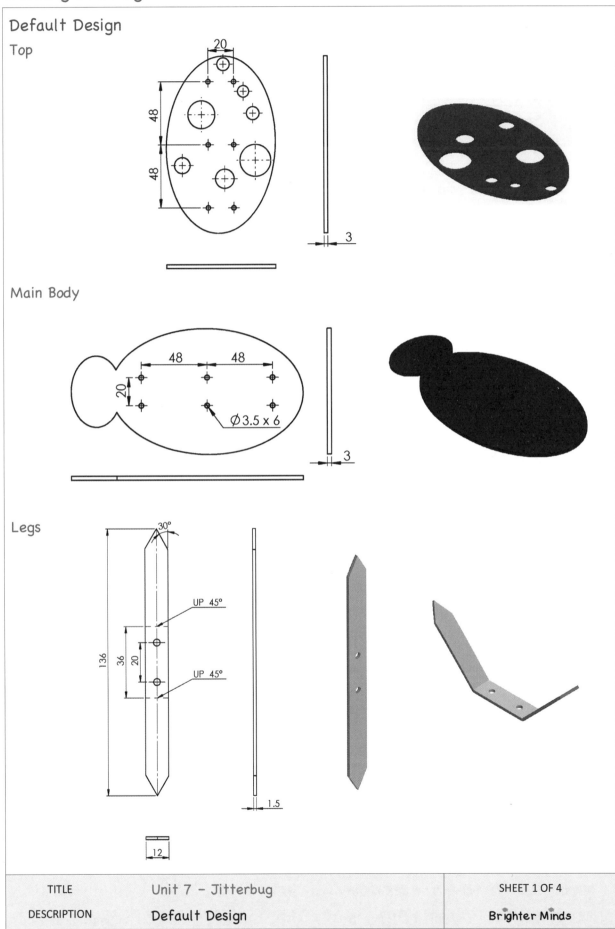

Main Body

Ø3.5 x 6

Legs

30°

UP 45°

UP 45°

TITLE	Unit 7 – Jitterbug	SHEET 1 OF 4
DESCRIPTION	Default Design	Brighter Minds

Default Design continued

Exploded View

Cam

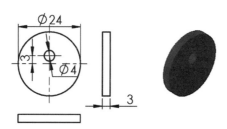

Circuit Diagram

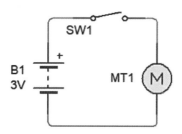

Assembled View

Bill of Materials

ITEM	PART	DESCRIPTION	QTY.
1	TOP	3mm Red Acrylic	1
2	MAIN BODY	3mm Black Acrylic	1
3	LEGS	1.5mm Aluminium	3
4	DC MOTOR	3V, Medium Torque	1
5	MOTOR MOUNT	Plastic, Self Adhesive	1
6	CAM	3mm Red Acrylic	1
7	REDUCER	Plastic 4mm – 2mm Reducer	1
8	3V BATTERY BOX	Includes 1 x Switch	1
9	PAN HEAD BOLT	M3 x 10	6
10	CAP NUT	M3	6
11	OPTIONAL CONTROL CONSOLE (not shown)	To be designed by Student	1

TITLE	Unit 7 – Jitterbug	SHEET 2 OF 4
DESCRIPTION	Default Design	Brighter Minds

Your Concept Sketches (Follow the Project Storyboard Activities before attempting these)

TITLE	Unit 7 – Jitterbug	SHEET 3 OF 4
DESCRIPTION	Your Concept Sketches	Brighter Minds

Your Design Drawings (Follow the Project Storyboard activities before attempting these)

TITLE	Unit 7 – Jitterbug	SHEET 4 OF 4
DESCRIPTION	Your Design Drawings	Brighter Minds

Project Storyboard

LEARNING GOALS OF THIS PROJECT

- Learn to incorporate a **DC motor**, **mechanism** and **batteries** into a mixed-materials project
- Provide an opportunity for **design** e.g. the body, battery housings, a control console

A different project that has similar goals to the above could be substituted for our default design

DESCRIPTION OF THE DEFAULT DESIGN

- Our default design resembles a **ladybird**, and consists of three main sections:

  1) A red **acrylic top** plate with different-sized holes, so you can see through to the black 'spots' of the ladybird underneath

  2) A black **acrylic main body**

  3) Three **aluminium** leg plates that form **six legs** when bent and fastened to the main body

- The three sections are **joined** with nuts and bolts as shown in the drawings
- The **motor** is housed under the body and an off-centre **cam** is attached to the motor spindle
- The **motor** is powered by **two AA batteries**. The batteries are housed in a **battery box**

  (a battery box comes with an integrated on/off switch)

DESIGN OPPORTUNITIES IN THIS PROJECT

- You can **design your own body** and/or **legs**. (The outer dimensions of the body are not provided in the default design). However, we recommend you **keep the same sizes and spacings of the holes** that attach the legs to the body

- You will need to <u>design one of the following</u>:
  - (a) **Design** a method to **hold the battery box in the Jitterbug**, OR
  - (b) **Design** a **separate control console** - this would contain the batteries plus a separate switch, and control your Jitterbug at a distance using **long wires**
- You could also **incorporate a micro:bit** into your control console, e.g. to make **sounds** to accompany your Jitterbug movements

More details on these options are provided in the project storyboard activities on the next pages.

YOUR PROJECT DESIGN CONSTRAINTS

- Your design should be based on an **insect or creature**
- Your design should incorporate a **motor** with a **cam** or other mechanism for movement
- We recommend you **use the same spacing and size of the 6 holes** used to attach the legs to the body (this creates space for electronic components underneath)
- If you are building a **control console**:
  - It should incorporate a **battery holder** and a **switch**
  - You could incorporate a **micro:bit** in the control console
  - Ideally, the **visual design** of your control console should match in with the visual design of your Jitterbug, i.e. be part of the same **theme**

Project Planning Activities

Activity 1 – Decide How Much Design You Will Do

In consultation with your teacher, and considering the equipment, materials and time you have, **tick** which **design and manufacturing options** you are going to pursue in the table below:

I will be manufacturing the default supplied designs for the Jitterbug legs and body	☐
I will be creating my own design for the legs	☐
I will be creating my own design for the body	☐
I will be designing how to incorporate a battery box in the main body	☐
I will be designing a separate control console to house the batteries and a switch	☐
I will be incorporating a micro:bit in my control console	☐
I will be making a different but similar project	☐

Activity 2 – Project Schedule / Gantt Chart   *See Project Management on page 165*

In the table below, **list** the main tasks you think will be needed to design and build this project. For each task, tick or shade-in the week(s) you think the task might be completed in.

TASK	WEEK				
	1	2	3	4	5

Analysis Activities – Understanding the Default Design

Activity 3 – Interpreting Drawings

What is the name of the **drawing view** that shows how a product is **assembled**?

_____

Activity 4 – Understanding the Mechanical Design

1. Why do think **aluminium** was chosen as the material for the legs?

   _____

   _____

2. Why do you think a thickness of **1.5mm** aluminium was chosen for the legs rather than a thickness of 1mm or 2mm? _(Hint: think about strength and elasticity)_

   _____

   _____

   _____

Activity 5 – Understanding the Mechanisms

| See cams on pages 177-8 |

1. **Research** cams and explain what a **cam** is, and what cams are typically used for:

   _____

   _____

   _____

2. **Sketch** the cam used in this project, also showing the motor spindle, here:

3. **Explain** why a **cam** might cause the Jitterbug to **vibrate**:

   _____

   _____

4. **Explore** how you might **attach the cam to the motor spindle**:

| See page 179 |

   _____

   _____

Activity 6 – Understanding the Motor Mechanical Attachment

1. How do the working drawings suggest to **attach the motor holder to the body**?

_____

2. **Explore** and describe an **alternative method** of attaching the motor holder to the body:

_____   *Sketch:*

_____

_____

_____

_____

Understanding the Electronics

Activity 7 – Understanding the Motor Circuit

See Electronics on Page 180

The circuit diagram for the Jitterbug is shown in the working drawings.

1. **Name** an **electronic component** that you could add to this circuit, that would allow you to **adjust the speed of the motor**:

Component: _____

2. **Sketch** an updated circuit diagram that would allow you to **control the speed** of the motor:

3. **Consider** using this **updated circuit** in a **control console** for your Jitterbug

Activity 8 – Adding More Electronics

If you wish to include **LEDs** in your design, e.g. for eyes or spots, **modify** the motor circuit diagram provided to also include output LEDs. **Sketch** the modified circuit diagram below:

See page 121

Activity 9 – Testing your Electronics

We suggest temporarily **wiring up and testing your electronic circuit** (e.g. using a breadboard or crocodile clip cables) to ensure it works **before** you incorporate the circuit in to your project.

Design Activities

Carry out the tasks below according to the amount of design work you chose to undertake in Activity 1.

Activity 10 – Concept Sketches

- On separate paper, draw some free-hand **concept sketches** for designs for your Jitterbug
- Ensure the **battery** and **electronic components** will fit in the **body** or in a **control console**
  - **Measure components** if you need to, to ensure they will fit
  - Consider using **existing holes** when designing holders / housing solutions for items
  - Consider **sticky pads** for joining items together
- Ask your **teacher or peer to review your designs**, and update your designs as required
- **Transfer / draw** your favourite concept sketch in the '**Your Concept Sketches**' section of the working drawings pages. Include important **dimensions** on those sketches.

Activity 11 – Final Design Drawing

Accurately draw your final **design drawings** to scale in the '**Your Design Drawings**' section of the working drawings area. Ensure your drawing uses the required **technical language**.

Manufacturing Activities

Activity 12 – Planning for Manufacture – Legs

Name **two** different pieces of **equipment** that could be used to **bend the aluminium legs**:

1. _____

2. _____

Activity 13 – Manufacture - Legs

Mark out and manufacture your Jitterbug **legs** now

Activity 14 – Planning for Manufacture - Body

Identify the **processes** and **tools** required to manufacture the **Jitterbug Body** part(s):

_____

_____

_____

_____

Activity 15 – Manufacture - Body

Mark out and manufacture your Jitterbug **body** now

Activity 16 – Planning for Manufacture - Cam

1. **Explain** how you will mark out and manufacture the **cam**

_____

_____

2. The **cam** must fit onto the **spindle** of the 3V DC motor. The spindle of the motor is **2mm** in diameter, however the cam has a **4mm** diameter hole. **Explain** how the cam can be attached to the motor spindle: *(Hint: consult the working drawings)*

See Page 179

_____

Activity 17 – Manufacture - Cam

Mark out and manufacture the **cam** for your Jitterbug now

Activity 18 – Assembly - Cam and Motor

Assemble the **cam** to your **motor**. **Assemble** the **motor** and **cam** to the Jitterbug **body**.

Activity 19 – Manufacture - Battery Holder or Control Console

Mark out and manufacture your body **battery holder** or external **control console** now.

Activity 20 – Planning the Electronics Assembly

See Circuit Assembly, page 144

1. **Name** the **process** that you will use to make the **electrical connections** between the **electronic components:**

_____

2. Identify **two safety precautions** you should take during this process:

Safety Precaution 1: _____

Safety Precaution 2: _____

Activity 21 – Electronics Assembly

Solder your electrical connections now.

See page 144

Project Testing and Evaluation

Activity 22 – Project Testing and Evaluation

1. What results did you get when you first tested your project? _____

_____

2. What **modifications** did you make to improve the project?

_____

_____

2. Place tick marks in the table cells below to **indicate** how you felt you used your time:

TASK	In this task, I spent...		
	Too Little Time	Enough Time	Too Much Time
Planning			
Understanding the Project			
Deciding how much Design to Do			
Designing			
Manufacturing			
Correcting Errors			
Surface Finishing			
Testing and Modification			

Project Assessment

Student Self-Assessment

In this project, I gained the following new **skills** and **knowledge**:

1. _____

2. _____

3. _____

I **evaluate** my project to have **turned out well** in the following areas:

_____

_____

If I were to carry out this project again, I would **modify** or **improve** the following aspects:

_____

_____

_____

_____

On a scale of 1 to 10, I would give my project a **score** of...

Peer Assessment

I felt the following design and manufacturing processes were **good**:

_____

_____

_____

I felt the following project areas could be **improved**:

_____

_____

_____

Teacher Feedback on Project

Teacher comments on student's project:

| Not Graded | Partially Achieved | Achieved | Merit | Higher Merit | Distinction |

Learning Topics for Unit 7

Processes and Principles

Project Management

> **Project management** is the way in which we **organise**, **schedule**, **track** and **manage projects** so that they can be completed in the required **time** with the desired **results**

What is a Project?

A **project** is not a continuous activity. A project has:

- a defined **beginning** and **end**
- a set of **goals** (i.e. outcomes to be achieved at the end)

Typical Project Phases

Engineering projects can typically be broken down into three large phases (tasks): **design, manufacturing** and **testing**. Each of these phases needs to be planned and managed.

TYPICAL ENGINEERING PROJECT PHASES

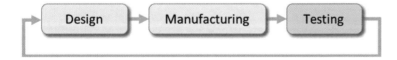

Design → Manufacturing → Testing

The diagram is drawn as a loop because one or more re-designs may be needed after testing. However, all activities will be planned, and so the project will still have a definite end.

How to Plan a Project

1. **Break down** the project into **smaller tasks** - *this is called a **work breakdown** (see below)*
2. **Estimate** how long each task will take
3. **Schedule** the tasks on a **timeline** - *this is called a **Gantt Chart** (see below)*

Work Breakdown

> A **Work Breakdown** breaks your project down into **smaller, more manageable tasks**
> that can be completed in a specific timeframe

You can create a **work breakdown structure** (WBS) in two main ways:

- by **drawing a tree diagram** showing how each large task breaks down into many smaller tasks
- by creating a **list of tasks and sub-tasks** like the below. You can add **time estimates** for each task

Example Work Breakdown

No.	TASK	SUB-TASK	SUB-SUB-TASK	ESTIMATED TIME
	DESIGN	Analyse Brief		1 hour
		Carry out Research		2 days
		Create Concept Designs		1 day
		Create Final Design		
	MANUFACTURE	Manufacture Legs	Mark Out	0.25 hour
			Cut Shape	0.25 hour
			Drill Holes	0.25 hour
		Manufacture Body	etc	

Gantt Charts

Once you have used a work breakdown to identify the **tasks** required, you can create a **project schedule**. One common way of doing this is to arrange your tasks visually along a **timeline**, in the sequence that they need to be carried out. This is called a **Gantt chart**. A simplified example is shown below.

> A **Gantt Chart** shows project **tasks** as **horizontal bars** along a **timeline**

Specialised software packages like Microsoft Project are available to create Gantt Charts,
but you can create simple ones as free-hand drawings, or using Word or Excel grids / tables.

TASKS	WEEKS					
	1	2	3	4	5	6
PLANNING TASKS						
Create a Project Schedule / Gantt Chart	▪					
Ensure all Tools and Materials available	▪					
DESIGN TASKS						
Create Concept Designs		▪				
Create Final Design		▪				
MANUFACTURING TASKS						
Manufacture the Legs		▪				
Manufacture the Body		▪				
Manufacture the Control Console			▪			
Manufacture the Cam			▪			
Assemble all the Mechanical Parts				▪		
Solder the Electronic Circuit				▪		
TESTING AND RE-WORK TASKS						
Test the Jitterbug				▪		
Make required changes					▪	
Re-test					▪	
Write up Project Evaluation						▪

The Design Process

A **design process** is a **set of steps** that engineers follow to help them create **good solutions**

Design is a Cycle

You don't just design once - you create an **initial design**, **test** your design, and go back and **improve** it. Designing involves **continuous improvement**.

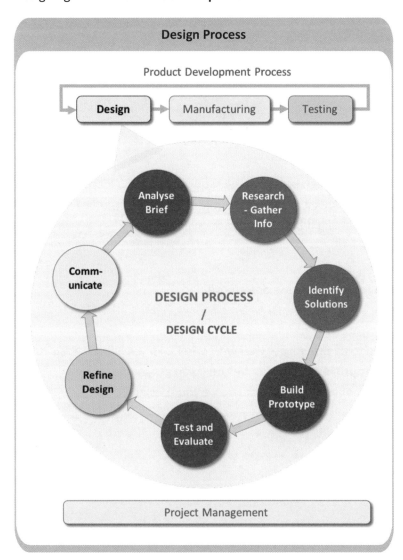

1. Analyse the Brief

The **first design step** is to **really understand** what your project or product is all about, e.g.:

- What am I being asked to do?
- What problems am I trying to solve?
- What should the product do?
- What size & weight should it be?
- How important are its looks?
- Who is going to use it?
- Is it safe for users?
- Is it environmentally-friendly?
- How much can it cost?
- Will I be able to make it?
- How long does it have to last?

You should look at these and other **design factors** in this stage. We'll learn more about design factors later. After examining the design factors, write down the **requirements** for your product. For example: the product should do X, the product should be Y, etc.

2. Research / Gather Information

Research existing solutions to the same or similar problems to get ideas. Use the **internet**, **talk** to other people, ask **users** of similar products what they would like. Also use this time to **investigate** what **materials**, **equipment**, **tools** and **skills** you might need, have available, or may need to acquire.

3. Identify Solutions

Come up with **multiple ideas and designs** – not just one idea. Sketch a lot. Test how well these design ideas match with the design factors and requirements you identified earlier. Get reviews from other people. Select the best design ideas.

4. Build a Prototype

A **prototype** is a **simple version** of a product or idea that you **build** in order to **test the design**

Rather than wait until you build the full product – which could be expensive and take some time – instead **build a simple easy quick version** of it and test that.

For example, you could make the important parts of your design out of **cardboard**. Sometimes you can only find problems when you see things.

Benefits of Prototyping
- **Identifies weaknesses in design** at an early stage
- Help to **sell** and **communicate** the product to others
- Can **test** aspects that can't be tested without a physical product
- **Allows design modifications** to be made before going to production (manufacturing)
- **Reduces cost** and **time**

5. Test and Evaluate

Evaluate your design and prototype against your design brief and the requirements you identified earlier. Ask peers and real users to **review** your designs. Does it do what it should? Have you forgotten something? Are there things you can change to make it better? Record any findings.

6. Refine your Design

Modify your design to fix or improve issues found during the design evaluation.

7. Communicate

Throughout the design process you will need to communicate well with others. For example, when working in industry, you will need others to **approve** your design before it can get manufactured. You can and should use several different types of **media** to communicate your designs:

Examples of Design Communication Media
- Engineering Drawings
- Physical Prototypes
- 3D CAD Software Models *(see later)*
- Presentations
- Videos
- Meetings – face-to-face, video calls

Go Around the Design Cycle Again

It often happens that you didn't get the design quite right the first time around, and you may need to go around the design circle again. Better to improve the design than to build the wrong product.
Look at the brief and requirements again, carry out more research, talk to more users, try a different approach, create a new design and prototype, review that and incorporate the feedback in to your next design.

Project Management of the Design Cycle

You will also need to **schedule** and **track** your **design** work. **Estimate** how much time you will need for design tasks – such as research, creating an initial design, building a prototype, and reviewing and updating your designs. Create a design schedule and track your progress against it.

Design Factors

> **Design factors** are a set of **aspects to consider** when creating good designs

- Design factors are like a checklist of **different question areas** to help ensure you have considered your design from enough **viewpoints**
- Design factors help both when **designing a new product** and when **evaluating an existing design**

Design Factor	Explanation and Example Questions
FUNCTIONALITY (USAGE)	<ul><li>What does this product need to **do**? How does this product need to **behave**?</li><li>Does it need to work with **other products**?</li><li>**Who** will use it? Are there **different types of users** with different needs?</li><li>**Where** will it be used? What are the different **scenarios** that it will be used in?</li><li>What **size** and **weight** does it need to be?</li><li>How **strong** does it need to be - what are the **maximum loads** and **stresses**?</li><li>How will it be **powered**?</li><li>How **reliable** does it need to be?</li><li>Can **extra features** be added to it later if necessary?</li></ul>
SAFETY	<ul><li>What safety **hazards** and **risks** might there be from this product? (e.g. from electricity or sharp edges, what happens if it breaks or is swallowed?)</li><li>Does it come in **contact with people**, particularly with **children**?</li><li>What specific **safety features** do I need to build in to this product?</li></ul>
ENVIRONMENT	<ul><li>How much **energy** will this product use? How can this be **reduced**?</li><li>What is the **environmental impact** of this product at its **end-of-life**?</li><li>What is its **working environment**? (E.g. **outdoors**? **inside the body**?)</li><li>Is the product at risk of **corrosion**? How can corrosion be **minimised**?</li></ul>
LOOKS (AESTHETICS)	<ul><li>How important are **looks** for this product?</li><li>How will this product be **presented** to users and others?</li><li>What kind of **surface finish** is needed?</li></ul>
EASE OF MANUFACTURE	<ul><li>How would such a design **be manufactured** ?</li><li>What **processes** would be needed? Are these available & **cost-effective**?</li><li>Are there very high quality and high **tolerances** required on the parts?</li><li>Will a lot of **testing** be required to manufacture this product correctly?</li></ul>
COST	<ul><li>What is the maximum **price** that this product can cost to make?</li><li>What would it cost to manufacture a **large quantity** of this design?</li></ul>
MATERIALS	<ul><li>What **types of materials** would suit this product?</li><li>What types of material(s) would **meet all the requirements** of functionality, safety, environment, looks, manufacturability and cost?</li></ul>

Computer-Aided-Design (CAD)

> **Computer-Aided Design (CAD)** is the use of **computer software** to produce **engineering drawings** and **3D models**

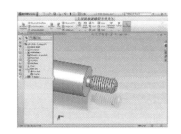

Solidworks is a common CAD software application used in many schools. Many other CAD packages are used in industry.

Advantages of CAD software

- **Easy to create**, **modify** and **store** technical drawings
- CAD software comes with **libraries** of thousands of parts
- CAD software can run **checks** on drawings to ensure they are correct and consistent
- It is easier to **visualise the product** using CAD - you can create a **3D model** and view it from **different angles**
- You can test how multiple parts would be **assembled**
- CAD software can generate instructions for **3D printers**, **laser cutters** and **CNC machine tools** to build the parts

Activities – Practicing Design, Sketching and Design Evaluation

Design Activity 1 – Evaluation

Evaluate the design of the hoverboard shown, under the following **design factors**:

Functionality:

Aesthetics (looks):

Safety:

Materials Used:

Environmental Impact:

Ease of Manufacture:

Cost:

Design Activity 2

Design a simple **steering system** for this wooden kart.

Sketch your design on top of the image shown.

Describe how the steering system works:

_____

_____

Design Activity 3

Sketch a design for a **postbox** that can be **fixed to a wall.**

It should have a **slot** for letters, a **decorative** feature, and provide protection from the **weather**.

Illustrate how the postbox can be **fixed** to the wall.

Suggest a **material** for the postbox:

_____

Suggest a **surface finish / coating**:

_____

Design Activity 4

Sketch a design for a **waste bin** that is **environmentally-friendly**.

List the design **features** that make your bin environmentally-friendly:

_____

_____

_____

_____

Design Activity 5

Sketch a design for **charging stand** for your **phone**. This should keep your phone off the floor and the wires tidy, while your charger is plugged into a wall socket.

Describe and **justify** your design under the following **design factors**:

Functionality:

_____

_____

Materials:

_____

_____

Aesthetics (looks): _____

Safety: _____

Design Activity 6

Sketch a design for a **bus shelter**.

The shelter should provide **seating** for 4 people and space for **passenger information** and advertising.

Indicate on the sketch the **materials** you have selected.

Indicate on the sketch **how the seating is attached** to the shelter.

Describe any other useful features.

Design Activity 7

Sketch a design for a **stand** that will hold a rectangular **advertising board** upright on the footpath.

(for example a restaurant menu board)

The stand should prevent the adverting board from falling over, and also ideally allow the advertising board to be **easily removed** from the stand, and replaced.

Prototyping Methods

CARDBOARD	• **Light**, **cheap**, **easy** to **fold**, **cut** and **shape** • **Strong** enough for many prototyping applications • Can be **joined** using a variety of methods: **tape**, **glue**, **staples**	
3D PRINTER	• Takes instructions from a **digital file** and manufactures a part by **depositing layer upon layer** of material (usually **thermoplastic**) • The digital file required by 3D printers can be generated by **CAD software**	Moving Plastic Depositor
LASER CUTTER	• Takes cutting instructions from a **digital file** and cuts material using a laser • Can cut complex shapes **very quickly** • The digital file required by laser cutters can be generated by **CAD software**	

Prototyping Activity 1 – Phone Charger Stand

Build a **prototype** of the **phone charging stand** you designed earlier in Design Activity 5. We recommend using **cardboard**, however decide with your teacher on an appropriate prototyping method.

Prototyping Activity 2 – Discuss Pro and Cons

THINK	By yourself, think about: • **three positives** (pros) of prototyping • **three negatives** (cons) of prototyping
PAIR	**Discuss** your ideas with a **peer**. Do your positives and negatives match?
SHARE	One of you **share your ideas** with the whole group. As you **listen** to the ideas of the group, feel free to **contribute** to the group discussion in a respectful manner.

Materials

Research Activity – Materials

Research the following types of materials using the internet, for homework and/or in class with your teacher. **Describe** them under the headings listed below:

Material	Description	Main Properties	Examples, Applications
WOOD			
CERAMICS			
COMPOSITES			
SMART MATERIALS			

Revision Activities – Materials, Marking Out & Joining

Revision Activity 1 - Plastics

1. Give two properties of **acrylic**:

   Property 1: _____

   Property 1: _____

2. Explain why you think the **legs** of the Jitterbug were **not** made from acrylic:

   _____

3. Explain why it is **not** recommended to use a **scriber** on acrylic:

   _____

Revision Activity 2 - Metals

List the **three categories of metals**, their main features and examples, using the table below.

Metals Category	Main Features and Properties	Example Metals

Revision Activity 3 – Marking Out

Sketch:

Demonstrate using **notes** and **sketches** the importance of working from a **datum edge**:

_____

_____

_____

_____

Revision Activity – Joining

Describe the differences between **temporary** and **permanent joints** and give 2 examples of each:

Type of Joint	Description	Examples
TEMPORARY JOINTS		1. _____ 2. _____
PERMANENT JOINTS		1. _____ 2. _____

Joining

Pop Rivets

Pop riveting is a type of **permanent joint** used to join thin **sheet metal** together. **Holes** are first drilled through the pieces to be joined. The **pop rivet** goes through the hole from the front side, and a **pop rivet gun pulls** it. The pop rivet **expands** on the far side of the metal, squeezing the metal pieces together.

POP RIVETS

- Suitable for joining **sheet metal**
- **Drill a hole** through both pieces to be joined
- **Clamp** the metal pieces together, lining up the holes
- **Insert** the long thin **pin** side of the pop rivet in the gun
- Insert the **short thicker** part of the rivet **in the hole**
- **Squeeze** the handle of the gun several times
- The **gun** pulls the **pin** that runs through the middle of the pop rivet, which **enlarges** the tail side of the rivet, pulling the pieces together
- The pin **breaks** (pops) off when enough pressure has been created

INSERTED IN DRILLED HOLE

PULLED BY POP RIVET GUN

ADVANTAGES of POP RIVETS	DISADVANTAGES of POP RIVETS
- Very **fast** - Only need access to **one side of the material**	- **Visible** on the surface of joints

Mechatronics

Mechanisms

Refresh your existing knowledge of mechanisms by completing the questions below.

Revision Activities – Mechanisms

1. Draw the **symbol** for meshing spur **gears** in the box opposite.

2. Indicate a **driver gear** and a **driven gear** on the symbol drawing.

3. **Tick** which word indicates the **driver** gear:

   Input ☐   Output ☐

   Symbol for meshing Spur Gears:

4. **Research** and list **four** everyday products that use **gears**:

   (a) _____   (b) _____

   (c) _____   (d) _____

5. **Research** and list **four** everyday products that are, or use **levers**:

   (a) _____   (b) _____

   (c) _____   (d) _____

Cams and Followers

You used a **cam** in the Jitterbug project to create movement and vibration.
A cam is usually used with a **follower**.

> A **cam** is an **irregular rotating shape**, designed to make sliding contact with a **follower**, which causes the follower move back-and-forth in a **reciprocating motion**

| CAM and FOLLOWER | <ul><li>A **cam-and-follower** mechanism changes **rotary motion** into **reciprocating motion**</li><li>Used in **car engines** to raise and lower the valves – see Unit 10</li><li>Also used in **weaving machines**, **toys, printers**</li></ul> | FOLLOWER — RECIPROCATING MOTION (output) — ROTARY MOTION (input) — CAM — FOLLOWER — CAM |

Types of Cams

PEAR	ECCENTRIC	HEART	SNAIL / DROP

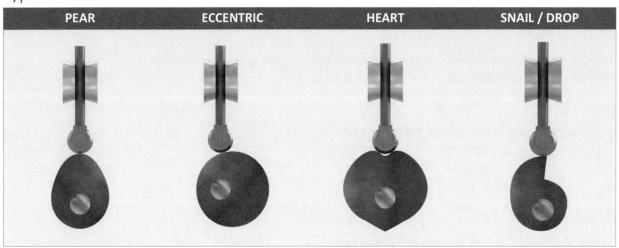

Types of Followers

FLAT	POINT / KNIFE	ROLLER	OFFSET

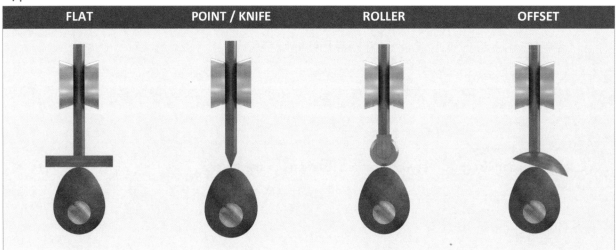

Electronics

Battery Holders and Battery Boxes

BATTERY HOLDER	• Holds two AA or AAA batteries **in series** *Which way round do you insert the batteries?*[1] • If each battery provides 1.5 volts, how many volts does a populated battery holder provide?[2] • Contains **holes** to allow screwing to workpiece • Does **not** provide a built-in on/off switch	
BATTERY BOX	• Holds two AA or AAA batteries **in series** • Contains an **on/off switch** built in to the cover • The built-in switch is **useful for saving space** as you don't need to wire a separate switch	

1. *Negative / flat side of the battery to the spring*
2. *Three volts*

Revision Activity – LED Circuits

1. Explain what happens if you connect a **9V** power source to an **LED**:

_____

2. Identify the electronic **component** required to prevent this from occurring:

_____

Output Components – Motors

DC Motors

There are many different types of motors. We use **DC motors** because they are **simple**, **cheap** and operate at safe **low voltages**. We will see other types of motors in Unit 11.

Device	Description	Images
DC MOTOR	• DC motors work based on the supplied voltage, and they are sold to work at **different operating voltages** – for example 3V, 6V, 9V etc • Select the **correctly-rated motor** for your voltage supply • DC motors **don't need a resistor** to limit the current because they generate enough resistance themselves • **Higher voltage motors** will usually have higher output speeds and **higher output torque** (turning force)	
INLINE DC MOTOR or **GEARED DC MOTOR**	• DC motors rotate at very **high speeds**. If you wish to reduce the speed, use an **inline or geared motor** • This type of motor comes with a **built-in gearbox** _(usually containing a worm wheel – see Unit 10)_ • The built-in gearbox **reduces the output speed** and **increases the output torque** (turning force) • A **high-torque motor** will rotate a **heavy load** on the spindle. A low-torque motor will not _We see the inline motor again in Units 9 and 10, where we use it to power our projects_	

Motor Accessories

SLEEVE REDUCER	• The **spindle** on a small DC motor is typically **2mm in diameter** • Many components such as gears have a **4mm diameter** hole • We can use sleeve **reducers** to push onto the spindle to **change the diameter** from 2mm to 4mm	

Process Components

Variable Resistors

VARIABLE RESISTOR	• The resistance of a **variable resistor** is changed by **turning** a **knob** or **screw** • The resistance can go from **zero ohms** (Ω) to the **maximum value** that is written on the component • Used in **dimmer lights**, **volume control** (e.g. a car radio), heat controls • Note, there are 3 connections on a **potentiometer** – use the **middle** connection and one of the **side** connections to use it as a **variable resistor** • Can be used to **reduce the speed of a DC motor** but needs to be a low resistance value, e.g. 50Ω

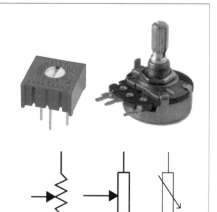

DC Motor Speed Control using a Variable Resistor

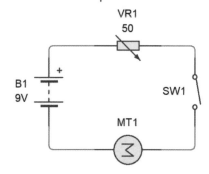

You can place a variable resistor **in series** with a DC motor to control the speed of the motor, as shown in the circuit opposite.

For this to work, the variable resistor should have a very **low maximum resistance**, e.g. 50 to 100 ohms.

Electronics Activities – Understanding Motor Circuits

Activity – Experimenting with Motor Circuits

1. Using a **breadboard, build** the **motor circuit** shown on the Jitterbug working drawings
   (i.e. a 3V battery holder connected to a SPST switch connected to a 3V DC motor)

2. **Modify** the circuit by replacing the SPST switch with a **PTM** switch.
   Explain the difference in the behaviour of the circuit:

   _____

3. **Explain** what would happen if you replaced the PTM switch with a **PTB** switch:

   _____

4. **Connect** the SPST switch and a **variable resistor** between the battery and the motor.
   (Use a low-resistance variable resistor - 50 to 100 ohms). What happens when you twist it?

   _____

5. Why do you think we did not use an **inline motor** for the Jitterbug?

   _____

micro:bit Programming

In this section, we use the micro:bit to **measure light levels**, make **music**, and get **two micro:bits** to **communicate** with each other using **radio** signals.

Return to the micro:bit makecode editor

- Go to **makecode.microbit.org**
- Click on an existing project or '**New Project**' to bring you into the **makecode editor**

---

micro:bit Programming - Measuring Light Levels

The micro:bit is able to measure the light level around it using its LEDs. LEDs are normally used to create light, but when they are configured a certain way in a circuit, they can also be used to **detect light**.

Useful Code Blocks

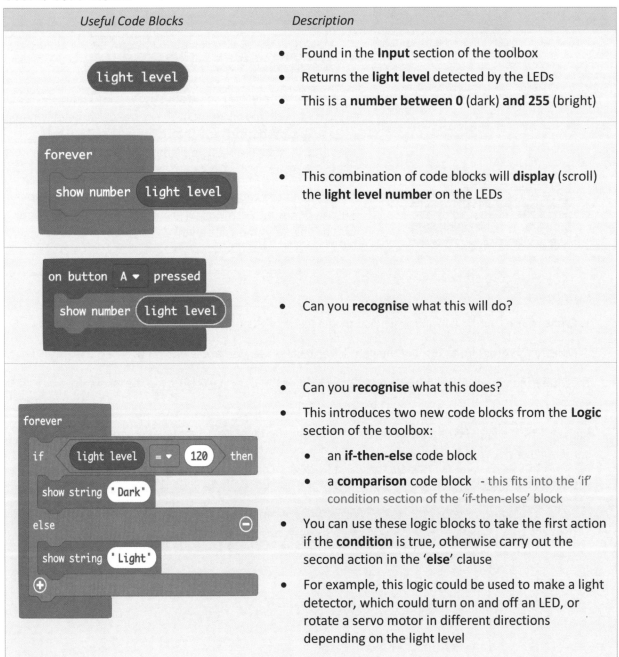

Useful Code Blocks	Description
light level	• Found in the **Input** section of the toolbox • Returns the **light level** detected by the LEDs • This is a **number between 0** (dark) **and 255** (bright)
forever show number light level	• This combination of code blocks will **display** (scroll) the **light level number** on the LEDs
on button A ▼ pressed show number light level	• Can you **recognise** what this will do?

forever
if light level = ▼ 120 then
show string "Dark"
else
show string "Light"
	• Can you **recognise** what this does?
	• This introduces two new code blocks from the **Logic** section of the toolbox:
	  • an **if-then-else** code block
	  • a **comparison** code block - this fits into the 'if' condition section of the 'if-then-else' block
	• You can use these logic blocks to take the first action if the **condition** is true, otherwise carry out the second action in the '**else**' clause
	• For example, this logic could be used to make a light detector, which could turn on and off an LED, or rotate a servo motor in different directions depending on the light level

Code Block	Description
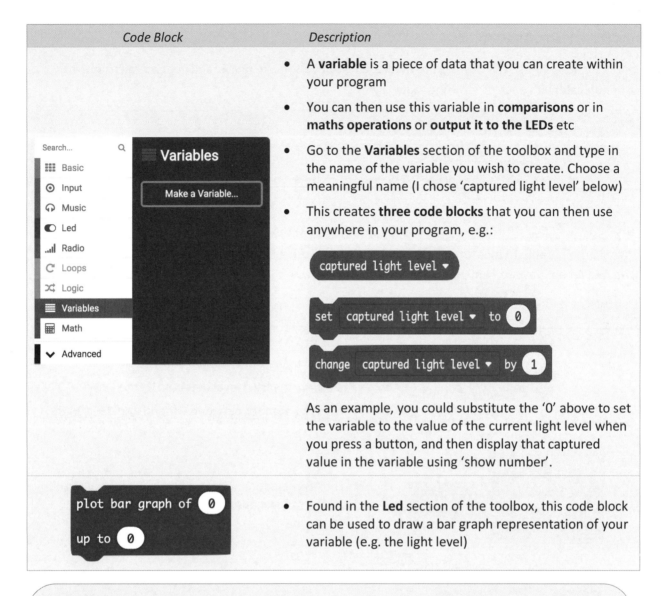	• A **variable** is a piece of data that you can create within your program • You can then use this variable in **comparisons** or in **maths operations** or **output it to the LEDs** etc • Go to the **Variables** section of the toolbox and type in the name of the variable you wish to create. Choose a meaningful name (I chose 'captured light level' below) • This creates **three code blocks** that you can then use anywhere in your program, e.g.: As an example, you could substitute the '0' above to set the variable to the value of the current light level when you press a button, and then display that captured value in the variable using 'show number'.
plot bar graph of 0 up to 0	• Found in the **Led** section of the toolbox, this code block can be used to draw a bar graph representation of your variable (e.g. the light level)

Programming Activities – Light Levels

1. **Create** a program to continuously display the value of the **light level** on the LEDs.

2. **Modify** the program to display the light level value when you press button **B**.

3. **Modify** the above program to display "I'm afraid of the dark" when button **A** is pressed.

4. Using a **variable** and a **Maths** code block, modify the above program to continuously display the value of the **light level divided by 28**. This brings the displayed light level down to one digit between 0 and 9.

5. **Change** the program to display a **bar chart** of the current light level on the micro:bit LEDs.

Record your progress by ticking the appropriate cells below:

Activity Number	Too Difficult	Partially Completed	Completed
1			
2			
3			
4			
5			

micro:bit Programming – Making Music

The micro:bit can be programmed to output music signals at **Pin 0**. You can hear these music signals by connecting a set of headphones to the micro:bit, as follows:

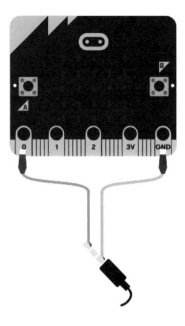

- Connect one end of a crocodile clip cable to the **GND** pin on micro:bit. Connect the other end to the **shank** of your headphone jack plug (the metal part closest to the plastic handle)

- Connect a second crocodile clip cable between **Pin 0** and the **metal tip** of your headphone jack

  Make sure the metal crocodile clips do not touch each other

- Note the sound will only come through one speaker

> WARNING – LOUD LEVELS
>
> - The sounds from the micro:bit can be loud
> - Test with the headphones away from your ears

Check out the following code blocks, and others, in the **Music** section of the toolbox:

Useful Code Blocks

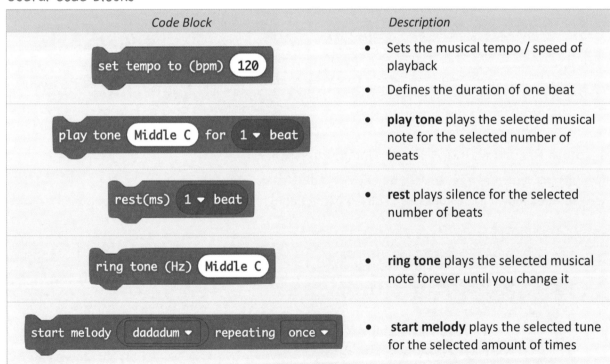

Code Block	Description
set tempo to (bpm) 120	• Sets the musical tempo / speed of playback • Defines the duration of one beat
play tone Middle C for 1 ▾ beat	• **play tone** plays the selected musical note for the selected number of beats
rest(ms) 1 ▾ beat	• **rest** plays silence for the selected number of beats
ring tone (Hz) Middle C	• **ring tone** plays the selected musical note forever until you change it
start melody dadadum ▾ repeating once ▾	• **start melody** plays the selected tune for the selected amount of times

Programming Activities – Music

> Activity 1 – Jitterbug Song and Name
>
> 1. Create a **chirpy tune** for your Jitterbug, which plays when **button A** is pressed.
>
> 2. Give your Jitterbug a name, and **scroll this name** across the micro:bit LEDs.

Activity 2 – Name that Tune

1. Build this program and press button A.

2. Name the tune, then build the rest of it.

Record your progress by ticking the cells below:

Activity	Too Difficult	Partially Completed	Completed
1			
2			
3			

Activity 3 – Light Music

1. Build this program and press button A.

2. Explain what it does.

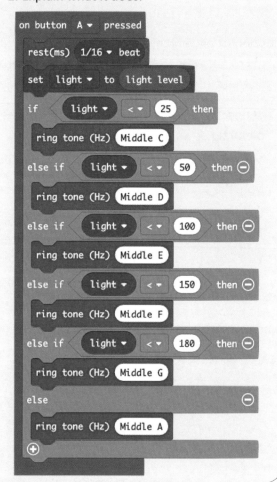

micro:bit Programming – Radio Communication

micro:bits can send messages to each other using radio signals.

Check out the following code blocks and others in the **Radio** section of the makecode toolbox.

Useful Code Blocks

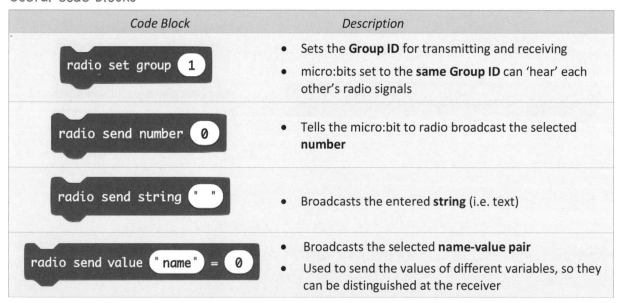

Code Block	Description
radio set group 1	• Sets the **Group ID** for transmitting and receiving • micro:bits set to the **same Group ID** can 'hear' each other's radio signals
radio send number 0	• Tells the micro:bit to radio broadcast the selected **number**
radio send string " "	• Broadcasts the entered **string** (i.e. text)
radio send value "name" = 0	• Broadcasts the selected **name-value pair** • Used to send the values of different variables, so they can be distinguished at the receiver

Code Block	Description
on radio received `receivedNumber`	• Runs the enclosed code block **when a number is received** by radio • The number received is available in the '**receivedNumber**' variable, for use in other code blocks
on radio received `receivedString`	• Runs the enclosed code block when a **string** (i.e. text) is received by radio • The string received is available in the '**receivedString**' variable, for use in other code blocks
on radio received `name` `value`	• Runs the enclosed code block when a **name-value pair** is received by radio • The name-value pair received is available in the '**name**' and '**value**' variables, for use in other code blocks

Programming Activities – Radio Communication

Programming Activities – Radio Communication

- **Pair-up** with another student, or group of students
- You'll need **two or more micro:bits**, and transmitter and receiver parts in your programs
- You'll need to set your **radio group IDs** to the same number in order to communicate

ACTIVITY 1 – **Create** a program / programs which:
- **transmits** a **number** via radio when **button A** is pressed
- **displays** any number on the LEDs that is received by radio
- **clears** / blanks the LED display when **button B** is pressed

Each micro:bit should transmit a different number, so you know where it came from.
Download and test.

ACTIVITY 2 – **Modify** the above program to transmit and display different **text messages** between micro:bits.

ACTIVITY 3 – **Modify** the programs to transmit and display different **images** (LED icons) between micro:bits when button A is pressed.

ACTIVITY 4 – **Modify** the programs to transmit and display different images (LED icons) **when the micro:bit is shaken**

Record your progress by ticking the appropriate cells below:

Activity Number	Too Difficult	Partially Completed	Completed
1			
2			
3			
4			

Unit 7 Revision

Unit 7 Revision Questions

1. Explain what project management is, and why it is important.

2. Explain what work breakdown means, and why it is useful.

3. Explain what a Gantt Chart is, and what it is used for.

4. Explain why research is an important step in the design process.
   In your answer, also reference your own project experiences.

5. (a) Explain the term prototyping;
   (b) Give three advantages of prototyping;
   (c) List three common methods used for prototyping.

6. (a) Demonstrate what evaluation is in the context of the design process, and why it is important.
   Include references from your own project experience.
   (b) Describe a number of different ways of evaluating a design.

7. List five design factors that should be considered when designing.

8. (a) Explain what CAD stands for;
   (b) Give two advantages of CAD.

9. (a) Explain what a composite material is;
   (b) Give two examples of composite materials.

10. (a) Explain what a smart material is;
    (b) Give two examples of smart materials.

11. (a) Explain the process of pop riveting;
    (b) For what types of materials and applications is pop riveting suitable?
    (c) Give two advantages of pop riveting;
    (d) Give one disadvantage of pop riveting.

12. (a) Explain what a cam is;
    (b) What is the name of the component that is almost always paired with a cam?
    (c) Give one typical application of cams in industry;
    (d) What type of motion transformation is provided by a cam-and-follower mechanism?

13. Explain the difference between a battery holder and a battery box.

14. (a) Explain the difference between a DC motor and an inline DC motor;
    (b) Which type of motor would you use to drive a heavy load?

15. (a) Explain what a variable resistor is;
    (b) Give two common applications for a variable resistor;
    (b) Draw the electronic symbol for a variable resistor.

16. What method, other than crocodile clips, could be used to connect external components to a micro:bit?

17. What micro:bit makecode code blocks can be used to wirelessly send a text message from one micro:bit to another?

Salt and Pepper

Unit 8 – Salt & Pepper Shakers

Unit Objectives

PROJECT	Design and manufacture **copper salt and pepper shakers** plus a **stand**

- Learn how to use a **lathe** safely, understand the parts and operations
- Learn how to join copper pieces by **soldering**
- Learn about **ferrous metals and alloys**, types of **steel** and **how steel is made**

Content

PROCESSES AND PRINCIPLES	**Materials**	• Ferrous metals and alloys • Iron and steel production, furnaces, heat treatment
	Workholding	• Vee-block
	Measurement	• Inside calipers
	Drilling	• Parallel and taper shank bits, hole saw
	Lathework	• Lathe parts, cutting tools, angles and speeds • Parallel turning, facing off, parting off, drilling, taper turning, chamfering, knurling
	Joining	• Soldering copper parts
		• Threaded Bar
DESIGN	• Design of a stand/holder for the shakers, modification of existing shakers	
MECHATRONICS	• No new mechanisms, electronics or micro:bit programming in this unit	

Learning Outcomes from this Unit

PROCESSES AND PRINCIPLES	DESIGN APPLICATION	MECHATRONICS
1.1, 1.2, 1.3, 1.4, 1.7, 1.8, 1.9, 1.10, 1.11, 1.12, 1.13	2.3, 2.5, 2.7, 2.8, 2.9, 2.12	

Suggested Timeframes

START TIME	YEAR 2	September		DURATION	6-7 weeks

Working Drawings

Default Design

Salt and Pepper Shakers

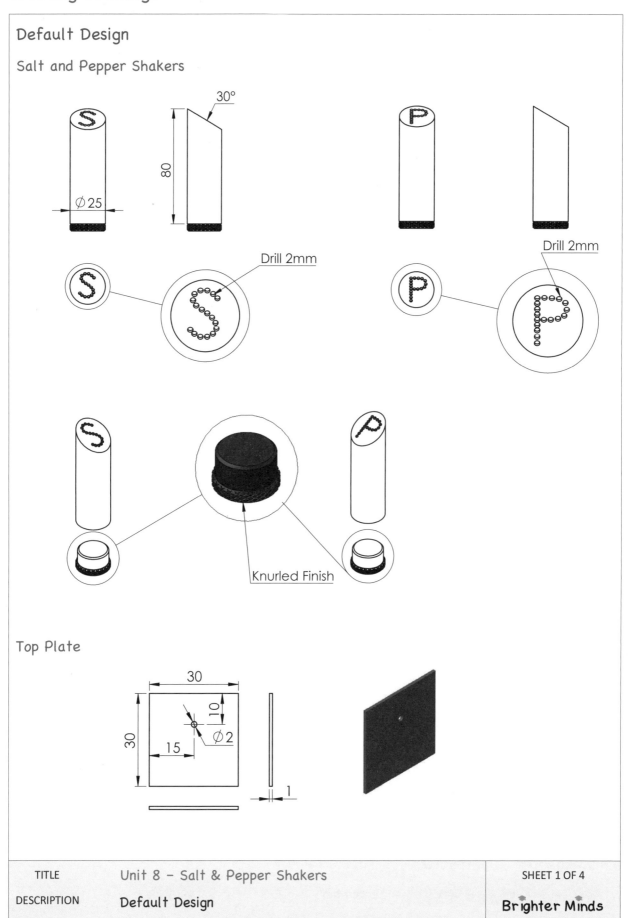

Top Plate

Default Design

Stoppers

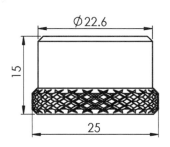

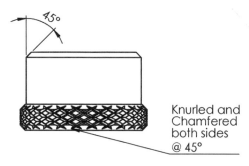

Knurled and Chamfered both sides @ 45°

Example Shaker Stand (Design Your Own)

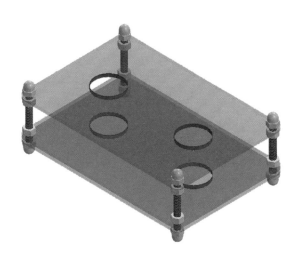

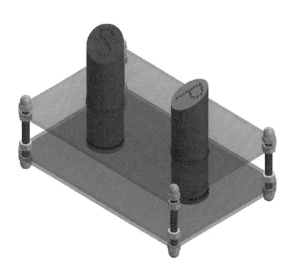

Bill of Materials

ITEM NO.	PART	DESCRIPTION	QTY.
1	SHAKER BODY	Ø25mm Copper Cylinder / Pipe	2
2	SHAKER TOP	1mm Copper Plate	2
3	STOPPERS	Ø25 Nylon Black Bar / Cylinder	2
4	SHAKER STAND	3mm Transparent Acrylic	2
5	THREADED BAR	M5	4
6	HEX NUT	M5	8
7	CAP NUT	M5	8

TITLE	Unit 8 – Salt & Pepper Shakers and Stand	SHEET 2 OF 4
DESCRIPTION	Default Design	Brighter Minds

Your Concept Sketches for the Stand (Follow the Project Storyboard Activities)

TITLE	Unit 8 – Salt & Pepper Shakers and Stand	SHEET 3 OF 4
DESCRIPTION	Concept Sketches for Shaker Stand	Brighter Minds

Your Final Design Drawings for the Stand (Follow the Project Storyboard Activities)

TITLE	Unit 8 – Salt & Pepper Shakers and Stand	SHEET 4 OF 4
DESCRIPTION	Final Design Drawings for the Shaker Stand	Brighter Minds

Project Storyboard

Project Description

LEARNING GOALS OF THIS PROJECT

- Learn how to **use a lathe** to shape cylindrical parts
- Learn how to **solder copper** sheets and pipes
- Provide an opportunity for **design** within the project

A different project that has similar goals and outcomes to the above could be substituted for ours

DEFAULT DESIGN - DESCRIPTION

- The default design project consists of:
    - A copper **salt shaker** - with holes in the top and a nylon **stopper** at the bottom
    - A copper **pepper shaker** - with holes in the top and a nylon **stopper** at the bottom
    - A **stand** for the shakers – we have provided an example but encourage your own design
- The shaker bodies are made from **copper pipe**
- The top plate is made from copper, **soldered** to the shaker body and then shaped to fit
- The **stoppers** are made from a single piece of **nylon** and are patterned (**knurled**) for grip

DESIGN OPPORTUNITIES IN THIS PROJECT   (See Project Storyboard Activities)

- You can design **your own drilling pattern** on the top plate of each shaker
- You can **modify** the salt and pepper **shakers** if you wish. For example, it would be simpler to make them with a flat circular top, rather than with a sloped elliptical top
- You can design your own **knurling pattern** on the nylon stopper
- You are encouraged to **design your own stand / holder** for the salt and pepper shakers:
    - You can make the stand from **one or more** pieces
    - You can choose your own **material**, or use a **number of different materials**

SOME DESIGN THOUGHTS

- Users should be able to **distinguish between the salt and the pepper** shakers
- We suggest the holes on the tops of the salt and pepper shakers could be diameter **2mm**
- One option for the design of the stand / holder - but not the only one - is to make **25mm holes** for the shakers to sit into

Understanding and Choosing Materials

Activity 1 – Materials

(1) List **two properties** associated with **copper**:

Property 1: _____

Property 2: _____

(2) Give **two reasons** why you think **copper** might be a **good choice** for salt and pepper shakers:

(i) _____

(ii) _____

Manufacture the Shaker Bodies

Activity 2 – Preparing for Manufacture

In the default design, the copper cylinder needs to be **cut at 60°** relative to side of the pipe

(1) **Explain** how you could **mark out** the required cut **angle** on the copper cylinder:

_____

_____

_____

(2) **Explain** how you could **cut** the copper cylinder to the required angle:

_____

_____

_____

(3) **Explain** how you would **finish** the edge of the copper after cutting it:

_____

_____

Activity 3 – Manufacture the Shaker Bodies

Cut the copper pipes to size, and finish the edges

Design and Manufacture the Shaker Tops

Activity 4 – Design the Shaker Tops

1. **Sketch** two designs for how you would like the **tops of your salt and pepper shakers** to look when completed (i.e. the final shape and the hole pattern).   *Hint: shape may be elliptical*

<u>DESIGN 1</u>   <u>DESIGN 2</u>

Salt Top   Pepper Top   Salt Top   Pepper Top

2. My selected design is Design Number: _____

I chose this design because: _____

_____

Activity 5 – Manufacture the Shaker Tops

Mark out, cut and drill your **top plates** now

Note - the top plates can be cut larger than the cylinder tops (they can be left square). The top plates can be soldered to the cylinder tops, and then later shaped to become flush with the cylinders.

Join the Shaker Tops to the Shaker Bodies

Activity 6 – Preparing for Manufacture

(1) List the equipment you will need to **solder** the top plate to the body:

See page 209

_____

_____

(2) **Explain** why **flux** is required in the soldering process:

See page 209

_____

_____

Activity 7 – Solder the Shaker Tops to the Bodies

Solder the unshaped / square **top plates** to the tops of the **cylinders** now

Activity 8 – Planning the Top Shaping and Finishing

1. After you have soldered the shaker tops to the shaker bodies, **describe** how you will **shape and finish the shaker tops** to become flush with the cylinders: *(consider use of a lathe, see p211)*

_____

_____

2. Explore how you will **clamp** the soldered cylinder securely while shaping the top plate.

Activity 9 – Complete the Shaker Bodies

Shape and finish the top plates to match the shape of the shaker bodies.

Manufacturing the Stoppers

Activity 10 – Understanding the Stopper Design

See page 215

1. Explain **why** the shaker stoppers are **knurled**:

_____

2. Name one piece of **marking out equipment** that is also **knurled**:

_____

Activity 11 – Understanding the Lathe

See Lathe pages 211-5

(A) **Learn about the lathe**. Follow teacher instructions. *(Complete H&S passport on page 20)*

(B) List **two safety precautions** you will take when using the lathe:

1. _____   2. _____

(C) Name the **lathe processes** you will use to shape your **stoppers**:

1. _____   2. _____

3. _____   4. _____

Activity 12 – Manufacture the Stoppers

Manufacture the shaker stoppers now. Ensure they **push-fit** tightly in the shaker bodies

Design a Shaker Stand / Holder

You may skip this and manufacture the stand shown in the working drawings, or design your own below.

Activity 13 – Concept Designs for Your Shaker Stand

On the 'Concept Sketches' page in the working drawings area, using free-hand, **sketch** three different **concept design ideas** for a shaker stand.
If you wish, practice your design ideas on separate paper before transferring to the book.

- Think about how the shakers will be **held**, and how easily they can be **removed**
- Think about including **additional features** in your stand, e.g. a napkin holder
- Remember the **dimensions** of the salt and pepper shakers
- Think about **different materials**
- Think about the **manufacturability** of your stand:
    - how will the parts be **shaped**?
    - how will the parts be **joined**?
- Consider your **time constraints**

Activity 14 – Prototype your Shaker Stand

1. If time allows, choose your favourite concept design and make a **cardboard model** of it.

2. **Test** your cardboard model with your manufactured shakers and **evaluate** your design.
Ask your teacher or a peer to **review** your prototype and design and make suggestions.

3. List any **modifications** you made to your design as a result of prototyping and reviewing:

_____

_____

_____

Activity 15 – Materials Selection for your Shaker Stand
Identify and **justify** your choice of material(s) for your shaker stand:

Material(s): _____

Reason(s): _____

_____

Activity 16 – Final Drawing for your Shaker Stand

In the '**Final Design Drawing**' page in the working drawings area, accurately **draw** and **dimension** your design.

Manufacturing the Shaker Stand

Activity 17 – Planning the Stand Manufacture

Your stand may contain two **25mm diameter holes** to hold the shakers.
Explain how you could best create these two large holes:

See Drilling page 210

Name of tool / equipment: _____

Process: _____

Activity 18 – Manufacture the Shaker Stand

Mark out and **manufacture** your **shaker stand** now

Post-Manufacturing Evaluation

Activity 19 – Evaluate the Shaker Manufacture

Describe any **difficulties** you had in **manufacturing the shakers**, and any **actions** that **helped**:

_____

_____

_____

_____

Activity 20 – Evaluate the Stand Manufacture

1. Describe **how you manufactured your stand**:

_____

_____

_____

_____

2. Describe **how your stand functioned** and what you might do differently to **improve** it:

_____

_____

_____

Project Assessment

Student Self-Assessment

In this project, I gained the following new **skills** and **knowledge**:

1. _____

2. _____

3. _____

I **evaluate** my project to have **turned out well** in the following areas:

_____

_____

If I were to carry out this project again, I would **modify** or **improve** the following aspects:

_____

_____

_____

_____

On a scale of 1 to 10, I would give my project a **score** of...

Peer Assessment

Identify **manufacturing processes** that were carried out to a **high standard**:

_____

_____

_____

Identify **manufacturing skills** or **design skills** your peer could **improve** upon:

_____

_____

_____

Teacher Feedback on Project

Teacher comments on student's project:

Not Graded	Partially Achieved	Achieved	Merit	Higher Merit	Distinction

Learning Topics for Unit 8

Processes and Principles

Materials – Ferrous Metals and Alloys

Revision Activities

See page 104, 202

(1) Explain what an **alloy** is:

_____

(2) Name **two alloys** that you know:

(i) _____ (ii) _____

(3) Explain why **alloys can have advantages** over pure metals:

_____

FERROUS METALS

- **Ferrous metals** predominantly contain **iron**, and this makes them **strong**
- **Steel** is a **ferrous alloy** of **iron** and **carbon**
- **Steel** is the most-commonly-used metal in the world
- Most of the **equipment** you use in the Engineering room is made from **steel** – e.g. drill bits, cutting tools, hammer heads, scribers, files. This is because steel is **strong** and **hard**

Later in this section, we'll learn about **different types of steel**, and **how steel is made**.

FERROUS METALS and ALLOYS

- **Contain IRON**
- **Strong**, usually **magnetic**
- **Corrode (rust) easily**
- **Iron does not exist naturally as a pure metal**, but it becomes very useful when **alloyed with carbon** - to make **steel** *(see next page)*

Material Properties particularly relevant to Ferrous Metals

Property	Explanation		Examples
STRENGTH	A strong material requires a large force to make it deform plastically or fracture. A strong material will **support a large load** without deforming permanently. The strength of a material depends on the direction that the force is applied:		
	COMPRESSIVE STRENGTH	Materials that are **strong under compression** can support large compressive loads without deforming plastically or breaking, e.g. **concrete**.	**Concrete**
	TENSILE STRENGTH	Materials that have **high tensile strength** can withstand large pulling forces without deforming plastically or breaking, for example **steel cables**.	**Steel**
ELASTICITY	An **elastic** material can be deformed a long way from its original shape and will still **return to that original shape**. Elasticity is highly useful in **steel springs** and rubber seals.		**Rubber, Spring Steel**
BRITTLENESS	A brittle material breaks easily when impacted. When hit, a brittle material doesn't deform elastically or plastically - it goes straight to fracture (breaking) Note: **strong materials can also be brittle**. For example, construction bricks are very strong in compression (i.e. they will support a heavy load) but they will shatter easily when tipped with a hammer!		**Cast Iron, Glass, Ceramics, Concrete**
TOUGHNESS	A **tough material** is **difficult to break by impacting it**. It is **impact-resistant** – it absorbs the energy of the impacts by deforming. It will only fracture under very high energy impacts. **A tough material is both strong and not brittle**. You need tough materials in applications where they can receive lots of impacts – e.g. car axles, motorway safety barriers.		**Mild Steel / Low-Carbon Steel** *(see later)*
HARDNESS	A **hard** material is **difficult to scratch or indent** – i.e. it **resists plastic deformation** of its surface. Hard materials keep their **surface finish** without scratching.		**Diamond, Tungsten Carbide**
CORROSION-RESISTANCE	**Corrosion** means the surface of the material oxidises with the air. **Ferrous metals** like iron and steel **corrode (rust) easily**. **Non-ferrous metals** and **plastics** do **not** corrode easily.		**Ferrous Metals corrode**

Ferrous Alloys – Irons and Steels

As mentioned earlier, iron does not exist naturally on its own (iron oxidises quickly to make iron oxide), so all the useful ferrous metals are **ferrous alloys** – i.e. iron combined with another metal or element. The most common ferrous alloys are **cast iron** and **steel**, which are alloys of **iron and carbon**.

Iron and Steels

- **Irons** and **steels** are alloys of **iron** and **carbon**

- The **carbon** comes from the **iron and steel-making process** *(see later)*

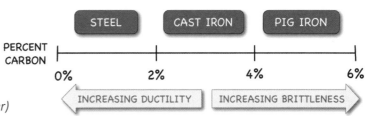

Irons and steels are classified according to the **percentage of carbon** they contain. The **more carbon** in the alloy, the **harder** and **more brittle** the material will be.

Irons – High Carbon Content (> 2.1%)

Type of Iron	% Carbon	Description	Applications
PIG IRON	> 4%	• Pinkish, **very brittle** metal • Made from **iron ore** using a **blast furnace** *(see later)*	• Too brittle to use • **Used to make cast iron and steel**
CAST IRON	2.1% - 4%	• Made from **pig iron** using a **cupola furnace** *(see later)* • **Easily cast** into different shapes • **High compressive strength** • **Resistant to wear** • More **brittle** than steel • **Rusts** easily	• Cookware • Vice bodies • Engine blocks • Crankshafts • Machine tools • Brake pads

Steels

> **Steel** is an **iron-carbon alloy** where the **carbon percentage is less than 2.1%**

Steel is made by removing carbon from pig iron – we'll see how this is done shortly.

Plain Carbon Steels - Low to High Carbon Content (< 2.1%)

> **Plain carbon steels** are composed primarily of **iron** and **carbon**, and are common and cheap

Carbon Steel	% Carbon	Description	Applications
LOW-CARBON STEEL *(MILD STEEL)*	0.03% - 0.25%	• **Tough, ductile, malleable** • Easily machined (cut) • Rusts easily *(Properties page 103)*	• **Sheet metal**, cans • Car bodies • Nuts, bolts, nails
MEDIUM-CARBON STEEL	0.25% - 0.6%	• **Stronger** and **harder** than mild steel • Good **mix of strength** and **toughness** • **Machinable** (e.g. using lathes, drills)	• **Gears**, crankshafts • Axles • Railway tracks • Structural beams

Carbon Steel	% Carbon	Description	Applications
HIGH-CARBON STEEL	0.6% - 1.5%	• **Strongest** and **hardest, most brittle** • **Difficult** to **machine** and **weld** • Can be **heat-treated** *(see later)* to **harden** the surface further for tools and bearings	• **Cutting tools** • Hammers, chisels, files • Springs • Ball bearings

Alloy Steels

Alloy steels contain **more alloying elements** than just carbon – to create desirable properties

Alloy Steel	Composition	Description	Applications
STAINLESS STEEL	Low-carbon steel plus 11% **chromium**	• High **resistance to corrosion** • **Shiny** surface	• **Cutlery**, utensils • Medical and dental instruments
HIGH-SPEED STEEL (HSS) / TOOL STEEL	High-carbon steel plus 18% **tungsten** plus **cobalt**	• **Retains hardness** and cutting edge with high-speed and high-temperature cutting	• **Drill bits** • Lathe cutting tools • Hacksaw blades
SPRING STEEL	Medium-to-high carbon, plus **manganese**	• **High elasticity** • **Hard** surface	• **Springs**, clips • Music wire/strings

Coated / Plated Steels

Coated Steel	Plating Metals	Description	Applications
GALVANISED STEEL	**Mild steel** coated or plated with **zinc**	• **Resistant to corrosion** • Outer layer of **zinc** prevents inner layer of **steel** from rusting	• **Roof panels** • Ladders
TINPLATE	**Mild steel** coated or plated with **tin**	• **Resistant to corrosion** • **Non-toxic** - safe for food	• Food and drink **cans**

Difference between Alloys and Composites

- The coated / plated materials above, such as **tinplate** - are **composites** – because they are composed of **two separate materials bonded together**
- **Alloys** are not composites - they are a **single material** the whole way through. The elements that make up an alloy are thoroughly mixed together at a **molecular level** to create one single material

Activities – Ferrous Metals and Alloys

Activities

1. Steel is an alloy of **iron and** _____

2. What type of steel is used to make **sheet metal**? _____

3. What type of steel is a **drill bit** made from? _____

Production of Ferrous Metals and Alloys

OVERVIEW OF THE PRODUCTION OF IRON AND STEEL

- **Iron ore** comes in different mineral forms (e.g. hematite, magnetite, limonite and iron pyrite). It is mined, crushed and separated to form **concentrated iron ore**

- A **blast furnace burns** the **concentrated iron ore**, along with coke, limestone and blasts of hot air, to create **pig iron** and **slag** (waste)

- A **cupola furnace** burns the cooled **pig iron** with more coke, limestone and air, to remove more carbon and create **cast iron** (and more slag)

- A **basic oxygen furnace** takes the **molten pig iron** straight from the blast furnace and forces high-pressure **pure oxygen** into it using a **water-cooled oxygen lance**. This burns off large amounts of carbon to create molten **steel**

- An **electric arc furnace** is another way to make steel. It takes the **molten pig iron** from the blast furnace (or it can use **scrap /recycled steel**). It uses its **electrodes** to create high-voltage **electric arcs**. This creates huge heat that burns off carbon to form **molten steel**

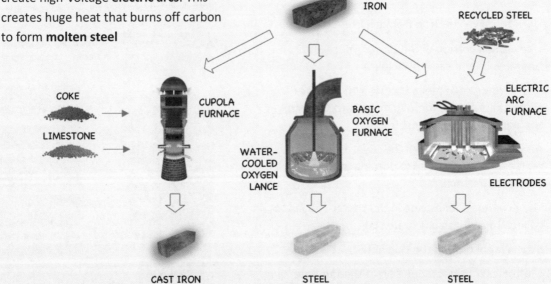

- When the metal is hot and soft, it can be **cast**, **forged**, **extruded** or **rolled** into desired shapes
- The process of using **heat** and **furnaces** to create metals is called **smelting**
- Even though the waste from these furnaces is treated, these furnaces are very **environmentally-unfriendly** and produce **large amounts of carbon dioxide and solid waste** (slag)

Furnaces used to produce Iron and Steel

THE BLAST FURNACE — PIG IRON

CHARGING BELLS

CHARGE (INPUTS)

CONCENTRATED IRON ORE · COKE · LIMESTONE

GAS OUTLET

REFRACTORY BRICK LINING

STEEL SHEEL

BURNING FURNACE

TUYERES (AIR NOZZLES)

MOLTEN SLAG

SLAG HOLE

MOLTEN PIG IRON

▶ VIDEO

TAP HOLE

- Makes **pig iron** from **iron ore**
- The **charge** (inputs) is loaded in through the top **charging bells**
- The **charging bells** are a system of double doors that **prevent the heat escaping**
- **Air** is **blasted** in through the **tuyeres** *(air nozzles)* to **burn the coke** more fiercely
- Chemical reactions take place that cause **molten pig iron** to sink to the bottom
- The molten pig iron is tapped off at the **tap hole**
- The **limestone** in the charge is used to collect impurities and make **slag** (waste)
- The **slag** floats on top of the molten pig iron and is tapped off at the **slag hole**
- The **walls** are made from **refractory brick** to contain the immense heat
- Produces large amounts of **waste** – solid **slag**, **carbon dioxide** and other gases

THE CUPOLA FURNACE — CAST IRON

- Used to make **cast iron** from pig iron
- Like a small version of the blast furnace and operates on the same principle
- The **burning coke melts the pig iron** and the chemical reactions **remove more carbon from the pig iron**, creating **cast iron**
- **Air** is pumped in through the **tuyeres** *(air nozzles)* regularly to keep the coke burning and the temperatures high
- The powdered **limestone** in the charge is used to collect impurities and create **slag**
- **Slag** is tapped off at the **slag hole**
- **Molten cast iron** is tapped off at the **tap hole**

Watch the Brighter Minds videos to see the furnaces in action. Take the quizzes.

CHARGE (INPUTS)

PIG IRON · SCRAP IRON/STEEL · COKE · LIMESTONE

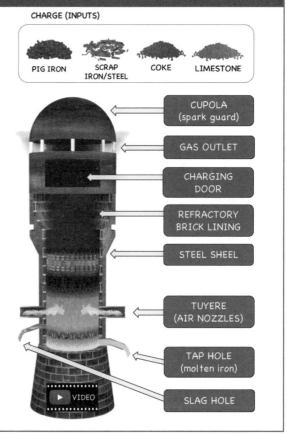

CUPOLA (spark guard)

GAS OUTLET

CHARGING DOOR

REFRACTORY BRICK LINING

STEEL SHEEL

TUYERE (AIR NOZZLES)

TAP HOLE (molten iron)

▶ VIDEO

SLAG HOLE

THE BASIC OXYGEN FURNACE   STEEL

CHARGE (INPUTS)

MOLTEN PIG IRON (FROM BLAST FURNACE) · SCRAP IRON / STEEL · LIME (FLUX)

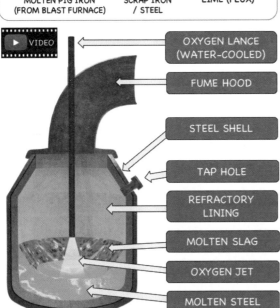

- ► VIDEO
- OXYGEN LANCE (WATER-COOLED)
- FUME HOOD
- STEEL SHELL
- TAP HOLE
- REFRACTORY LINING
- MOLTEN SLAG
- OXYGEN JET
- MOLTEN STEEL

- Makes **steel** from **molten pig iron**
- It does this by **blasting pure oxygen** into the molten pig iron to **burn off more carbon** to create the **steel** (< 2.1% carbon)
- The **fume hood** is first removed / swivelled off
- **Molten pig iron** - coming straight from the blast furnace - is **poured in** the top
- **Lime** is added to collect impurities and make **slag** (waste)
- The **fume hood** is replaced
- The **water-cooled oxygen lance** is lowered into the furnace
- **Oxygen** is pumped in at **supersonic speed** for a short time
- The fume hood is removed
- The furnace is **tilted** and the **molten steel is poured out the tap hole**
- The furnace is then **tilted back the other way** and the **molten slag is poured out** the opening

THE ELECTIC ARC FURNACE   STEEL

- Makes new **steel** from **scrap iron and steel**
- **High-voltage electrodes** create electric arcs which create huge amounts of heat to melt the metal and **burn off excess carbon**
- The **roof** and carbon **electrodes** are **lifted off** the furnace
- **Scrap metal** is lowered into the furnace
- **Lime** is added to collect impurities and make **slag** (waste)
- The **roof** and electrodes are **placed back** on the furnace
- High voltage applied to the electrodes creates **electric arcs** which melts the metal and **burns off any excess carbon**
- The **roof** and electrodes are **removed** again
- The furnace is **tilted** and the **molten slag is poured out** through the inspection door
- The furnace is tilted forward and the **molten steel** is **poured out** the **tapping spout**

CHARGE (INPUTS)

SCRAP IRON/STEEL · MOLTEN PIG IRON (OPTIONAL) · LIME (FLUX)

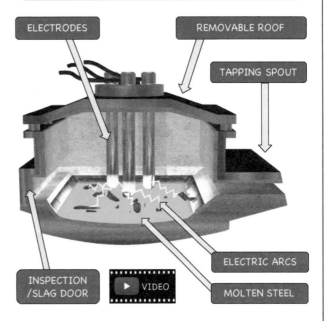

- ELECTRODES
- REMOVABLE ROOF
- TAPPING SPOUT
- ELECTRIC ARCS
- INSPECTION /SLAG DOOR
- ► VIDEO
- MOLTEN STEEL

Research Activity – Iron and Steel Production

Watch the Brighter Minds **videos** on the **four furnaces** involved in iron and steel production.
For each furnace:

- **draw** a simple **sketch** of the furnace, and **label** the main parts
- **write** out your own **notes** on the furnace:
  o list the **inputs** (charge) and the **outputs** of the furnace
  o write out a number of bullet points describing **how the furnace operates**

Revision Activities – Metals

1. Circle the **non-ferrous** metals in this list:

   Copper   Steel   Brass   Cast Iron   Aluminium

2. Circle the **strongest metal** in the list below:

   Copper   Steel   Bronze   Aluminium

3. Circle the **two metals** that are the **most ductile** in the list below:

   Copper   Mild Steel   Gold   Cast Iron   Aluminium

4. Circle the **hardest** metal in this list:

   Copper   Mild Steel   Gold   Cast Iron   Aluminium

5. Circle which of these metals is the **most brittle**:

   Copper   Steel   Cast Iron

6. Circle which of these steels is the **hardest**:

   High-Carbon Steel   Low-Carbon Steel   High-Speed Steel

7. Circle which of these steels would be the most suitable to make **thin sheet metal** from:

   High-Carbon Steel   Low-Carbon Steel   High-Speed Steel

8. Circle which of these steels would be the most suitable to make **cutting tools** from:

   High-Carbon Steel   Low-Carbon Steel   High-Speed Steel

9. Circle which of these metals is the **lightest**:

   Mild Steel   Tin   Aluminium   Cast Iron

10. Circle the **materials** that are **corrosion-resistant** in this list:

   Copper   Mild Steel   Tinplate   Gold   Cast Iron   Aluminium

Materials – Heat Treatment of Metals

> **Heat treatment** is used to **change the properties** of metals and **alloys**

- Heat treatment is widely used on **steels** and on some **non-ferrous alloys**
- Heat treatment can make metals **harder** or **softer** depending on the process used (see below)
- Heat treatment **does not melt** or change the shape of the metals
- Heat treatment works because it **re-organises the crystal structures** within the metal

3 Stages of Heat Treatment

THREE STAGES OF HEAT TREATMENT

HEATING → 'SOAKING' → COOLING

HEATING - The metal is **heated** to a defined **temperature**, using a furnace or a flame

SOAKING - The metal is **kept at that temperature** for a defined period of time

COOLING - The metal is **cooled** at a defined **rate** in a certain **medium** – e.g. air, water, oil or a furnace

Types of Heat Treatment

There are many different types of heat treatment - some of the most common are shown below.

Process	Applications	HEATING	SOAKING	COOLING
HARDENING	Used to create a **hard surface on steel**, e.g. for **cutting** (blades, chisels, drill bits, punches), or for increased **scratch-resistance**	**High temp**: > 750°C for steel (cherry red)	15 min to 1 hr depending on thickness	**Rapid** cooling by **quenching** the metal in water, oil or brine*
TEMPERING	Used to **remove excess brittleness** from steel that has just been **hardened**	**Low temp**: 175-375°C for steel (yellow to blue)	No. of hours depending on ductility required	**Medium fast** natural cooling in **air**
ANNEALING	Creates the **most ductile** (softest) version of the metal. Used on **steels** and **copper**. Often used before hardening to get the best results.	**High temp**: > 750°C for steel (cherry red)	No. of hours depending on thickness of material	**Very slowly** over many hours by reducing temp of furnace
NORMALISATION	Used on steels to **relieve internal stresses** and create a **strong** and **ductile** (i.e. tough) material. Faster process than annealing.	**High temp**: > 750°C for steel (cherry red)	No. of hours depending on thickness of material	**Medium fast** natural cooling in **air**

*Quenching Media for Hardening

1. **BRINE** (salt and water) – gives the **fastest cooling** and the **hardest** and **most brittle** results.
2. **WATER** – gives a medium-fast cooling with a **less hard** result, but with less risk of metal cracking.
3. **OIL** – gives the **slowest** cooling and **least hard and brittle** result. Safety hazard - produces **fumes**.

Manufacturing Processes

Workholding

VEE BLOCK AND CLAMP	• Used to **clamp cylindrical parts** like bars or pipes while working on them • The **V-shaped block** can accommodate **different diameter workpieces** • The screws tightens down to **clamp** the workpiece against the vee-block 

Measurement

INSIDE CALIPERS	• Used to capture the **inside dimension** of an object e.g. the internal diameter of a **cylinder** • The **distance** between the calliper points is then **measured** using a ruler or Vernier callipers • The **nut** and **spring** keep the callipers in a fixed position while the distance is being measured 

> ### Revision Activity - Measurement
> Name a **piece of equipment** other than the above that can accurately **measure internal and external diameters** and the **depth of a hole**:
>
> _____

Joining – Threaded Bar

THREADED BAR	• **Long headless bolts** - come in metre lengths • Cut to size with a **hacksaw** • Used where standard bolts are too short • Come in a wide variety of threads: M3, M4, M6, M8 and M10 etc. • Also known as a **stud** • Can also be used as **axles** for school projects 

Joining - Soldering

> ### Revision Activity
> **Explain** the two main purposes of **flux**:
>
> *Purpose 1: (hint: oxidisation)* _____
>
> *Purpose 1: (hint: flow)* _____

Joining Copper Pieces by Soldering

In Unit 6 you used **soldering** to create permanent **electrical connections**. You can also use **soldering to join copper pipes** and plates together. The process is similar, but different tools and techniques are used:

SOLDERING LARGE COPPER PARTS	SOLDERING SMALL ELECTRICAL CONNECTIONS
• Uses a **gas torch** to provide more heat • Uses a **separate flux** and **solder** • The **lead-free solder** is thicker and a different composition to electrical solder • The **flux** comes as a separate **paste**. It is an **active flux** which contains chemical cleaners	• Uses a **soldering iron** to provide the heat • Uses thin **cored solder** – where the flux is contained inside an outer tube of solder • The **flux** is a **passive flux** which is **non-corrosive** and suitable for electrical connections *See Soldering Electronics Circuits page 144*

Steps to Join Copper Pipe and Copper Plate by Soldering

STEP 1	• **Clean** the areas to be joined, with sandpaper
STEP 2	• **Apply flux paste** to the joint areas. *Flux helps the solder **flow** and **stops the metals oxidising** (which could ruin the joint)*
STEP 3	• **Place** the copper pipe on top of the copper sheet **in a safe area** – *see safety notes* • Place a small amount of **solder** inside the pipe
STEP 4	• **Heat** the joint area with the **flame** - *see safety notes* - until the solder **melts**. Remove heat. • Solder is drawn into the gap between the metals by **capillary action** and solidifies quickly
NOTES on joining two pipes	• To **solder two pipes**, clean and **flux** the joint areas, place one pipe **inside** the other. **Heat** the joint area and **touch** the stick of solder on the joint area, where it will **melt** and be 'sucked' inside the pipes by **capillary action**

SAFETY NOTES – GAS TORCH

- Ensure **gas torch** is maintained and in **good working order**
- Ensure there is a working **fire extinguisher** in the room in a known location
- Wear **safety gloves** and **safety goggles**
- Work in a **safe area**, where the surrounding environment cannot be burned by the flame
- Use a **brazing hearth** if possible to contain the flames
- **Turn off the flame** as soon as possible – do not leave the flame on when not in use
- **Never point flame** at anyone or mess with the flame

Drilling

Drill Bits

PARALLEL SHANK Drill Bits	• **Parallel shank** drill bits are held in a **drill chuck** • Available up to diameter 13mm • Drill bits are made from **High-Speed Steel** (HSS)	
TAPER SHANK Drill Bits	• A **morse taper shank** drill bit fits directly into the **spindle** of the pillar drill (or lathe) using a **friction fit** • The **chuck must be removed** in order to gain access to the spindle • Taper shank drill bits are generally used to drill **larger holes** 13mm and above	
MORSE TAPER SLEEVE	• A **morse taper sleeve** is used to make up the **difference in size** between a thin **taper shank** drill bit and the **spindle** • A **'drift' tool** is used to remove the drill bit from the sleeve afterwards	
HOLE SAW	• A **hole saw** is special type of drill bit used to **cut large holes** • It has saw **teeth** around its circumference • It has a **pilot drill bit** in the middle, to ensure the drilling is **centred** before the saw teeth engage with the material • Can be used in a pillar drill or cordless drill	

Drilling Activity - Think-Pair-Share

Think about the following questions, pair up with another student, and share your thoughts.

1. <u>How</u> would you **change the rotation speed** of a **pillar drill**?

_____

_____

2. <u>Why</u> would you need to **change the rotation speed** of a drill?

_____

_____

The Lathe

- A **lathe** is a **machine tool** used to carry out **turning** and related operations on **metals** or **plastics**
- The **workpiece** is usually cylindrical and is clamped in a **chuck** and rotated
- The **cutting tool** is moved slowly against the workpiece to **cut away** the desired material
- A lathe can be controlled **manually** or via **Computer Numerical Control (CNC)**

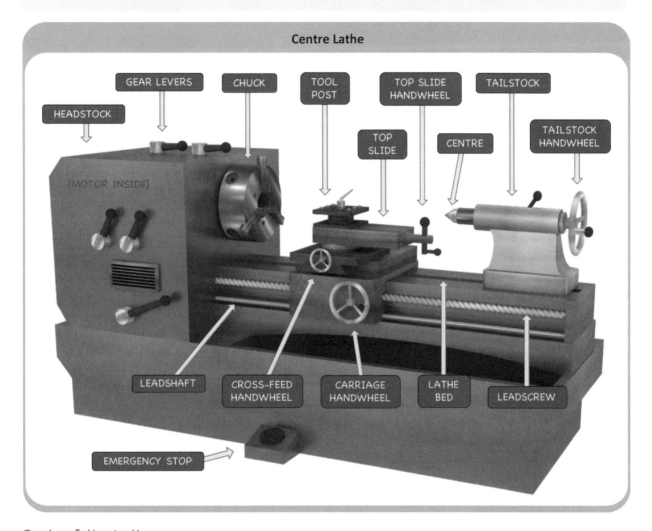

Centre Lathe

Parts of the Lathe

Part	Description
HEADSTOCK	The **headstock** houses the **motor** and **gears** which turn the main **spindle** and **chuck**
CHUCK	The **chuck** is attached to the **motor spindle** and clamps the **workpiece**

3-JAW CHUCK	4-JAW CHUCK
Self-centering - all three jaws close at the same time	Each jaw is closed **independently**, so it can hold **non-cyclindrical** shapes

Part	Description
TOOLPOST	The **toolpost** holds the **cutting tool** **4-WAY TOOLPOST** / **QUICK CHANGE TOOLPOST** Can hold up to four cutting tools. Tools are bolted down. / Has a lever to allow quick changing of different-sized tool holders and tools.
CARRIAGE AND SLIDES	• The **toolpost** is mounted on the **top slide** (also called a **compound rest**) and can be rotated to the desired cutting tool angle. • The **top slide** sits on the **cross-slide**, which can be moved at 90° to the lathe axis • The cross-slide sits on the **carriage**, which slides left-to-right along the lathe axis • The carriage can be moved **manually** via the handwheel, or the leadscrew can be engaged with the main spindle so that the cutting tool is **automatically** fed from right to left at a defined rate (thread cutting) TOOLPOST TOP SLIDE CROSS SLIDE APRON CARRIAGE
TAILSTOCK	• The **tailstock** is at the opposite end of the lathe to the headstock • The tailstock can also **hold tools** such as **drill bits** and **reamers**, which operate on the rotating workpiece • The **barrel** of the tailstock contains a **taper** to allow tapered tools to be held on a **friction-fit** (i.e. without the need for a tailstock chuck) • The handwheel wheel moves the barrel and releases the tool from the barrel • For safety, ensure the tailstock is always locked to lathe bed with the lever
TAILSTOCK CHUCK	A **tailstock chuck** fits into the **tailstock barrel** on a taper fit, and can be used to hold **small** and straight-shaft **tools** like **drill bits**.

Lathe Safety

Safety Features of the Lathe	Safety Precautions to be taken when Operating a Lathe
• **Emergency Stop** button • **Braking** mechanism on chuck • **Interlocking Chuck Guard** • **Chip Screens** • **Leadscrew Guard** • **Rigidity** to minimise vibrations	• Ensure work is **securely clamped. Remove chuck keys!** • Ensure all **safety guards** (chuck, chip, splash) **are in place** • Ensure stopping controls are **unobstructed** • Use the **correct speeds** for materials, use **low spindle speed** when taper turning and knurling • **Minimise vibration**

Lathe Tools

CUTTING TOOL (SINGLE-POINT)	Lathes use **single-point cutting tools**. Cutting tools come in a variety of materials, shapes and sizes designed for different jobs. They are usually made from one piece of **HSS** (high-speed steel), or contain **tungsten-carbide** inserts. *Cutting tools must be on-centre before cutting.*	
PARTING -OFF TOOL	A **parting-off tool** is a sharp narrow tool for cutting fully through the workpiece (and separating it into two parts). It can also be used to create **undercuts** – cylindrical **grooves** in the workpiece.	
MORSE TAPER DRILL BIT	Many **drill bits** for lathes have a **tapered shank** so that can be gripped in the tapered tailstock barrel without the need for a tailstock chuck.	
CENTRE DRILL (OR SLOCOMBE)	A **centre drill** is a **drill bit** used to create a **small conical hole** in the end of the workpiece, either as a pilot hole for drilling, or so that the workpiece can be supported by a **centre** held in the **tailstock**. The shank of the centre drill is a large diameter so that the bit doesn't flex.	
KNURLING TOOL	A **knurling tool** makes a diamond- or other-shaped **pattern** on the **surface** of the workpiece. Knurling creates a **grip** surface on metal surfaces. Knurling is commonly seen on metal **darts**.	

Cutting Tools – Rake and Clearance Angles

The **angles** on a cutting tool are important in the functioning of the cutting tool.

RAKE ANGLE	• The **rake angle** is the angle between the **cutting face** and **workpiece surface** • The rake angle applies the deforming force and **shapes the chip** (waste) • **Positive** rake angles are used for **ductile** materials, **negative** for **hard** materials
CLEARANCE ANGLE	The **clearance angle** prevents the bottom of the tool scraping the cut surface

Rake and Clearance Angles

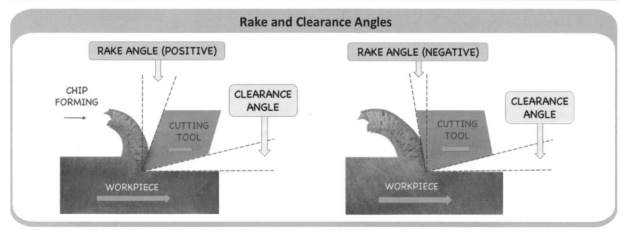

Using the Lathe

Lathe Operations

Operation	Description
PARALLEL TURNING	<ul><li>**Parallel turning** (or just '**turning**') creates a smaller-diameter cylinder, removing a thin layer of material</li><li>The **workpiece** is clamped in the **chuck** and rotated</li><li>The **cutting tool** is **fed** right-to-left, parallel to the axis of rotation, manually or automatically</li><li>Long workpieces can be supported using *steadies* or a *tailstock centre*</li></ul> 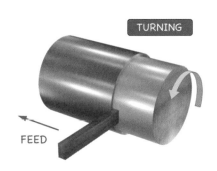

FACING / SETTING THE TOOL ON-CENTRE

FACING	SETTING THE TOOL ON-CENTRE
<ul><li>**Facing** produces a **flat surface** on the **end** of the workpiece</li><li>The cutting tool cuts with the **front edge**</li><li>The tool is **fed inwards only**, at right angles to the axis of rotation</li></ul>	<ul><li>The **cutting edge** of the tool must be **aligned** with the **centre axis** of the workpiece before machining</li><li>If the tool is **too high**, the rake and clearance **angles** will be incorrect, causing rubbing and poor surface finish</li><li>If the cutting tool is **too low**, cutting angles will be affected and **the cutting edge cannot reach the centre** of **the workpiece**, leaving an **uncut** piece</li></ul>

FACING

FEED

CUTTING TOOL TOO HIGH

TOO LARGE RAKE ANGLE

TOO SMALL CLEARANCE ANGLE

CUTTING TOOL TOO LOW

TOOL CAN'T REACH THE CENTRE TO FINISH THE FACING!

| **PARTING-OFF** | <ul><li>**Parting-off** means **cutting the workpiece into two pieces**</li><li>This is done by moving a **parting-off tool** inwards in a straight line, to cut a narrow **groove** from the surface to the centre</li><li>The height of the tool must be in line with the centre axis of the workpiece</li></ul> 
PARTING OFF
FEED |

Operation	Description	
TAPER TURNING	**Taper turning** creates a **conical shape** on the workpiece. ***OFFSETTING THE TOP SLIDE*** Used for **short tapers**. The workpiece is held in the chuck. The top slide is rotated to form an angle with the axis of rotation. The cutting tool is fed along the axis of the top slide using the top slide handwheel.	TAPER TURNING – OFFSETTING THE TOP SLIDE FEED
DRILLING	• A **drill bit** is held in the **tailstock**, using a **taper fit** or a **tailstock chuck** • The workpiece is rotated and the drill bit is **fed** into the centre of the work piece using the tailstock wheel • A **centre drill** is used to drill a **pilot hole** first to ensure drilling starts on centre	DRILLING USING THE TAILSTOCK ROTATED VIA CHUCK HELD IN TAILSTOCK
KNURLING	• **Knurling** creates a **pattern** on the workpiece • Used on **darts** and **tool handles** to provide a **grip** • SAFETY WARNING: Knurling generates a lot of **heat**. There is a risk of **personal burns** or cutting fluids *(used to lubricate and cool the cutting)* going **on fire**	
CHAMFER-ING	• **Chamfering** creates a small **angled edge** (usually 45°) • Carried out for **safety** reasons to **remove sharp edges** or to **improve appearance** • It can be carried out using a **chamfering tool** and a straight cross-feed, or by **angling** a suitable **cutting tool** using the **top slide**	

Cutting Speed

Cutting speed is the **LINEAR speed that a cutting edge travels across the material surface**

For a machine tool to cut correctly, it must cut at the **correct cutting speed**. The correct cutting speed is **dependent on the type of material**. You can look up cutting speeds, or your teacher will tell you.

Spindle Speed

Spindle speed is the **ROTARY speed (RPM)** associated with a rotary tool **like a drill or lathe**

When you are cutting with a lathe or drill, you will often need to know what **spindle (rotary) speed** will give you the desired linear cutting speed. The RPM required is **dependent on the diameter of the workpiece** or hole being cut. *(This is because for a given RPM, the linear cutting speed will be higher for larger diameter workpieces).* You can **calculate the spindle speed** you need using this formula:

$$N \text{ (spindle speed in RPM)} = \frac{S \text{ (cutting speed in m/sec)} \times 1000}{\pi \times D \text{ (diameter in mm)}}$$

Research Activity – CNC Lathes

Research **CNC lathes** and contrast them with **manual lathes**. In your report or presentation, consider the following: basic operation, accuracy, speed/time required, workforce required, cost, suitability for different types of work, advantages, disadvantages.

Unit (8) Revision

Unit 8 Revision Questions

1. Explain the following terms: brittleness, elasticity, hardness.

2. Name two ductile metals.

3. Explain what an alloy is.

4. Give three characteristics of a ferrous metal.

5. Explain what steel is, and give three reasons why steel is so widely used.

6. Explain what corrosion is, and give three ways of limiting its effect.

7. Give one application for each of the following:

   (i)   Cast Iron
   (ii)   Low-Carbon Steel
   (iii)   Medium-Carbon Steel
   (iv)   High-Carbon Steel
   (v)   Galvanised Steel
   (vi)   Stainless Steel

8. Explain the term smelting.

9. Name the type of furnace that is used to make pig iron. List what it uses as inputs (charge).

10. Name two types of furnaces that make steel.

11. List the input charge that is used to make steel (i.e. what is steel is made from).

12. Name three different types of heat treatment. For each type of heat treatment:

    (a) Explain what that type of heat treatment does;

    (b) Give one application for that type of heat treatment.

13. Explain what a hole saw is, what it is used for, and how it is used.

14. Explain what a Morse taper sleeve is used for. Communicate your answer with the use of a sketch.

15. Explain what outside callipers and inside callipers are used for.

16. Describe the equipment needed, and the steps required to solder two pieces of copper together.

17. How is oxidation prevented from affecting joints that are being soldered?

18. Name three safety features on a lathe.

19. Describe each of the following lathe processes with the use of text and sketches:

(a) Facing-off	(c) Taper Turning	(e) Drilling
(b) Parallel Turning	(d) Parting-off	(f) Knurling

'Tis the Season

Unit 9 – 'Tis the Season

Unit Objectives

PROJECT	Design and make a **moving festive figure** for Christmas or other occasion

- Build a **peg-and-slot** mechanism powered by a DC motor. Understand **linkages**
- Learn and apply the joining techniques of **tapping and threading**
- Learn about **forces** and **structures**
- Learn how to DC motors from a **micro:bit** using an **expansion board**

Content

	Materials	• Working with brass
PROCESSES AND PRINCIPLES	**Structures**	• Types of forces: compression, tension, shear, torsion • Structures: arches, triangulation, struts, ties, beams
	Cutting	• Scroll saw, bandsaw
	Drilling	• Blind hole, tapping size hole
	Joining	• Tapping and threading
DESIGN APPLICATION	• Designing to a theme, incorporating new joining techniques, new mechanisms, designing the electronics housing	
MECHATRONICS	**Mechanisms**	• Peg-and-slot, crank-and-slider, linkages
	micro:bit	• Controlling DC motors using a DC Motor Driver Board

Learning Outcomes from this Unit

PROCESSES AND PRINCIPLES	DESIGN APPLICATION	MECHATRONICS
1.1, 1.2, 1.3, 1.4, 1.7, 1.8, 1.9, 1.10, 1.11, 1.12, 1.13	2.3, 2.5, 2.6, 2.7, 2.8, 2.9, 2.10, 2.11, 2.12	3.3, 3.6, 3.7, 3.8, 3.9, 3.10

Suggested Timeframes

START TIME	YEAR 2	Mid October

DURATION	8-9 weeks

Working Drawings

Default Design

Assembled View

Bill of Materials

NO	PART	DESCRIPTION	QTY.
1	FRAME	1mm Brass Sheet	1
2	BASE	6mm Transparent Acyrlic	1
3	FRAME-BASE SCREWS	M5 x 6mm Pan Head	2
4	MOTOR	3V Inline (geared) DC motor	1
5	MOTOR BOLTS	M3 x 25mm	2
6	MOTOR NUTS	M3 Hex Nut	2
7	FULCRUM THREADED BAR	Ø6mm Round Bar (aluminium, mild steel, brass)	1
8	SPACER FOR FULCRUM BAR	Ø8 Brass Round Tube	1
9	NUT FOR FULCRUM BAR	M5 Hex Nut	1
10	MOTOR-DRIVEN DISC	6mm Transparent Acyrlic	1
11	PEG FOR DISC	Ø6 Round Bar (aluminium, mild Steel, brass)	1
12	SLOTTED ARM	6mm Transparent Acyrlic	1
13	REINDEER / FESTIVE FIGURE	2mm Aluminium or 5mm Acrylic	1
14	REINDEER NOSE *(optional)*	LED Top or Red Acrylic	1
15	REINDEER BOLT	M5 x 12mm Pan Head	1
16	REINDEER NUT	M5 Hex Nut	1
17	BATTERY BOX *(not shown)*	To contain 2 x AA Batteries	1
18	BATTERIES *(not shown)*	AA size	2

Exploded View

TITLE	Unit 9 – 'Tis the Season	SHEET 1 OF 6
DESCRIPTION	Default Design – Assembled & Exploded Views	Brighter Minds

Default Design

Base

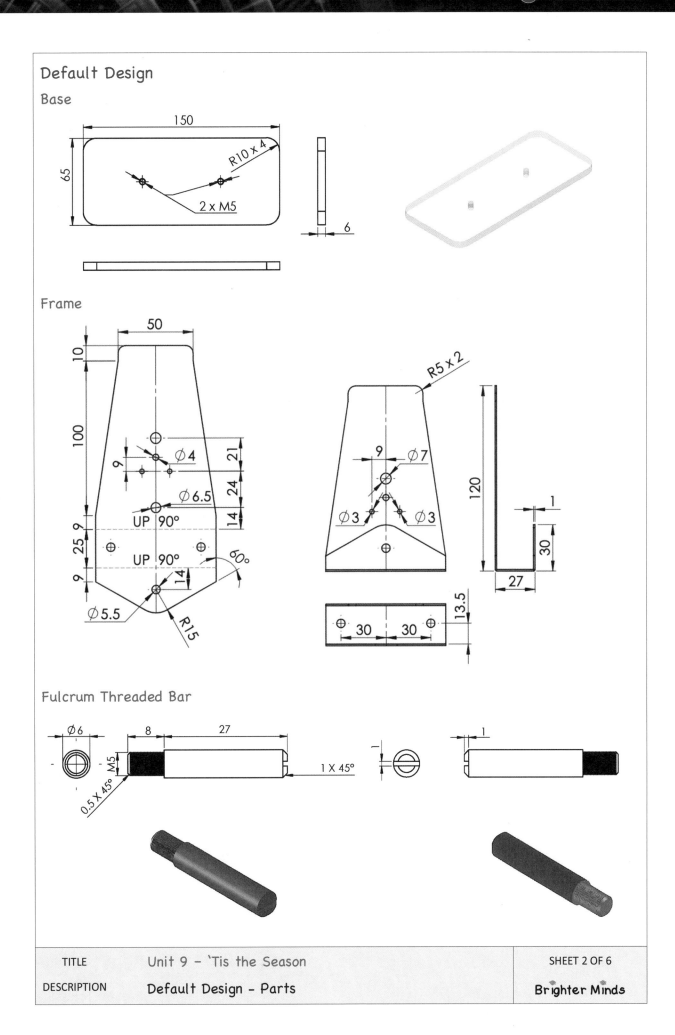

Frame

Fulcrum Threaded Bar

TITLE	Unit 9 – 'Tis the Season	SHEET 2 OF 6
DESCRIPTION	Default Design - Parts	Brighter Minds

Default Design

Spacer for Fulcrum

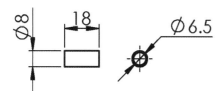

Disc

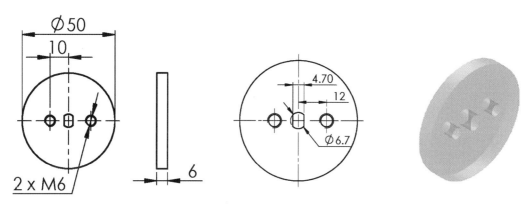

Laser cutter file available

Slotted Arm

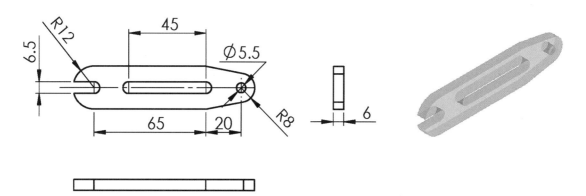

Threaded Peg

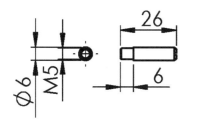

TITLE	Unit 9 – 'Tis the Season	SHEET 3 OF 6
DESCRIPTION	Default Design - Parts	Brighter Minds

Default Design
Circuit Diagram

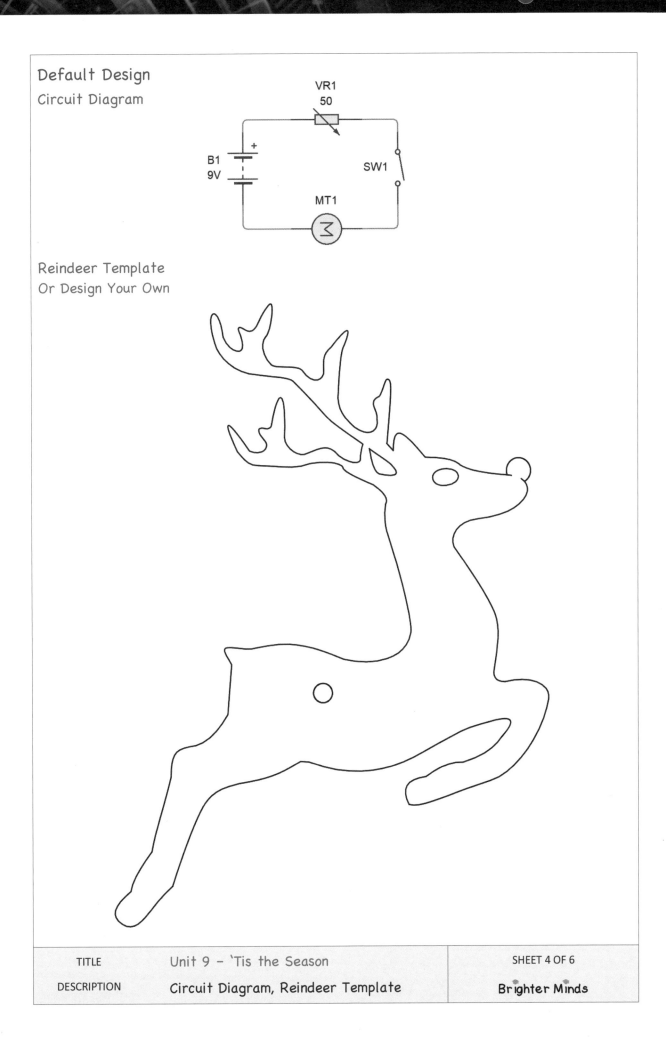

Reindeer Template
Or Design Your Own

TITLE	Unit 9 – 'Tis the Season	SHEET 4 OF 6
DESCRIPTION	Circuit Diagram, Reindeer Template	Brighter Minds

Your Design Drawings   (Follow the Project Storyboard Activities before attempting these)

TITLE	Unit 9 – 'Tis the Season	SHEET 5 OF 6
DESCRIPTION	Your Design Drawings	Brighter Minds

Your Design Drawings (Follow the Project Storyboard Activities before attempting these)

TITLE	Unit 9 – 'Tis the Season	SHEET 6 OF 6
DESCRIPTION	Your Design Drawings	Brighter Minds

Project Storyboard

Project Description

LEARNING GOALS OF THIS PROJECT

- Apply your **design** skills to develop a **festive-themed mechatronic project**
- Use a **motor-driven mechanism** such as a **peg-and-slot** to create **movement**
- Learn how to carry out the joining techniques of **threading** and **tapping**
- Provide a project that requires a **high level of accuracy and precision** to manufacture

We have provided a default design that can be modified. Alternatively, you could substitute or design a different project that uses similar technologies and has similar learning outcomes.

THE DEFAULT DESIGN

Our default design option, as shown in the working drawings, consists of the following:

- A **two-part body** is composed of an acrylic **base** and a bent brass upright **frame**
- The acrylic base is **tapped** to take the bolts securing the frame to the base
- An inline 3V DC **motor** is secured with nuts and bolts to the rear of the frame
- The **motor spindle** protrudes through a hole in the frame to the front
- An **acrylic disc** mounts on to the D-shaped motor spindle using a **push-fit hole** in the disc
- A protruding **peg** is attached to the disc by **threading** the peg and **tapping** a hole in the disc
- The **fulcrum** bar for the slotted arm is mounted at the bottom of the frame by **threading** one side of the round bar / cylinder, pushing it through the frame holes and the hollow spacer, and securing it with a nut to the front of the frame
- A **slotted arm** is manufactured to slot over the disc **peg** and hinge on the **fulcrum**
- The **spacer** keeps the slotted arm vertical and in the right place
- A **festive figure** attaches to the top of the slotted arm using a bolt and nut. It **rocks side-to-side** (oscillates) as the motor and disc turns, and as the peg slides inside the slotted arm
- The suggested **circuit** uses a 9V battery, a switch and a variable resistor to adjust the speed

DESIGN OPPORTUNITIES IN THIS PROJECT

- You can **design** your own **festive figure** to be moved by the **peg-and-slot mechanism**
- You can **design** your own **base** and **frame** to match your festive figure
- You will need to **design** a way to mechanically **house the electronic circuit** and wiring
- You could consider adding **LEDs** or **sound** to your project
- You could consider powering the motor with a **micro:bit** rather than with an electronic circuit To do this, you will need to use a separate **micro:bit DC Motor Drive Expansion Board.** *See the micro:bit programming section at the end of this unit*
- You could design a different project that has similar technologies and learning outcomes

Analysis Activities - Understand and Plan Your Project

Activity 1 – Choose Your Motor Circuit

- Before you can incorporate the electronics into your project, you will need to **decide on the circuit that you will use to power the motor**
- We suggest you **build** and **test** a prototype of the **basic motor circuit first** e.g. using crocodile clip cables, before building the rest of the project – for the following reasons:
  - depending on the type of components you have available, you might have to experiment with resistance values, battery voltage and motor type to ensure the motor turns slowly enough to operate your festive figure
  - when the prototype works, you then know which components you have to incorporate into the design of your project
- If you wish to use a **micro:bit** to control the motor, you will need to use a micro:bit **DC motor drive expansion board** *(see page 238)* in addition to the micro:bit board itself

Activity 2 – Decide How Many Parts you will Design or Redesign

- Decide if you are basing your project on our **default design** or using a **different design**
- Decide whether you will be building the default **reindeer** figure or **designing your own**
- Decide whether you will be **modifying the frame and base** to suit your figure
- Decide what approach you will take to **house the electronic circuit** that you decided above in Activity 1. You could consider either:
  1) **integrating** the electronic components into the existing design by **modifying the base** and/or **frame**, and/or by adding **additional parts**; OR
  2) **designing** a separate **control console** box to house the battery and electronic components apart from the motor

Discussion Activity 3 – Understand How You Will Manufacture the Project

Discuss the following in groups, or with your teacher and class:

- What **materials** will you use, if they are different than the default design? Justify your choices.
- How will you create an internal **thread** in the **base** for the frame bolts to screw into? Make a list of the **equipment** you will need for this.
  What **size hole** will you need to drill initially to create an M5 thread?

  See Joining pages 234-5

- How will you **bend** the frame? What equipment will you need?
- How will you manufacture the **fulcrum threaded bar** and the **threaded peg?** Make a list of the **tools** and equipment you will need.
- When manufacturing the **disc**, should you: (1) **create the shape first** and then drill the holes; OR (2) **drill the holes first** and then create the shape? Justify your choice.
- How will you **mark out** and **manufacture** the **slotted arm**? What **tools** will you need?
- How do you plan to **manufacture** the **reindeer** / your own **festive figure**?

  See Cutting on page 232

- What **sequence** will you **manufacture** the parts in?
- What **sequence** will you **assemble** / connect the parts in?
- How will you create the **electrical connections**? What equipment will you need?

Activity 4 – Create a Project Plan / Schedule - Gantt Chart

(1) Fill in the list of tasks you think will be required for this project below

(2) Tick or shade-in with a pencil the week(s) in which you expect to start and complete each task

TASKS	WEEKS					
PLANNING TASKS	1	2	3	4	5	6
Choose and Test Your Motor Circuit	√					
Decide how many Parts you will Design	√					
Ensure you have the Tools and Materials	√					
DESIGN TASKS						
MANUFACTURING TASKS						
ASSEMBLY TASKS						
TESTING AND RE-WORK TASKS						

Design Activities

Activity 5 – Concepts and Prototypes

- First create free-hand **concept sketches** for your designs on separate paper
- Consider **prototyping** your designs using **cardboard** to test how will work
- Ask your teacher or peer to **evaluate** your chosen design(s)

Activity 6 – Design Drawings

- Accurately **draw**, with **dimensions**, your chosen designs in the '**Your Design Drawings**' section of the working drawings pages at the beginning of this unit

Manufacturing Activities

Activity 7 – Manufacturing

1. **Mark out** and **manufacture** the mechanical parts of your project

2. **Assemble** the mechanical parts and electronic components
   - *Think about the best order to assemble the parts*
   - *Can you test the parts / sub-assemblies as you assemble them?*

3. **Connect / wire** the electronic components

4. **Test the overall project** and **improve it** if needed

Post-Manufacturing Reflection

Activity 8 – Project Evaluation

Evaluate your project under the headings below.

TASK	How did this task progress for you? What was difficult about this task?	What advice would you give to someone starting this task for the first time?
PLANNING, Managing Your Time		
DESIGN Tasks		
MANUFAC-TURING Base Frame Fulcrum Disc Peg Arm Figure		
ASSEMBLY and WIRING		
TESTING and REWORK		

Project Assessment

Student Self-Assessment

In this project, I gained the following new **skills** and **knowledge**:

1. _____

2. _____

3. _____

I **evaluate** my project to have **turned out well** in the following areas:

_____

_____

If I were to carry out this project again, I would **modify** or **improve** the following aspects:

_____

_____

_____

_____

On a scale of 1 to 10, I would give my project a **score** of…

Peer Assessment

I felt the following design and manufacturing processes were **good**:

_____

_____

_____

I felt the following project areas could be **improved**:

_____

_____

_____

Teacher Feedback on Project

Teacher comments on student's project:

Not Graded	Partially Achieved	Achieved	Merit	Higher Merit	Distinction

Learning Topics for Unit ⑨

Processes and Principles

Materials - Forces and Structures

Types of Forces

Materials, and **structures** made from those materials, are designed to **withstand forces** acting on them.
It is useful to know more about **forces** so that better materials and structures can be designed.
One thing that makes a big difference with the ability of materials and structure to withstand forces,
is the **direction** forces are applied in.

Type of Force	Illustration	Description
COMPRESSION		• **Compressive forces** act to **push** or squash a material together, to make it smaller • The material shown is **under compression**
TENSION		• **Tensile forces** act to **pull** a material apart • The material shown in **under tension**
SHEAR		• **Shear forces** act inwardly (like compression) but shear forces are **not in line** / directly opposite each other • This can cause the material to break by **shearing**, i.e. by **sliding** against itself

Type of Force	Illustration	Description
TORSION		• **Torsion forces** come about through **two opposing twisting forces** acting on a material • **Axles** experience torsion forces all the time
BENDING	Compression Tension	• Bending is a **combination of tension and compression** forces • In a **beam** supporting a heavy load, the top half of the beam is in **compression** and the **bottom** half is in **tension**

MATERIALS REACTION TO FORCES = PROPERTIES

- How a material behaves when an external force is applied defines its **mechanical properties** e.g. its strength, elasticity, hardness and brittleness. These properties arise as a result of the internal atomic structures and internal forces and resistances within the material.

- A material can be strong against one type of force, but weak against another. For example, **concrete** is strong in compression but weak in tension. This is why **steel**, which is strong in tension (think of suspension bridges) is combined with concrete to provide more **tensile strength**. **Composite materials** are designed to combine the best properties of multiple materials.

Structures - Resisting Forces

When we make something out a particular material, the strength of that structure is not only determined by the properties of the material, but also by the **shape of the structure**.

Choosing Good Shapes

- We can make structures made from a certain material **stronger**, by **choosing good shapes**.
- A stronger structure means the structure is **better able to resist the forces** acting on it, and not bend or break. We'll see some examples of good structures next.

Structures that Increase Strength

ARCHES

It's not a coincidence that many bridges are made using **arches**. An arch is able to support more weight than a straight beam of the same width - because an arch is **harder to bend** downwards than a straight beam.

An arch only has to sustain **compressive forces**, and stone and concrete are good at that. An arch also **transfers the load** from the middle onto the stronger **sides**.

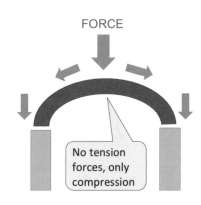

FORCE

No tension forces, only compression

TRIANGULATION

A common way to increase the strength of structures is to use **triangulation**, i.e. creating triangular structures that use bracing **struts** or **ties** *(see below)*. One example is a **bicycle frame**.

Q1. Which shelf bracket is stronger – left or right?

Q2. Is the diagonal element on the right bracket a strut or a tie?

> **A strut** is any member of a structure that is in **compression**.
> A **tie** is any member of a structure that is in **tension**.

If we **join lots of triangle shapes together** we can create extremely **strong** structures or **frames** that are still relatively **light**. Think of the **roof** of a **stadium** or the body of a lifting **crane**.

BEAMS

Beams are **long straight structures** used to **support heavy loads**, e.g. the weight of a roof or a floor in a building. We can make a solid beam stronger by making it **thicker** and **larger**. However, this also makes it much **heavier**.

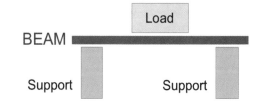

However, if we make the **beam** in one of the **shapes** *(or sections)* shown below, the beam becomes **stronger** while remaining relatively **light** and cheap. *This is because the vertical part of the beam stops the beam bending in the vertical direction, and the horizontal part of the beam stops it bending in the horizontal direction.*

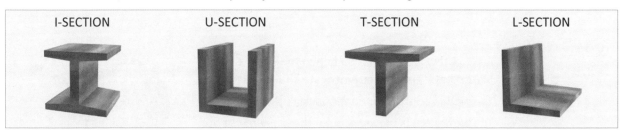

I-SECTION · U-SECTION · T-SECTION · L-SECTION

Tubular Sections

Making a single piece of material **hollow** also keeps most of its strength while making it much **lighter**.

ROUND · SQUARE · RECTANGULAR · HEXAGONAL · L-SECTION

Solid Sections

Metals can also be purchased in different **solid sections** *(cross-sections)*

ROUND · SQUARE · RECTANGULAR · HEXAGONAL · L-SECTION

Activity – Structures

Name **two** of the **structural techniques** mentioned on the previous page used to make this bicycle both **light** and **strong**.

Technique 1: _____

Technique 1: _____

More Material Properties

FATIGUE	• **Fatigue** is the **weakening of a material by applying repeated alternating forces.** The repeated movement spreads cracks throughout the material • For example, if you bend a metal paper clip back-and-forth many times, it will become **brittle** (due to a process called work-hardening) and **break** • Fatigue is a major concern for **airplane maintenance**, as the **constant flexing** of the wings and other parts can cause weaknesses with potentially catastrophic results

Cutting

The following cutting tools are often used to cut **intricate or complex shapes**.

SAFETY

Power tools such as scroll saws and band saws are **dangerous** and the **appropriate PPE** (personal protective equipment) must be worn. *See Unit 2 Health and Safety.*

SCROLL SAW	• A scroll saw is an electrical bench tool with a **fine blade** that is used to **cut intricate shapes** • The blade **reciprocates** continuously **up-and-down** • The **workpiece** is **moved around** the blade to cut out the detailed shape • Usually used to cut **acrylic** and **wood** • Can be used to cut **thin sheet metal** using the correct blade, slow speed and careful attention	
BAND SAW		• A **bandsaw** is used to cut larger pieces of material • It uses a **continuous loop** blade that moves in one direction only around two internal **pulleys** *(see mechanisms in Unit 10)* 

LASER CUTTER	• Cuts material using a high-powered **laser** light • Can cut complex shapes **very quickly** • Takes its cutting instructions from a **digital file** which can be generated from **CAD** software	

Drilling

> ### Revision Activity - Drilling
> Demonstrate the difference between a **countersunk** and a **counterbored** hole below using **annotated sketches**:

More Hole Types

BLIND HOLE	• A **blind hole** is a hole that does **not go all the way through** a workpiece • Can be carried out accurately on a **pillar drill** (or cordless drill) using the drill's **depth gauge** • A blind hole is often **tapped** *(see below)* to take a **bolt**, when you don't want the bolt coming out on the other side of the part	Blind Hole 
TAPPING SIZE HOLE	• A **tapping size hole** is the hole that is drilled before **tapping** the hole, i.e. cutting a thread inside the hole (see below) • The thread is cut into the wall of the drilled hole using a **tap** *(see below)*	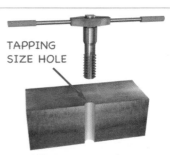 TAPPING SIZE HOLE

Joining

> ### Revision Activity - Joining
> Identify **three** different **types of adhesives**, highlighting the differences between them.
>
> 1. _____
>
> 2. _____
>
> 3. _____

Threading

> **Threading** is the process of creating a **screw thread** on the **outside** of a cylinder. It is carried out using a tool called a **die**. After threading, a nut can be screwed onto the threaded cylinder.

Threading Tools

DIE CIRCULAR SPLIT DIE BUTTON DIE	• A **circular split die** is used to cut external **threads** on round bars or pipes • The thread **size** is indicated on the top of the split die • Made from a hard material like **high-speed steel (HSS)** 
DIE HOLDER or DIE STOCK	• A **die stock** or die holder is used to hold the **die** during the threading process • Has **two arms** to help turn the die • Can hold dies for different thread sizes 

Threading Process

HOW TO THREAD A CYLINDER	• Choose the correct diameter cylinder. Also to match the desired nut (e.g. M5, 5mm) • **Cut** the cylinder to the required **length** • **Clamp** the cylinder in a bench vice in a vertical / plumb position • **Taper** / bevel the top of the cylinder using a file so that the die will sit on top of the cylinder • Choose the **correct die size** and **thread** 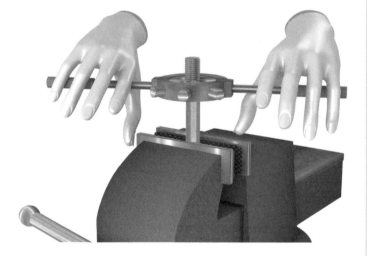 • Using the handles on the die holder, press down and **turn the die clockwise** to cut the thread • After 3 clockwise turns, and if the die becomes difficult to turn, **turn the die counter-clockwise.** This will help break off and remove any build-up of swarf (waste material) inside the die. Then resume cutting the thread by turning clockwise again. • **Very important** - keep the die **extremely level** to ensure an even thread is created

Tapping

Tapping is the process of creating a **screw thread** on the **inside** of a pre-drilled cylindrical **hole**. Tapping is carried out with a tool called a **tap**. After tapping, a bolt can be screwed into the hole.

Tapping Tools

TAPER TAP	• The first **5-6 cutting edges** are tapered, making it easy to start the tap in the hole • You won't be able to complete a long thread with a taper tap because of the taper. You'll need to use a **second tap** or **bottoming tap** afterwards (see below)
SECOND TAP / PLUG TAP	• Has a **shorter taper**. Used on its own, or after the taper tap , to complete the threading process in deeper holes
BOTTOMING TAP	• Used to **thread blind holes**, as the cutting edges extend the whole way to the tip • **Difficult to start** the threading with a bottoming tap because it has no taper • Start the thread with a **taper tap** and finish it with the bottoming tap • Alternatively, you could drill a small **countersunk** shape at the top of the hole to guide the tap into the hole
TAP WRENCH **OR** **TAP HOLDER**	• **Holds** your chosen tap type and size • Provides **two arms** to allow you to twist the tap into the hole

Tapping Process

HOW TO TAP A HOLE	• **Drill** a hole **smaller** than the diameter of the desired bolt or screw. For example, to tap a thread for a M4 bolt, drill a Ø3.2 or Ø3.5 hole • **Clamp** your drilled workpiece in the vice and **ensure that it is level** • Spray a little oil e.g. WD40 into the hole as lubrication • Place the **correct type and size tap** into the tap wrench • Place your tap inside the hole **ensuring it enters straight** • Tap the hole by **turning the tapping wrench clockwise** for **three** rotations and **anticlockwise for one**. This helps remove the waste from the threads of the tap • **Keep the tap straight** (plumb) to ensure a straight and even thread is created

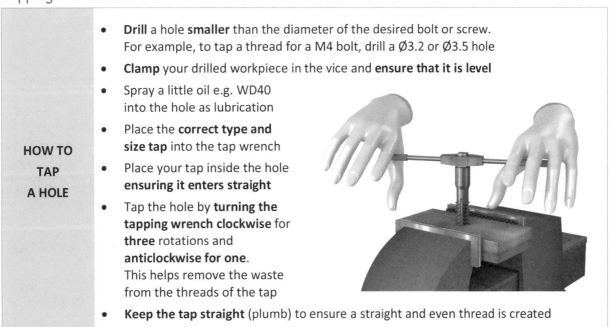

Mechatronics

Mechanisms

Mechanism	Description
PEG-AND-SLOT MECHANISM (QUICK-RETURN MECHANISM)	• A **peg-and-slot** mechanism converts **rotary motion** into **oscillating motion** • A **peg** is rotated via a disc usually connected to a motor or engine • The **peg** fits in to a **slot** in a **shaft** • The shaft **pivots** around a fixed **fulcrum** at one end • As the **peg** rotates, it slides up and down in the **slot**, rocking the **arm** left-to-right (and back again) around its fulcrum • The peg-and-slot mechanisms is also called a **quick return** mechanism. This is because the top of the shaft will move **quickly in one direction** (when the peg is close to the fulcrum), while it will move **slowly in the other direction** (when the peg is furthest from the fulcrum) Oscillating Motion / Slotted Arm / Rotary Motion / Peg / Slot / Fulcrum (Fixed Pivot)

CRANK AND SLIDER	• Converts **rotary motion** to **reciprocating motion**, and vice versa
	
	• *Applications:*
	  ○ **Cars:** The **reciprocating** motion of the **pistons** is changed into the **rotary** motion of the **engine** using a **crankshaft** (see later)
	  ○ **Air Compressors**: Via a crank, the **rotary** motion of a **motor** creates a **reciprocating** motion in a **piston**, which can compress the air in a tank with the help of one-way valves Crank / Slider / Rotary Motion / Reciprocating Motion

Revision Activity – Mechanisms

Describe a cam with the aid of a sketch: *(Hint: see Unit 7)*

Description: *Sketch:*

_____

_____

_____

_____

Linkages

A **linkage** is a set of **connected levers** used to **transmit linear motion** over a distance.

Linkage	Description	
PARALLEL-MOTION LINKAGE	• A **parallel-motion linkage** uses **two fixed** pivots and **two moving pivots** to ensure all **sides remain parallel to each other** • Used in some **toolboxes** and **sewing boxes** - to ensure the **drawers stay level** with the box when you lift them out	
REVERSE-MOTION LINKAGE	• **Reverses the direction** of **linear motion** • If the one arm is moved, the other arm will **move in the opposite direction** • You can **amplify** (increase) or **reduce** the amount of motion transferred from the input to the output **by moving the fixed pivot** (fulcrum) away from the middle of the middle lever	
BELL CRANK LINKAGE	• A bell crank linkage **changes the direction of linear motion by 90°** (makes it turn a corner) • The amount of motion and force transferred from input to output can be changed by **moving the position of the fixed pivot** (fulcrum) closer to one of the moving pivots (creating a lever effect) • *Applications* - **bicycle brakes**: When a cyclist pulls the brake handles, this pulls a cable which pulls one end of a bell crank. The other end of the bell crank is attached to the brake pads - via a pair of reverse-motion linkages - which pushes the brake pads onto the rim of the wheel.	

SCISSORS LINKAGE	• An input squeezing motion at the **base** causes the other end to extend out at **90 degrees** to the input motion (and vice versa)
	
	• *Applications:*
	  o **Lifting platforms** and **car jacks**:
	    The advantage of this mechanism is it doesn't have to be taller than the object that requires to be lifted
	  o **Shaving mirrors**	

micro:bit Programming

Controlling a DC Motor

A micro:bit cannot supply enough current to power a DC motor on its own. You need to use a **micro:bit DC Motor Drive expansion board**. You can buy various micro:bit expansion boards from various suppliers. *The one we describe here, and have tested our programs with, is from **Kitronik**.*

Connecting the micro:bit to the DC Motor Drive Board

Lay the motor drive board down flat. Pick up the micro:bit board and press the **pins** edge vertically down into the long **edge connector** on the motor drive board. The micro:bit can be inserted either way round in the edge connector and the motor drive outputs will still work.

FEATURES OF THE MICRO:BIT DC MOTOR DRIVER BOARD

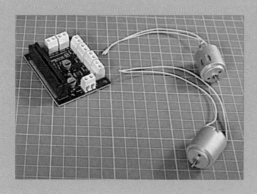

- Can power **two DC motors**, with **forward, reverse** and **stop** control
- Provides **terminal blocks** for easy connection of motors and inputs
- **Four inputs**
- Requires **4.5V to 6V power supply / batteries**
- **Provides 3V** to the attached **micro:bit** board
- **Dimensions**: L 67mm, W 53mm, H 18mm

Connecting a DC Motor to the Motor Drive Board

Use a DC motor rated 3V to 6V. Geared (inline) motors will provide useful lower speeds. Bare the ends of the motor wires, insert them into the terminal blocks marked Motor 1 or 2, and tighten the screws.

Adding the Motor Drive Code Blocks

Before you can program and send commands to the motor driver board with your makecode editor, you need to **add some new motor drive code blocks** into your makecode editor. You can do this with just a few clicks, as outlined below.

> Add the Motor Drive Code Blocks to makecode
>
> 1. Go to https://**makecode.microbit.org**
> 2. Select a **new project**. This opens the makecode editor
> 3. Select **Advanced** at the bottom of the toolbox menu
> 4. Select **Extensions**
> 5. Type in '**motor drive**' in the search box and click return
> 6. Select '**Kitronik motor driver**'
> 7. You now have a new '**Motor Driver**' item in your toolbox
> 8. Click on the **Motor Driver** menu item and you will now see **two new motor drive code blocks** which are explained on the next page

Useful Motor Control Code Blocks

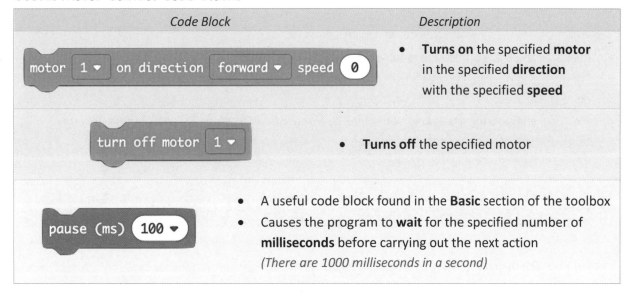

Code Block	Description
motor 1 ▼ on direction forward ▼ speed 0	• **Turns on** the specified **motor** in the specified **direction** with the specified **speed**
turn off motor 1 ▼	• **Turns off** the specified motor
pause (ms) 100 ▼	• A useful code block found in the **Basic** section of the toolbox • Causes the program to **wait** for the specified number of **milliseconds** before carrying out the next action *(There are 1000 milliseconds in a second)*

Worked Example – Controlling a DC Motor

Task: Rotate a motor at full speed for 5 seconds and then stop.

Solution:

- **Connect** your micro:bit, motor drive board, power supply and motor as outlined above
- **Create the code** opposite in the makecode editor
- **Download** to your micro:bit
- If the motor turns the wrong way, reverse the wires

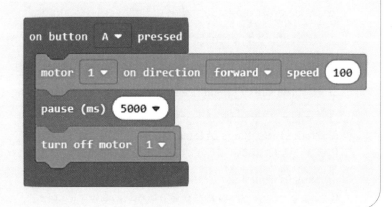

Motor Programming Activities

1. **Reduce the speed** of the motor in the above example
2. When **button B** is pressed, **reverse** the direction of the motor at **half speed** for **5 seconds**
3. Display '**Forward**' on the micro:bit LEDs when the motor is turning in the forwards direction, and display '**Reverse**' when the motor Is turning in the opposite direction
4. Connect **two external LEDs** to the micro:bit using jumper wires or crocodile clips. Light one LED when the motor turns one way, and the other LED when the motor reverses.

Record your progress by ticking the appropriate cells below:

Activity Number	Too Difficult	Partially Completed	Completed
1			
2			
3			
4			

Research Activity

Research Activity – Engineering Disciplines

- Research the main different **branches of engineering** that you could study and work in
- For each engineering area, describe the type of **projects** and **products** that engineers might work on in those areas
- Pick **two engineering areas** that you might be interested in **working in**, and **explain why** you think you might like to work in those areas

Unit 9 Revision

Unit 9 Revision Questions

1. Describe the difference between a compressive force and a tensile force.

2. (a) Describe two techniques used to increase the strength of structures.
   (b) Give examples of the use of each technique.

3. (a) Explain what beams are used for.
   (b) Name and sketch four types of beam cross-sections.

4. Describe three differences between a scroll saw and a bandsaw.

5. Name the mechanism used inside a bandsaw to move the blade around in a loop.

6. State three safety precautions to be adhered to when using a bandsaw or scroll saw.

7. (a) Explain what tapping means in an engineering context.
   (b) Name three types of taps.
   (b) Using text and sketches, explain how the tapping process is carried out on a workpiece.

8. (a) Explain what a blind hole is, and when It is used.
   (b) Explain how you would drill a blind hole accurately.

9. (a) Explain what threading means in an engineering context.
   (b) Name the hand tools used to carry out threading.
   (c) Explain using text and sketches how the threading process is carried out on a workpiece.

10. Name and sketch a mechanism that converts rotary motion to oscillating motion.

11. Name and sketch a mechanism that converts rotary motion to reciprocating motion.

12. Name a piece of measuring equipment that can be used to measure the depth of a blind hole.

13. (a) Using an annotated sketch, describe the operation of a parallel motion linkage.
    (b) Give one application for this mechanism.

14. A bell crank linkage is used on bicycles. Communicate using an annotated sketch how this mechanism works.

15. (a) Sketch a scissors mechanism.
    (b) Give one application for a scissors mechanism.

16. Why is a motor drive expansion board needed if you want to control a motor using a micro:bit?

17. What type of motion transformation is carried out by a peg-and-slot mechanism?

Unit (10)

Unit 10 – Motorised Vehicle

Unit Objectives

PROJECT	Design and manufacture a **motorised vehicle**

- Design and manufacture a project based on a **brief** and provided **circuit** options
  Working drawings are available in the Appendix but we encourage you to develop your own.
- Provide a project that **further improves your planning, design and manufacturing skills**
- Learn about **energy**, energy conversion, **engines**, more **gear** and **pulley mechanisms**
- Provide an opportunity to **research** and **evaluate** automotive design and technology
- Learn how to **radio control a vehicle** using two micro:bit boards
- Learn how to **form plastic** using a **vacuum former**

Content

PROCESSES AND PRINCIPLES	Materials	• Plastic forming using a vacuum former
	Energy	• Energy sources, energy conversion • Environmental impacts
DESIGN APPLICATION		• Designing from a brief, design selection and justification • Evaluation of existing designs
MECHATRONICS	Mechanisms	• Axles, gears, pulleys, wheels. Automotive mechanisms • Engines: two-stroke, four-stroke, electric and hybrid
	Electronics	• DPDT switches, reversible motor circuits
	micro:bit	• Radio control of DC motors

Learning Outcomes from this Unit

PROCESSES AND PRINCIPLES	DESIGN APPLICATION	MECHATRONICS
1.1, 1.2, 1.3, 1.4, 1.5, 1.6, 1.7, 1.8, 1.9, 1.10, 1.11, 1.12, 1.13	2.3, 2.4, 2.5, 2.6, 2.7, 2.8, 2.9, 2.10, 2.11, 2.12	3.3. 3.4, 3.5, 3.6, 3.7, 3.8, 3.9, 3.10

Suggested Timeframes

START TIME	YEAR 2	January		DURATION	8-10 weeks

Working Drawings

Default Design

*Working drawings for a **three-wheel car** are in the **Appendix** but we encourage you to design your own.*

Motor Control Circuits

Option 1 – Reversible Motor Circuit

Manual control of forward, stop and reverse using a DPDT switch. Can be used with one or two motors.

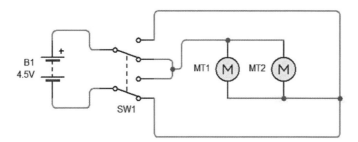

Note - the DPDT switches shown on this page also have a mechanical centre-off (stop) position

Option 2 – Reversible Motor Circuit with Speed Control and Steering Switches

Manual control of forward, reverse and stop using a DPDT switch; manual control of speed using the variable resistor; manual control of steering by briefly turning off the left or right wheel motor using the PTB switches. (This steering system best with two motorised front wheels and one rear free-wheeling castor wheel)

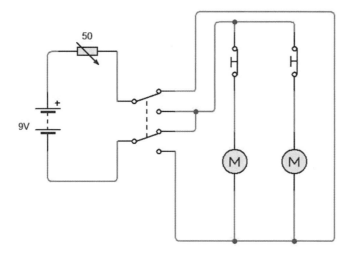

Option 3 – Radio Control using two micro:bit boards

micro:bit 1 sends radio instructions to micro:bit 2 which controls the left and right wheel motors via an micro:bit DC motor expansion board. See the micro:bit programming section at the end of this unit.

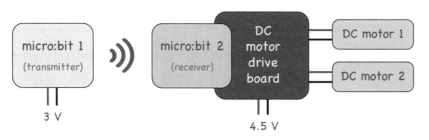

TITLE	Unit 10 – Motorised Vehicle	SHEET 1 OF 4
DESCRIPTION	Motor Control Circuit Options	Brighter Minds

Your Design Drawings for a Motorised Vehicle

TITLE	Unit 10 – Motorised Vehicle	SHEET 2 OF 4
DESCRIPTION	Your Design Drawings	Brighter Minds

Your Design Drawings for a Motorised Vehicle

TITLE	Unit 10 – Motorised Vehicle	SHEET 3 OF 4
DESCRIPTION	Your Design Drawings	Brighter Minds

Your Design Drawings for Motorised Vehicle

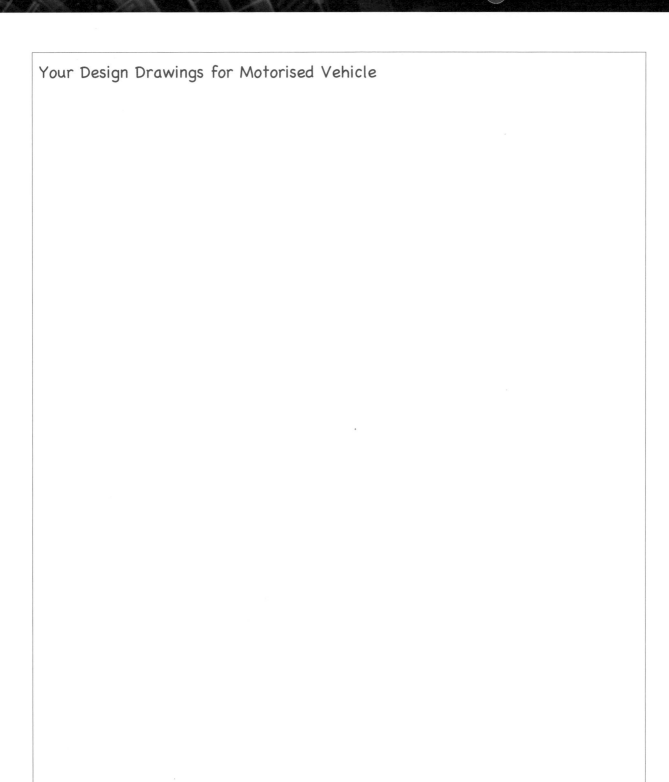

TITLE	Unit 10 – Motorised Vehicle	SHEET 4 OF 4
DESCRIPTION	Your Design Drawings	Brighter Minds

Project Storyboard

Project Description

LEARNING GOALS OF THIS PROJECT

- Design and manufacture a **motorised vehicle** from a **brief**.
  (Working drawings for a car are provided on page 313, however we encourage you to modify that design, or preferably develop your own design drawings based on the design brief, motor circuit options, and design ideas provided below)
- Further enhance your planning, design and manufacturing skills

PROJECT BRIEF

- Your brief is to design and build a small **motorised vehicle** on wheels, which can be moved in both **forward** and **reverse** directions using one or more electric **motors**
- Your vehicle will ideally be **steerable** – i.e. it can be turned left or right
- The **speed** of your vehicle will ideally be **controllable**
- The **movement** of your vehicle may be **controlled** in one of the following ways:
  a) Using **switches** and controls on the vehicle itself, or
  b) Using a separate **control console** that connects to your vehicle with long wires, or
  c) By **radio remote control** - using **2 micro:bit boards** and a **DC motor drive expansion board** *(see the micro:bit Programming section at the end of this unit)*
- The **physical design** of your vehicle may resemble conventional cars or trucks etc, or it may be something different and unique
- You may use **any suitable materials**
- Your final product should exhibit a **high quality of finish**
- **Decide** with your teacher whether to **work in groups** or **individually**
- **Communicate** your design using **drawings** and document and **justify** your design decisions

DESIGN SUGGESTIONS

- We suggest you **first choose the motor control circuit** you will be using *(see working drawings)*
- Choose a **type of motor** that will provide **slow speeds** and **high torque** (turning force)
- Think about how you could connect the motor spindles to the **wheels**

  See Mechanisms on page 263

- If you are building a **steerable** vehicle, one way to do that is to use **three wheels only**, or **two front wheels** and a **rear castor**, which is a small wheel on a swivelling vertical axle. Power the left and right wheels separately with their own DC motor, and temporarily stop one of the motors to turn left or right
- Consider making the **body shape** from assembled **metal** parts and/or **plastic** parts. Also consider making one or more body shapes from moulded plastic using a **vacuum former**

  See Vacuum Forming on page 252

Analysis Activities - Understand the Project and Choose between Options

Activity 1 – Decide How Much Design You Are Doing

- **Discuss the project brief** and project approach with your teacher
- **Decide** whether you will modify the **default design** or develop a completely **new design**
- **Understand** how much **time** you have
- **Decide** whether you are working in **groups** or **individually**

Activity 2 – Discuss the Design and Manufacturing Options

- Discuss the **design and manufacturing options** available to you:
  - What **material options** are available?
  - What **motor drive parts** are available or could be ordered?
  - What kind of **wheels** are available or could be ordered?
  - Is a **vacuum former** available, and can a suitable **mould** be purchased or made?
  - How might you **attach the wheels to the motors**, and how might you implement **steering**?
    (Hint: research the mechanisms later in this unit, and consider using two independently-controlled motors and stopping one briefly)
  - Decide whether you will be building a separate **control console** or implementing **remote radio control** using **two micro:bit boards** *(see micro:bit programming later in this unit)*
  - You could including **additional electronics** in your vehicle *(e.g. LED lights, a buzzer horn)*
  - Choose the **electronic circuit** you are going to use *(see working drawings also)*
  - Discuss the **assembly** and **joining techniques** you could use for the body and electronics
- You may wish to **research** similar projects to see how they were designed

Activity 3 – Create an Initial Plan (Gantt Chart)

- Once you have an overall concept of the type of project you will be making, create a **first draft Gantt Chart** showing the main tasks you think will need to be completed each week in order to complete the project
- **Update** this Gantt chart each week as you gain more knowledge about the design and the manufacturing tasks required, and as you get some tasks completed

Design Activities: Option A – Create a Full New Design based on the Brief

Activity A1 – Create Concept Sketches

- Think about an **overall theme** for your motorised vehicle (e.g. transport, racing, colours etc)
- On separate sheets of paper, create **free-hand concept sketches** for your vehicle designs
- Once you are happy with a final assembled view, then also **sketch the different parts** required
- Show how the **electronics** and any mechanisms are integrated into the mechanical design
- Consider **prototyping** your designs using **cardboard**
- Select your **favourite concept design** and ask your teacher or peer to review it
- **Update** your concept design drawings based on feedback received

Activity A2 – Design Communication – Final Drawings

- **Draw** accurately all the parts of your chosen design with **dimensions**, in the '**Your Design Drawings**' section of the working drawings pages at the beginning of this unit
- In consultation with your teacher, you could **present your design** to the class

Design Activities: Option B – Base Your Design on the Default Design (page 313)

Activity B1 – Discuss the Design and Manufacturing Options

- Discuss which parts of the **default design** you wish to keep, and which to **modify**
- You could choose to make some parts from moulded plastic using a **vacuum former**
- You could stay with the suggested **two right-angle geared motors** and **one rear castor**
- You could implement a **different wheel drive** system and redesign the parts accordingly
- You could consider adding a **front spoiler** to the car
- You could **incorporate additional electronics** into the car (e.g. LED lights)
- Decide if you will design and build a separate wired **control console** to control the car
- Decide if you are using two **micro:bit** boards and DC motor drive board to **radio control** the car - *see micro:bit Programming at the end of this unit*
- Finalise on your **full electronic circuit** and how you will incorporate it in your project
- Decide on the **materials** and **joining** techniques you will use

Activity B2 – Design Communication – Sketches and Drawings

- Create **free-hand concept sketches** for all **modifications** to the default design
- Ask your teacher or peer to **review**, and update afterwards as required
- Accurately **draw your final designs** including dimensions in the '**Your Design Drawings**' section of the working drawings at the beginning of this unit
- In consultation with your teacher, you could **present your modified design** to the class

Manufacturing the Design

Activity 4 – Planning – Create a More Accurate Gantt Chart

- Make a list of the **parts** you need
- Think about the **best sequence** to manufacture and assemble them in
- Consider building and testing the **central and risky parts of your project first**
- Allow some time for rework and modifications
- **Update** the **Gantt Chart** you produced earlier to show a **more accurate sequence of tasks** required to complete your project

Activity 5 – Manufacture, Assemble and Test

Manufacture and **Assemble** your Parts. Validate your electronics early. Test the Assemblies.
You may find it useful to **work from your Gantt Chart** and **tick off each task** as it is completed.
Update your Gantt Chart as required.

Project Reflection - Testing, Modification and Evaluation

Activity 6 – Project Testing, Modification, Evaluation

1. What **results** did you **observe** when you tested your project?

What worked well? _____

_____

_____

_____

What didn't work so well? _____

_____

_____

_____

_____

2. What **changes did you make** to get your project to function and/or look **better**?

_____

_____

_____

_____

_____

3. If you were to carry out this project again, what areas would you **spend more time on**?

_____

_____

_____

_____

_____

Project Assessment

Student Self-Assessment

In this project, I gained the following new **skills** and **knowledge**:

1. _____

2. _____

3. _____

I **evaluate** my project to have **turned out well** in the following areas:

_____

_____

If I were to carry out this project again, I would **modify** or **improve** the following aspects:

_____

_____

_____

_____

On a scale of 1 to 10, I would give my project a **score** of...

Peer Assessment

I felt the following design and manufacturing processes were **good**:

_____

_____

_____

I felt the following project areas could be **improved**:

_____

_____

_____

Teacher Feedback on Project

Teacher comments on student's project:

Not Graded	Partially Achieved	Achieved	Merit	Higher Merit	Distinction

Learning Topics for Unit 10

Processes and Principles

Forming of Plastics

Thermoplastics can be melted and reshaped. A **mould** can be used to define the new shape for the hot molten plastic while it cools and sets. Moulds are often made from **wood**, **plaster** or **metals**.

Plastics Revision Activities

1. Explain what 'forming' means (as distinct from shaping):

_____

_____

2. What category of plastics **cannot be melted and re-shaped**?

_____

4. Name a piece of **plastic forming equipment** that you have used already in previous units:

_____   See Page 74

3. Name **two specific types of thermoplastics** that are particularly **suitable for moulding**:

Thermoplastic 1: _____

Thermoplastic 2: _____

Vacuum Forming

A **vacuum former** pulls a **heated thermoplastic sheet** down over a **mould** to create that shape. Suitable plastics for vacuum forming are **acrylic**, polythene, polypropylene, **ABS** and **HIPS**.

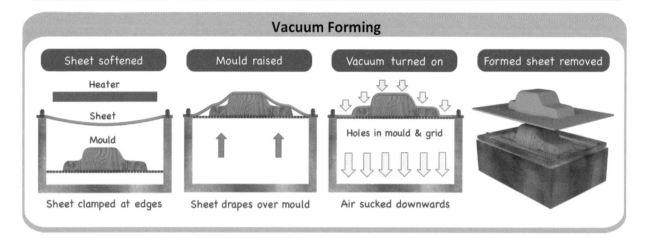

HOW TO USE A VACUUM FORMING MACHINE

1. Purchase or **make your own mould** e.g. from wood
    (Your mould should have vertical holes running through it at places where air could become trapped between the soft plastic sheet and the mould)

2. Place your **mould** in the vacuum former machine

3. **Clamp** a thin **sheet** of thermoplastic at the top of the machine above the mould

4. Turn on the **heater**. Wait 2 or 3 minutes until the plastic softens and becomes flexible

5. **Turn off** the heater

6. Use the lever to **lift up the mould** into the plastic sheet (until the lever locks in place)

7. Turn on the **vacuum pump**. The air is sucked out from the bottom of the unit, and the plastic sheet is pushed downwards by the room air pressure, to form around the mould

8. **Turn off** the vacuum pump. Remove the plastic when **cooled**, and **trim** off any excess

Mechatronics

Mechatronics and Energy

Energy

Modern life requires huge amounts of **energy** - to power our homes, transport, businesses and schools.

Energy is the **ability to do work**.
Energy comes in **different forms** – electrical, mechanical, chemical, heat, light, sound.

Energy cannot be created or destroyed, **it can only be converted from one form to another**.

Engineering and **mechatronics** provide the technology that is used **convert energy into convenient forms** - so that it can be generated, transported, stored and used where needed.

Sources of Energy

The energy that is used to power our homes and vehicles comes from a number of different sources. Sources of energy can be classified into **renewable** sources, and **non-renewable** sources.

RENEWABLE sources of energy	**NON-RENEWABLE** sources of energy
A **renewable** source of energy **can be replaced** – it does not get used up:	A **non-renewable** source of energy **cannot be replaced** once it has been used:
Examples of renewable sources:	*Examples of non-renewable sources:*
<ul><li>**Solar** power (from the sun)</li><li>**Wind** power, **wave** power</li><li>**Hydroelectric** (from rivers and dams)</li><li>**Biofuels / biomass**</li></ul>	<ul><li>**Fossil fuels** (coal, oil and gas)</li><li>**Nuclear power**</li><li>**Chemical batteries** (non-rechargeable)</li></ul>

Converting Energy from One Form to Another

Engineering and **mechatronics** are used to **convert energy from one form to another**.

Electricity is our most convenient form of energy because it can be **transported** very quickly from place to place, and it can be **converted** relatively easily to other forms of energy. This is why we generate and use a lot of electricity.

Generating Electricity

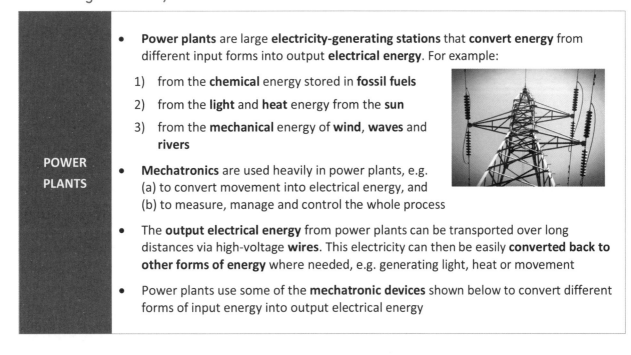

POWER PLANTS

- **Power plants** are large **electricity-generating stations** that **convert energy** from different input forms into output **electrical energy**. For example:

  1) from the **chemical** energy stored in **fossil fuels**
  2) from the **light** and **heat** energy from the **sun**
  3) from the **mechanical** energy of **wind, waves** and **rivers**

- **Mechatronics** are used heavily in power plants, e.g.
  (a) to convert movement into electrical energy, and
  (b) to measure, manage and control the whole process

- The **output electrical energy** from power plants can be transported over long distances via high-voltage **wires**. This electricity can then be easily **converted back to other forms of energy** where needed, e.g. generating light, heat or movement

- Power plants use some of the **mechatronic devices** shown below to convert different forms of input energy into output electrical energy

Mechatronic and Electronic Devices that convert other Energy into Electrical Energy

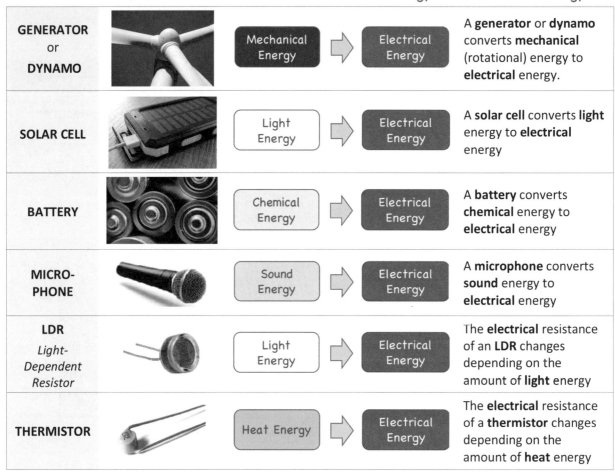

GENERATOR or **DYNAMO**		Mechanical Energy ⇨ Electrical Energy	A **generator** or **dynamo** converts **mechanical** (rotational) energy to **electrical** energy.
SOLAR CELL		Light Energy ⇨ Electrical Energy	A **solar cell** converts **light** energy to **electrical** energy
BATTERY		Chemical Energy ⇨ Electrical Energy	A **battery** converts **chemical** energy to **electrical** energy
MICRO-PHONE		Sound Energy ⇨ Electrical Energy	A **microphone** converts **sound** energy to **electrical** energy
LDR *Light-Dependent Resistor*		Light Energy ⇨ Electrical Energy	The **electrical** resistance of an **LDR** changes depending on the amount of **light** energy
THERMISTOR		Heat Energy ⇨ Electrical Energy	The **electrical** resistance of a **thermistor** changes depending on the amount of **heat** energy

Mechatronic and Electronic Devices that convert Electrical Energy to other Energy

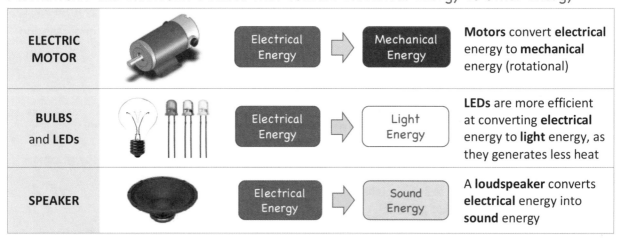

ELECTRIC MOTOR		Electrical Energy ⇨ Mechanical Energy	**Motors** convert **electrical** energy to **mechanical** energy (rotational)
BULBS and **LEDs**		Electrical Energy ⇨ Light Energy	**LEDs** are more efficient at converting **electrical** energy to **light** energy, as they generates less heat
SPEAKER		Electrical Energy ⇨ Sound Energy	A **loudspeaker** converts **electrical** energy into **sound** energy

Energy Conversion in an Internal Combustion Engine (see next section)

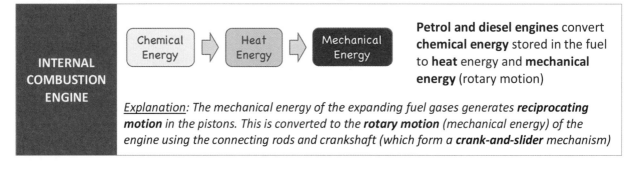

INTERNAL COMBUSTION ENGINE	Chemical Energy ⇨ Heat Energy ⇨ Mechanical Energy	**Petrol and diesel engines** convert **chemical energy** stored in the fuel to **heat** energy and **mechanical energy** (rotary motion)

*Explanation: The mechanical energy of the expanding fuel gases generates **reciprocating motion** in the pistons. This is converted to the **rotary motion** (mechanical energy) of the engine using the connecting rods and crankshaft (which form a **crank-and-slider** mechanism)*

Engines

> An **engine** or motor is a machine that **converts energy into mechanical energy**

The word "**engine**" usually refers to machines that **burn fuel** to create mechanical energy.
The word "**motor**" usually refers to machines that **convert electrical energy** to mechanical energy.

Internal Combustion Engines

> An **internal combustion engine burns fuel** (like petrol or diesel) **inside the engine**.
> The resulting hot expanding gases drive a **piston** which creates **motion** (mechanical energy)

*For example, a **steam engine** is **not** an internal combustion engine, because it burns fuel **outside** the engine to boil water to create steam. The steam is piped into the engine to drive the pistons.*

TYPES OF INTERNAL COMBUSTION ENGINE

There are many types of internal combustion engine, but the most common types:

- are fuelled by **petrol** or **diesel**
- have **one or more pistons**
- the pistons are operated using either a **two-stroke** system or a **four-stroke** system
  *(A **stroke** is one up or down movement of the piston)*

This gives us four common types of engine:

1) **Petrol two-stroke** engine
2) **Diesel two-stroke** engine
3) **Petrol four-stroke** engine
4) **Diesel four-stroke** engine

FOUR-STROKE ENGINES

- Fuel burns every **fourth** piston stroke
- Uses **valves** to steer gases in and out
- **Smoother, cleaner, fuel-efficient**
- Usually **water-cooled**
- Used in **cars, buses, trucks, trains**

TWO-STROKE ENGINES

- Fuel burns every **second** piston stroke
- **No valves**
- **Simpler, cheaper, louder, more polluting**
- Usually **air-cooled**
- Used in **chainsaws, boats, motorbikes**

PETROL ENGINES

- Use **spark plugs** to ignite the fuel/air
- **Cheaper** and **quieter** engine than diesel
- **More expensive** to run
- Used primarily in **cars**

DIESEL ENGINES

- **No spark plugs**   *(uses glow plugs to help start the engine in cold weather)*
- Fuel **injected** into very **hot compressed air**
- **Heavier** engines and so more **expensive**
- **Cheaper to run** because of fuel, efficiency
- Used in cars, **buses, trucks, trains**

The Four-Stroke Engine

> ### Activity – Engine Recognition
>
> 1. Which **parts** of the engine shown below tell us immediately that this is a **four-stroke** engine?
> 2. Which **part** of the engine below tells us that it is a **petrol** engine?

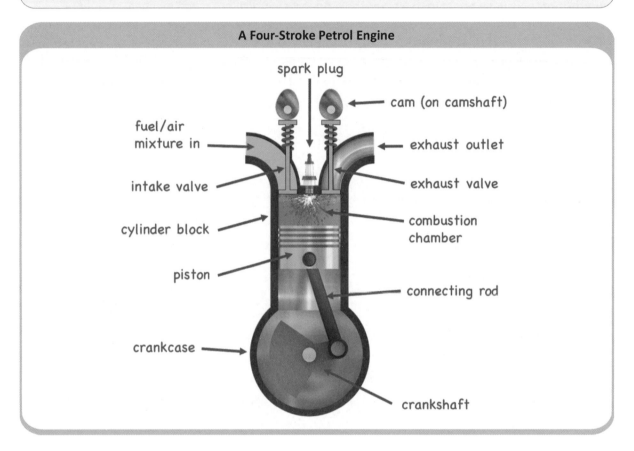

A Four-Stroke Petrol Engine

Operation of a Four-Stroke Engine

Stroke 1 **INTAKE STROKE** *(Suck)*	• The piston is moving **down** inside the cylinder • The **inlet valve** is **opened** by the **camshaft** *(see next section)* • The exhaust valve remains closed • The downward movement of the piston creates a vacuum in the cylinder which causes the **fuel/air mixture** to rush **into the combustion chamber** through the inlet value	fuel/air mixture sucked in
Stroke 2 **COMPRESSION STROKE** *(Squeeze)*	• The **piston** is moving back **up** the cylinder • The inlet and exhaust valves are **both closed** • The piston **compresses the fuel/air mixture** into the small space at the top of the cylinder • This makes the fuel/air mixture very **hot** and **combustible** (i.e. can catch fire and burn easily)	fuel/air mixture compressed

Stroke 3 **POWER STROKE** *(Bang)*	• At the top of the piston travel, the **spark plug ignites the fuel mixture** • The resulting explosion and **hot expanding gases** in the combustion chamber **drive the piston downwards** with great force	fuel/air mixture explodes
Stroke 4 **EXHAUST STROKE** *(Blow)*	• Due to the rotary movement of crankshaft, the piston starts to travel back **up** the cylinder • The camshaft opens the **exhaust valve** • The piston rises and pushes the **waste gases out of the exhaust valve** • At the top of the piston's travel, the camshaft **closes the exhaust valve** and **opens the intake valve** again. *We are now back to the start of the intake stroke, and the cycle repeats*	exhaust gases expelled

LUBRICATION: The crankcase holds **oil** which keeps the crankshaft, piston and cylinder **lubricated**. The piston and its rings prevent the oil escaping into the combustion chamber where it would burn.

4 CYLINDERS: Because a 4-stroke engine fires only on **every 4th stroke**, a 4-stroke engine usually has **4 cylinders** connected to the same crankshaft, at offset positions. The camshaft and electronics ensure a different cylinder fires on **every stroke**, keeping the engine **rotating smoothly at a constant speed**.

Parts of a Four-Stroke Engine

Part	Description	Image
CRANKCASE	• The crankcase houses the **crankshaft** *(see below)* • The crankcase contains **oil** to lubricate the crankshaft and the cylinder lining • The cylinder block is mounted on top of the crankcase • A typical four-stroke engine will have **four cylinders, four pistons** and **eight valves**	
CRANKSHAFT	• The crankshaft is an **rotating axle** with offset cranks that connect to the pistons via connecting rods • The crankshaft converts the **reciprocating motion** of the pistons into **rotary motion** of the crankshaft	
CONNECTING ROD	• Connects the **piston** to the **crankshaft**	
PISTON	• The piston **reciprocates** up and down inside the **cylinder** • Usually made from an **aluminium alloy** • The explosion and expansion of the fuel gases in the cylinder above the piston, pushes the piston down	

Part	Description	Image
GUDGEON PIN	• The gudgeon pin fits **inside the piston head** and acts as the **axle** for the **connecting rod** which connects the piston to the crankshaft	
PISTON RINGS	• Creates a gas **seal** between the piston and the cylinder • Also prevents the **lubricating oil** from the crankcase passing into the combustion chamber	
SPARK PLUG	• Used in a **petrol** engine to **Ignite the fuel / air** mixture • The engine electronics sends a **high voltage** pulse to the spark plug just as the fuel/air mixture is **compressed** • This creates a **spark** in the combustion chamber that **ignites the fuel/air mixture**, driving the piston down	
INLET VALVE	• The **inlet valve** opens to allow the combustion chamber to **fill with the fuel / air mixture** *(is sucked in by the piston moving downwards)*	
EXHAUST VALVE	• The **exhaust valve** opens to allow the **waste gases escape** out of the combustion chamber *(the exhaust is pushed out by the rising piston)*	
VALVE SPRING	• **Returns the valve** to the **closed** position after the valve has been pushed open by the **cam** *(see below)*	
CAM	• Each valve is opened and closed by an off-centre rotating **cam** (which is part of the camshaft) • The **cam opens the valve** at **just the right time** in the four-stroke cycle of the engine to let the gas mixtures in or out	
CAMSHAFT	• A camshaft is a rotating **axle that holds all the cams** needed. Two cams are needed for each cylinder • The camshaft is rotated in sync with the engine / crankshaft, via a **timing belt** or chain, so that the valves open and close at the correct times	
WATER COOLING SYSTEM	• Most four-stroke engines are **water-cooled** • The engine becomes very **hot** from the fuel explosions and **friction** of the pistons • Water is **pumped** and circulated through pipes / **holes in the engine block** • The heated water is **cooled** by passing it through very thin pipes in the **radiator** where it is **cooled** by air passing through the radiator • The cooled water from the radiator is recycled back to cool the engine block	

The Two-Stroke Engine

The two-stroke engine has a clever **simple construction** that doesn't need **valves.**

Instead, the **piston blocks and unblocks the inlet and outlet ports** as it moves up and down.

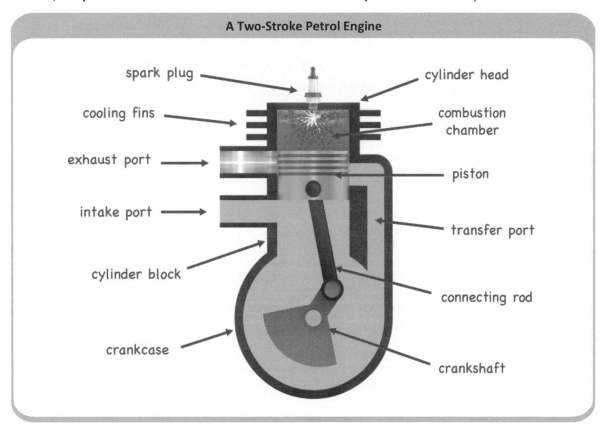

A Two-Stroke Petrol Engine

spark plug — cylinder head

cooling fins — combustion chamber

exhaust port — piston

intake port — transfer port

cylinder block — connecting rod

crankcase — crankshaft

Parts of a Two-Stroke Engine (different from the four-stroke)

INLET PORT	• The **inlet port** is a **hole in the cylinder wall** near the bottom of the piston travel • When the **piston** moves **upwards**, it **unblocks** the inlet port and creates a **vacuum** inside the crankcase, which **sucks** the fuel/air mixture into the crankcase
TRANSFER PORT	• The **transfer port** is an **internal tube** in the engine block that connects the **crankcase** to the **combustion chamber** • When the piston moves **downwards**, it blocks the intake port, **unblocks** the transfer port, and **pushes** the fuel/air mixture from the crankcase into the combustion chamber
OUTLET PORT	• The **exhaust port** is a **hole in the cylinder wall** towards the top of the piston travel • When the piston moves **downwards** and **unblocks** the **outlet port**, the **waste gases escape** out of the combustion chamber
AIR COOLING FINS	• Most two-stroke engines are **air-cooled**. This is because most two-stroke engines are **exposed to the air** and air-cooling is much **cheaper** than water cooling • The **cylinder block** is made with lots of **cooling fins** sticking out from it • This **increases the surface area** of the hot cylinder and therefore increases the amount of **heat** that can be **dissipated** (transferred) to the surrounding air • For example, if a two-stroke engine is used in a **motorbike** or **jet ski**, lots of cooling air is forced through the engine cooling fins as it moves, keeping it cool • However, it is **harder to control** the engine temperature with air-cooling

Operation of a Two-Stroke Engine

A **two-stroke** cylinder **burns fuel on every revolution**, i.e. **every two strokes**. This rate of burning is twice as fast a **four-stroke** cylinder, which only burns fuel on **every second revolution**.
So, a two-stroke cylinder has to do twice as much work (actions in parallel) on each stroke:

- On the **up-stroke**, the piston carries out the **intake** and **compression** actions
- On the **down-stroke**, the piston carries out the **power** and **exhaust** actions

Stroke 1 **UPSTROKE** *Intake +* *Compression* *(Suck and* *Squeeze)*	• The piston is **moving up** in the cylinder - driven around by the previous down-stroke – and it **unblocks the input port** • The **upward** movement of the piston creates a **vacuum** that sucks the **fuel/air mixture** into the **crankcase**, through the **inlet port** • As the piston rises further, it blocks the outlet port and **compresses the fuel/air mixture** in the combustion chamber *The fuel/air mixture was transferred into the combustion chamber by the previous down-stroke (see below)*
Stroke 2 **DOWN STROKE** *Power,* *Exhaust* *+ Transfer* *(Bang and* *Blow)*	• At the top of the piston travel, the **spark plug ignites the compressed fuel/air mixture** • The expanding gases **drive the piston downwards** • The downward movement of the piston **unblocks** both the **outlet port** and the **transfer port** • The continued **downward movement** of the piston blocks the intake port and **pushes the fuel/air mixture** out of the crankcase **into the combustion chamber** through the **transfer port** • The **pressurised fuel/air mixture** coming into the combustion chamber **forces the waste gases out of the outlet port**

Diagram labels: fuel/air mixture compressed; fuel/air mixture sucked in; fuel/air mixture explodes; exhaust gases pushed out by the incoming fuel/air mixture

LUBRICATION - OIL & FUEL MIXED: Because the **crankshaft** and **pistons** are moving parts, they must be **lubricated** with oil. However, there is no separation between the combustion chamber and the crankcase, as with the 4-stroke engine. So, **oil is mixed with the fuel and air** before it goes into the crankcase. This causes **oil to be burnt with the fuel**, which is wasteful and damaging to the **environment**. Also, because there are no valves, some **unburnt fuel** can end up in the exhaust gases, which is also wasteful and polluting.

Comparison of Two-Stroke and Four-Stroke Engines

Engine Type	ADVANTAGES	DISADVANTAGES	Applications
TWO-STROKE	• Simple, light • **Cheap** • **More power** for its weight	• More **air** and noise **pollution** • **Not fuel-efficient** • **Shorter life** (parts wear out due of poorer lubrication)	• Chainsaws • Motor boats • Off-road bikes • Jet skis
FOUR-STROKE	• **Fuel-efficient** • **Quieter** • **Less polluting**	• **More expensive** and **heavier** because of lots of parts	• Cars, Trucks • Buses, Trains • Trains

Other Engine and Vehicle Types

Name	Description	Picture

ELECTRIC MOTORS
 	
and
 	
ELECTRIC VEHICLES
	An **electric motor** uses **electrical energy** to produce **rotary motion**
	An **electric vehicle** contains a large **rechargeable battery** to power a large DC motor
	• Advantages:
	  ○ very **cheap** to run
	  ○ **zero emissions**, no air pollution
	  ○ **quiet**
	• Disadvantages:
	  ○ can be **expensive** to buy
	  ○ need to **recharge the battery** regularly
	  ○ may need to **replace the battery** after some years as it become less effective
		ELECTRIC CAR
		ELECTRIC MOTOR
		BATTERY

HYBRID ENGINES
 	
and
 	
HYBRID VEHICLES
	Hybrid vehicles have **BOTH** a **petrol or diesel engine AND** an **electric motor**
	• Advantages:
	  ○ Can **switch** to the petrol/diesel engine if the **battery runs out**
	• Disadvantages:
	  ○ **Expensive** to buy both engines
	  ○ The engine **still pollutes**
	Modern vehicles use **catalytic converters** to reduce toxic gas emissions
		HYBRID CAR
		Electric Motor / 4-stroke Engine
		Battery / Fuel Tank

Research Activities – Engines and Transport (for individuals or small teams)

1. List the inventors of the **2-stroke, 4-stroke** and **diesel** engines, and the **pneumatic tyre**

2. Research and document **four technologies** that are used in or with **modern internal combustion engines**, to improve their **performance, efficiency,** and **pollution levels**

3. Research and document **autonomous vehicles**, the **technologies** that enable them to work, and the **likelihood they will be adopted** in different transport systems

4. Create a **presentation** on the **environmental impact of different engine types**

Mechanisms

*Do you remember that **mechanisms** are used to change the **type**, **direction** and **speed** of motion?*

Name	Description	Picture / Symbol	Applications
CRANK and SLIDER	• Converts **rotary motion** to **reciprocating motion**, and vice versa	Crank · Slider · Rotary Motion · Reciprocating Motion	• **Engines** - reciprocating motion of the pistons is converted into rotary motion of the engine using the crankshaft • **Air compressors** - rotary motion causes the piston to pump air through valves
CAM and FOLLOWER	• Converts **rotary motion** to **reciprocating motion**	FOLLOWER · FOLLOWER · RECIPROCATING MOTION (output) · ROTARY MOTION (input) · CAM · CAM	• Used in **car engines** to open and close the valves
BEVEL GEAR	• Changes the **angle** of rotation by 90 degrees • Changes the **speed** depending on the ratio of teeth in each gear		• **Chuck key** • **Hand drill** • **Car drive shafts** • Hand whisk
WORM DRIVE	• **Non-reversible** - the worm can turn the worm wheel, but *the worm wheel cannot turn the worm* • **High gear ratio**: one full rotation of the worm only moves the worm wheel along by one tooth	Worm · Worm Wheel	• **Raising heavy loads without slipping** • Guitar string tuners • Tightening ropes • **Reducing motor speed** e.g. used in inline motors
GEARBOX	• A gearbox contains a set of **pairs of gears with different gear ratios** • You choose which gears are engaged by sliding the gears on their axles		• Used in **cars & machines** to change output speed and direction • A **clutch** can be used before a gearbox to allow the gears to be changed smoothly

Name	Description	Picture / Symbol	Applications
CLUTCH	• A **clutch c**onsists of **two plates** that can be **engaged** and **disengaged** to transmit or stop rotation from one axle to the other		• Used to **disconnect** a car **engine** from the **gearbox** and the **wheels** • Clutch allows cars to **change gear** smoothly • It also allows the engine to keep running when the car **wheels are stopped**
UNIVERSAL JOINT	• **Allows a rotating shaft to have a 'bend' or 'hinge' in it**, while continuing to rotate • Made from **two hinges** at 90 degrees		• **Allows car wheels to move up and down** on their suspension while staying connected to fixed central rotating drive shaft (axle) • Can connect a **drive shaft** from a **tractor** to a **trailer** that is moving up and down
BALL BEARINGS	• **Bearings reduce friction** between **rotating parts** • **Ball bearings** use **hard steel balls** to reduce friction between the inside (axle) and outside (axle support)		• **Car wheel axles** • **Bicycle** wheels • **Skateboard** wheels
ROLLER BEARINGS	• Roller bearings use **cylindrical rollers** instead of balls. • **Quieter** than ball bearings, and can **support heavier loads**		• Machine tools • **Fans**
CHAIN AND SPROCKET or **CHAIN DRIVE**	• Use a metal **roller chain** to connect two gears, which are called **sprockets** • **Strong** • **Doesn't slip** easily • However, needs **lubrication**		• **Bicycles** • Engine **timing chains** • **Forklifts** (the forks are lifted by the chain)
BELT PULLEY DRIVE	• Transmits rotary motion using a **belt** tensioned between **two pulley wheels** • **Lighter, quieter** and **cheaper** than a **chain** • **Doesn't need lubrication** • However, can **slip**		• **Washing machines**, driers, hoovers • Food processors • Sewing machines • **Toy cars**

Name	Description	Picture / Symbol	Applications
V-BELT PULLEY DRIVE	• Uses a V-shaped belt to **prevent the belt sliding off** the pulley wheels • Belt can **still slip** around the pulley		• **Industrial and machine tools** • Drills • Lathes
TOOTHED-BELT PULLEY DRIVE	• Uses a toothed belt and gears **to prevent the belt slipping** around the pulley		• Car **timing belts** • **Printers** • **Lathes**
STEPPED CONE PULLEY	• Used to **change speed** by **moving the belt** to different-diameter pairs of pulley wheels		• **Lathe** speed control • **Pillar drill** speed control

Axles, Wheels and Tyres

> A **axle** is a central **shaft** that allows a rotating part such as gear, pulley or wheel, to **rotate**.

Axle

Non-Rotating Axles: An axle may be fixed to the housing or body, and the rotating part(s) rotate(s) around the non-rotating axle.

Rotating Axles: Alternatively, the axle may be attached to the rotating part(s), and the axle rotates inside a fixed bracket or bearing that is attached to the housing or body.

Pneumatic Tyres

Pneumatic tyres are made from rubber or composites and are filled with pressurised air. They dampen shocks and vibrations from the road and provide a more comfortable ride to driver and passengers.

Wheels for Projects

You can buy **hobby wheels** with **solid rubber tyres** in various shapes and sizes. They can attach to your axles or motor spindles using a **push-fit** or **grub screw**. *(A **grub screw** is a small screw with no head)*. You can buy wheels that are specifically designed to attach to the spindle shapes (D-shafts) of inline geared electric motors.

Mechanisms Activitities

Mechanisms Activity 1

• If your engineering room has a **kit of mechanisms and axles** - experiment with them
• Make holes in **cardboard** boxes to hold the axles
• Learn how different mechanisms can be used to change the **speed**, **direction** and **type** of motion

Mechanisms Activity 2

1. Name **four mechanisms** that could be used to drive the **wheels** of a motorised vehicle from a **DC motor**:

Mechanism 1: _____   Mechanism 2: _____

Mechanism 3: _____   Mechanism 3: _____

2. Name a **mechanism** that could be used to change the direction of rotation by **90 degrees**:

_____

3. Name a **mechanism** that can be used to greatly **reduce the rotation speed** of a motor:

_____

4. Name a **mechanism** that **won't slip** or reverse when used to lift or pull heavy loads

_____

Example Mechatronic Solutions - Drive Systems

In engineering, the system used to power the wheels from an engine or motor is often called the **drive system** or **transmission**. Some useful drive systems for **projects** are shown below.

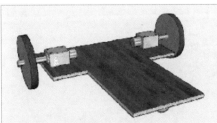

Individual Motor per Wheel	Worm Drive	Pulley Drive
Using **one motor for each wheel** has the advantage that if you use a swivel **castor** for a third wheel, you can **steer** the vehicle by changing the relative **speed** of the motors	The **worm drive** greatly **reduces the speed** of a fast motor and greatly **increases the torque** (turning power) supplied to the wheels	A **belt pulley** system can be an effective way to transfer rotary motion from a motor spindle to one or more axles

Research Activity

Research Activity - Mechanisms and Transport

Create a **presentation** on the **main mechanisms used in a car**.
Include the drive / transmission system and suspension system in your research.

Motor Vehicle Design

Design Evaluation Activities

Design Evaluation Activity 1

An **all-terrain vehicle** is shown.

1. (a) Name a **suitable material** for part **A**:

_____

  (b) Give **reasons** why that material is suitable:

_____

2. Give a **reason** why **pneumatic tyres** B are used on this vehicle:

_____

3. The **bonnet C** is made from **polypropylene**. Give **two reasons** why this material was chosen:

  (a) _____ (b) _____

3. Give two **reasons** why **LEDs** were chosen for the **headlights**:

  (a) _____ (b) _____

Design Evaluation Activity 2

Compare the **vintage car** and the **modern car** under the following headings:

1. Safety Features: _____

_____

_____

2. Design Features: _____

_____

_____

3. Environmental Impact: _____

_____

_____

Design Evaluation Activity 3

1. Describe **two design features** that enhance this racing car:

(a) _____

(b) _____

2. Give **two properties** of the **material** required to make the **body** of such a racing car:

(a) _____ (b) _____

3. Describe **two environmental impacts** of motor racing technology:

(a) _____

(b) _____

Electronics

Electronic Components

DPDT SWITCH	• A **Double-Pole Double-Throw (DPDT) switch** is composed of **two internal switches** that are **operated in parallel** / at the same time. Note the dashed line on the DPDT switch symbol • Each internal switch has one input connection and two output connections, which gives a total of **six connections on a DPDT switch**
SPEAKER or **LOUDSPEAKER**	• Converts input **electrical energy** to output **sound energy** • Installed in every phone, TV, radio and most computers

Electronic Circuits

Reversible DC Motor Circuit

A **reversible DC motor circuit** is shown below in both **schematic diagram** and **wiring diagram** forms.

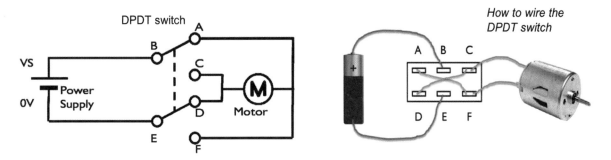

*The **schematic diagram** on the left shows the **electronic symbols** and their electrical connections.*
*The **wiring diagram** on the right shows the **physical connections** between the components.*

Reversible DC Motor Circuit Activities

1. What does DPDT **stand for**?

2. **How many connections** are there on a DPDT switch?

3. **Verify** that the **wiring diagram** and the **schematic diagram** shown above actually represent the **same circuit** - by checking all the connections to the lettered terminals on the DPDT switch are the same in both diagrams.

4. **Draw** the schematic diagram of the reversible motor circuit on a sheet of paper in free hand.

5. Using a **blue** pen or pencil, **trace out the route that the current would take** around the schematic circuit via the drawn position of the DPDT switch.

6. Using a **red** pen or pencil, trace out the route the current would take around the circuit **if the DPDT switch were moved to the other position**.

7. **Why** does the motor **reverse direction** when the switch is changed?

8. **Physically build the circuit** using a breadboard, crocodile cables, or soldering, and **test** it out.

9. If your school has electronic **circuit simulation software** like **Circuit Wizard** or Crocodile Clips, create and test the circuit using that.

Notes on the Reversible Motor Circuit:

o *You need to match the voltage of the battery/batteries to the rated voltage of the DC motor*

o *The physical connections to the battery / batteries will be different to those shown*

o *In addition to the two switched positions shown on the symbol, a DPST switch usually also has a physical 'centre-off' position, where no electrical connections are made inside the switch. If your DPDT switch does not have a 'centre-off' position, you can order DPDT CO (centre off) switches from a supplier, OR you can add an extra SPST switch between the battery and the DPDT switch to turn off the motor circuit.*

micro:bit Programming

Remote Control of DC Motors using Radio Waves

- In **Unit 7** we saw how micro:bit boards can communicate with each other using **radio waves**
- In **Unit 9** we saw how a **micro:bit** can control **DC motors** using a **DC Motor Drive Expansion Board**
- Putting these two things together, we can now **control DC motors remotely** using radio waves

First, we familiarise ourselves with the micro:bit code blocks needed, and then we get programming.

Revision Activity

Look back at Unit 9 **page 238**, which explains how to connect and set up your **micro:bit DC Motor Drive Expansion Board** with your **micro:bit** and **DC motor(s)**

Useful Motor Control Code Blocks

The code blocks for controlling the **motor drive board** can be found in the **Motor Driver** toolbox menu in the **makecode editor** *(once you have loaded the DC Motor Driver Extension - see Unit 9 page 238).*

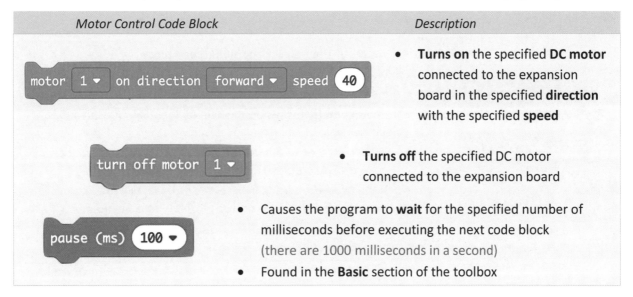

Motor Control Code Block	Description
motor **1 ▼** on direction **forward ▼** speed **40**	• **Turns on** the specified **DC motor** connected to the expansion board in the specified **direction** with the specified **speed**
turn off motor **1 ▼**	• **Turns off** the specified DC motor connected to the expansion board
pause (ms) **100 ▼**	• Causes the program to **wait** for the specified number of milliseconds before executing the next code block (there are 1000 milliseconds in a second) • Found in the **Basic** section of the toolbox

Useful Radio Control Code Blocks

These **code blocks** are found in the **Radio** section of the makecode toolbox. You need to create two micro:bit programs and download to two separate micro:bit boards.

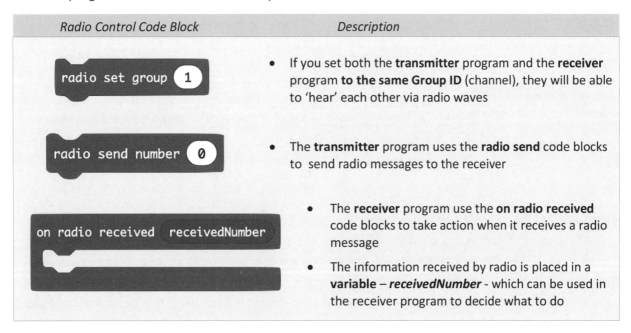

Radio Control Code Block	Description
radio set group **1**	• If you set both the **transmitter** program and the **receiver** program **to the same Group ID** (channel), they will be able to 'hear' each other via radio waves
radio send number **0**	• The **transmitter** program uses the **radio send** code blocks to send radio messages to the receiver
on radio received **receivedNumber**	• The **receiver** program use the **on radio received** code blocks to take action when it receives a radio message • The information received by radio is placed in a **variable** – *receivedNumber* - which can be used in the receiver program to decide what to do

The graphic below illustrates the basic concept of how a **transmitter micro:bit** and a **receiver micro:bit** communicate with each other using the **radio code blocks**.

Useful Logic Control Code Blocks

Logic control code blocks control the flow of a program. They decide which other code blocks are executed, and which are not. They are found within the **Logic** section of the makecode toolbox.

Logic Code Block	Description

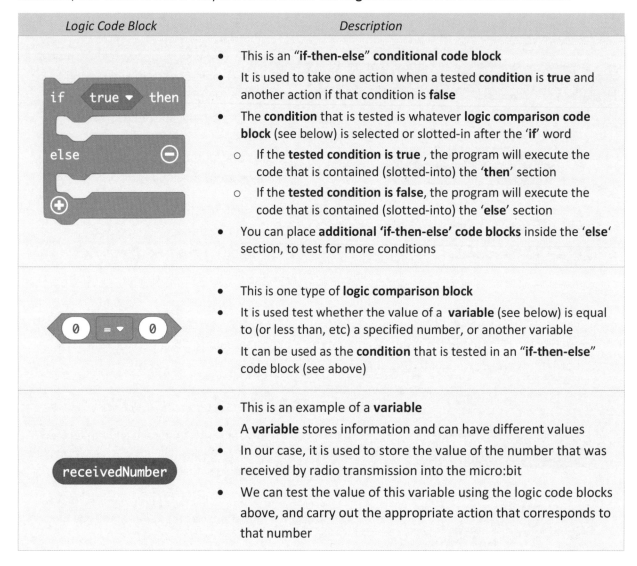	• This is an **"if-then-else" conditional code block**
	• It is used to take one action when a tested **condition** is **true** and another action if that condition is **false**
	• The **condition** that is tested is whatever **logic comparison code block** (see below) is selected or slotted-in after the 'if' word
	  ○ If the **tested condition is true** , the program will execute the code that is contained (slotted-into) the **'then'** section
	  ○ If the **tested condition is false**, the program will execute the code that is contained (slotted-into) the **'else'** section
	• You can place **additional 'if-then-else' code blocks** inside the **'else'** section, to test for more conditions

	• This is one type of **logic comparison block** • It is used test whether the value of a **variable** (see below) is equal to (or less than, etc) a specified number, or another variable • It can be used as the **condition** that is tested in an **"if-then-else"** code block (see above)
	• This is an example of a **variable** • A **variable** stores information and can have different values • In our case, it is used to store the value of the number that was received by radio transmission into the micro:bit • We can test the value of this variable using the logic code blocks above, and carry out the appropriate action that corresponds to that number

Using micro:bit Movements (Gestures) to send Radio Messages

We could send radio commands between micro:bits when we press buttons A or B (as we did in Unit 5). However, more usefully, we can use the movement of the micro:bit itself to send radio commands - for example by tilting the micro:bit up or down, left or right. This will be a useful way of remote-controlling the movement of our car later on. Detecting micro:bit movement is done using the **'on shake' code block**, as shown below:

Gesture Code Block	Description
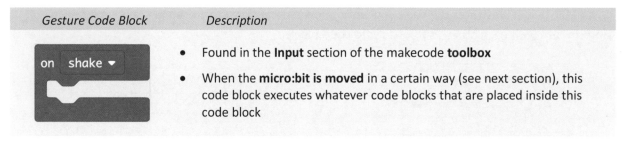	• Found in the **Input** section of the makecode **toolbox** • When the **micro:bit is moved** in a certain way (see next section), this code block executes whatever code blocks that are placed inside this code block

Gesture Code Block	Description
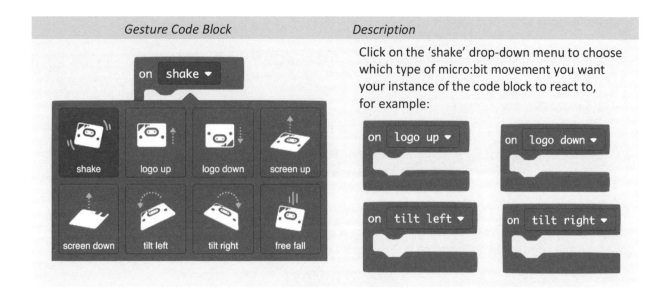	Click on the 'shake' drop-down menu to choose which type of micro:bit movement you want your instance of the code block to react to, for example:

Putting It All Together – Programming a Remote-Controlled Vehicle

Now that we've seen most of the **building blocks**, let's **put them together** to radio-control a motorised vehicle. Here is the scenario:

REMOTE CONTROL CAR SET-UP

- The car has **two motors**, one connected to a **left wheel**, the other to a **right wheel**
- The motors are connected to a **DC motor drive board**
- The **receiver micro:bit** is plugged into the **DC motor drive board**
- A **transmitter micro:bit** sends **numbered instructions** via radio to the **receiver micro:bit** to tell it how to control the motors
- You **tilt the transmitter micro:bit** forwards, backwards, left and right to make the car go in those directions

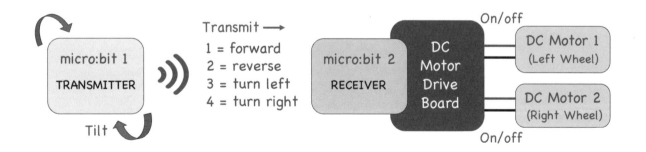

Here's the programming sequence we will be implementing:

TRANSMITTER		RECEIVER	
micro:bit movement	*Number sent*	*Receiver micro:bit action*	*Car action*
Tilt vertically, **logo up**	1	Turn both motors **on**, forward	Moves **forward**
Tilt vertically, **logo down**	2	Turn both motors **on**, reverse	**Reverses**
Tilt horizontally, to the **left**	3	Right motor **on**, left motor **off**	Turns **Left**
Tilt horizontally, to the **right**	4	Right motor **off**, left motor **on**	Turns **Right**

Programming Activities - Radio Control Your Vehicle Motors

Activity 1 - Create a Transmitter and a Receiver makecode Project

1. Go to https://**makecode.microbit.org**
2. Create **two new projects**
3. Save one project as a **transmitter** and the other project as a **receiver**

   Note – if you do not see a 'Motor Driver' menu item in your makecode toolbox, then install the DC motor makecode extension, following the instructions in Unit 9

Activity 2 - Send One Tilting Movement to the Receiver

1. In the **transmitter** project, create the following program:

2. In the **receiver** project, create the following program:

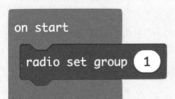 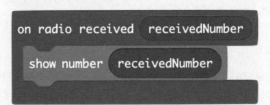

3. Make sure **each transmitter-receiver pair** of micro:bits uses a **different group ID** to avoid messages crossing
4. **Download** the programs to their respective micro:bits
5. **Tilt** the transmitter micro:bit to **logo up**, and test that the **receiver micro:bit displays a number "1"** in its LEDs

Activity 3 - Send All Tilting Movements to the Receiver

1. **Enhance** the **transmitter** project as follows: radio send number 2 on **logo down**, number 3 on **tilt left**, and number 4 on **tilt right**
2. **Download** the transmitter program to the transmitter micro:bit
3. **Tilt** the transmitter micro:bit in all directions and test that the **receiver micro:bit displays numbers 1 to 4** correctly

Activity 4 - Connect the Motors to the Receiver

- Plug the **receiver micro:bit** board into the edge connector in the **DC motor drive board**
- **Connect the two motors** to the Motor 1 and Motor 2 pins on the DC motor drive board
- **Connect the 4.5V power supply** / battery pack to the DC motor drive board

Activity 5 – Radio Control the Car in Forward and Reverse

1. Update the receiver program as follows:
2. Add an **if-then-else** block to the **on radio received** block
3. If the value of the received number is '**1**', **turn on both motors** fully in the forward direction:

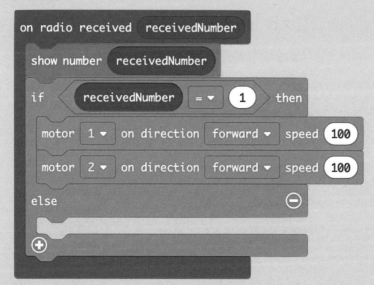

4. Add another **if-then-else** block into the **else** section above, test if the received number is **2**, and if so, **turn both motors on at half-power in the reverse direction**
5. **Download** the program to the **receiver micro:bit** board and test!

Activity 6 – Add Radio Control of Steering in the Forward Direction

1. **Add code to the receiver program to turn left**
   (Hint: Add another if-then-else block to the last 'else' section, test if the received number is 3, and if so, turn on the right motor full, and turn off or slow down the left motor)
2. Add code to the receiver program to **turn right**
3. **Download** the program to the **receiver micro:bit** board and test

Activity 7 – Further Refinement of your Radio Control program

1. Consider **how to steer the car in reverse** *(Hint: you could use a variable to record the current direction of travel, so that you know what way to control the motors)*
2. **Stop the car using button A** on the transmitter micro:bit
3. **Stop the car using a different movement** of the transmitter micro:bit
4. Display an **arrow indicating which way the car is moving** on the receiver micro:bit **LEDs**
5. **Connect external LEDs** to the vehicle, and turn them on when button B is pressed on the transmitter micro:bit
6. Turn **on front or rear vehicle lights** (LEDs) depending on which way the vehicle is moving

Unit 10 Revision

Unit 10 Revision Questions

1. Name two materials suitable for forming in a vacuum former.

2. List the steps required to use a vacuum former.

3. Name two materials suitable for making a mould for a vacuum former.

4. Give three sources of renewable energy and three sources of non-renewable energy.

5. Identify the energy conversions taking place in a bulb, a motor, and a battery.

6. List two applications of a two-stroke engine, and two applications of a four-stroke engine.

7. A two-stroke engine is shown. Answer the following questions:

   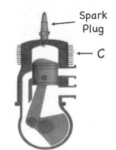

   a) Explain the purpose of the spark plug.

   b) Name part C and explain its function.

   c) Give the purpose of each of the 3 ports in a two-stroke engine.

   d) How is the piston connected to the crankshaft?

8. Explain what happens on the upward and downward strokes in a two-stroke engine.

9. Explain what happens in each of the four strokes of a four-stroke engine.

10. Give two advantages and two disadvantages of a two-stroke engine, and two advantages and two disadvantage of a four-stroke engine.

11. Explain the primary difference in operation between a petrol engine and a diesel engine.

12. Give one advantage and one disadvantage of the following engine types:
    (a) petrol, (b) diesel, (c) electric, (d) hybrid.

13. (a) Give two advantages of a worm drive
    (b) Sketch the symbol for a worm drive
    (c) Give two applications for a worm drive

14. What mechanism would you use to change the axis of rotation by 90 degrees?

15. Name one machine tool / manufacturing machine that uses a stepped-cone pulley system.

16. Give one advantage of a belt pulley system compared to a chain-and-sprocket system.

17. Give one advantage of a chain-and-sprocket system compared to a belt pulley system.

18. Name a mechanism that won't slip or reverse when used to lift and pull heavy loads.

19. Name the mechanism used to open and close the valves in a four-stroke engine.

20. Name the mechanism that converts rotary motion to reciprocating motion and vice versa.

21. In relation to a DPDT switch: (a) explain the abbreviation DPDT; (b) sketch the symbol of a DPDT switch; (c) give one application of a DPDT switch.

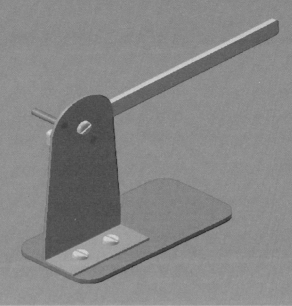

Stop/Go Barrier

Unit 11 – Stop/Go Barrier

Unit Objectives

PROJECT	Design and manufacture a controllable entrance **barrier**

- Learn to **design and manufacture based on a brief**. *Select the electro-mechanical system, materials, and create your own working drawings. One possible starting mechanical design is provided in the Appendix, but we encourage you to design your own.*
- Learn **lots more electronics**: servo motors, sensors, transistors, useful control circuits
- Control a **servo motor** with a **micro:bit**. Learn more **mechanisms** and useful **drive systems**
- Learn about **surface coatings** for metals

Content

PROCESSES & PRINCIPLES	Surface Finishing	• Surface coatings: plating, plastic, glass, paint, lacquer • Decorative techniques: Engraving
DESIGN	• Full design and manufacture of a mechatronic system from a brief	
MECHATRONICS	**Electronics**	• Input components: sensors: LDRs, thermistors • Process components: transistors, diodes, capacitors • Output components: servo motors, stepper motors • Circuits: Reversible DC motor circuit with limit switches, sensor circuits
	Mechanisms	• Additional gears & drives. Sample mechatronic solutions
	micro:bit	• Controlling a servo motor. Activation by light sensor

Learning Outcomes from this Unit

PROCESSES AND PRINCIPLES	DESIGN APPLICATION	MECHATRONICS
1.1, 1.2, 1.3, 1.4, 1.7, 1.8, 1.9, 1.10, 1.11, 1.12, 1.13	2.3, 2.5, 2.6, 2.7, 2.8, 2.9, 2.10, 2.11, 2.12	3.2, 3.3, 3.4, 3.6, 3.7, 3.8, 3.9, 3.10, 3.11

Suggested Timeframes

START TIME	YEAR 2	April		DURATION	6-8 weeks

Working Drawings

Your Concept Sketches for Your Barrier

TITLE	Unit 11 – Stop/Go Barrier	SHEET 1 OF 3
DESCRIPTION	Your Concept Sketches	Brighter Minds

Your Design Drawings for Your Barrier

TITLE	Unit 11 – Stop/Go Barrier	SHEET 2 OF 3
DESCRIPTION	Your Design Drawings	Brighter Minds

Your Design Drawings for Your Barrier

TITLE	Unit 11 – Stop/Go Barrier	SHEET 3 OF 3
DESCRIPTION	Your Design Drawings	Brighter Minds

Project Storyboard

Project Description

LEARNING GOALS OF THIS PROJECT

- **Design** and build a working model of a **movable barrier** based on the **project brief** below
- **Research** and **choose** appropriate **electro-mechanical solutions**, and **apply** them to the planning, design, manufacture, assembly, testing and evaluation of your project

---

PROJECT BRIEF

1. Your project should be based on the idea of a **barrier that can block or allow people or vehicles through**. It could be like a concert entrance system, or a car park barrier, or other.
2. You can move your barrier(s) in any direction - e.g. up and down, sideways, rotating, sliding.
3. You must use an **electro-mechanical control system** to open and close the barrier.
4. Your **control system** should ensure that the **barrier can rest at the open and closed positions**.
5. You can initiate the movement of the barrier in one of two ways:
   a) **manually** using a **switch**, OR
   b) automatically using a **sensor** – e.g. detect the presence of an object and trigger the barrier to open. Your control system should also close the barrier after the object has passed through

   See Circuits pages 289-290

6. Use one or more **surface coatings** in your project

   See Surface Coatings page 283

GENERAL DESIGN IDEAS / SUGGESTIONS

1. Early on, choose the **basic type of movement** and a general **physical shape** for your barrier. *We have included a basic idea for a beginning mechanical design in the Appendix, but we encourage you to develop your own*

3. Decide whether you are going use a simple **switch** or a more complex **sensor circuit** to activate your barrier. One way to implement sensor activation is to use something to **block and unblock light** shining on an **LDR** – see the sensor circuits later in this unit.

4. Choose which **electro-mechanical system** you will use to implement your chosen movement. Here are some options:

   - If you have access to a **micro:bit** and a **servo motor**, you could use these to accurately move the barrier between its open and closed positions. You can also use the micro:bit **LEDs** to display barrier messages;

     See micro:bit servo programming page 294

   - If you want to use a **DC motor**, remember:
     (a) you will need a **slow speed** for the barrier;
     (b) you can use **mechanisms** to move the barrier;
     (c) you will need **an automatic way to turn off the motor** when the barrier reaches its end (limit) positions.

     See Electronic Circuits, Limit Switches, Sensor Circuits on pages 289-90

Design Option A – micro:bit and Servo Motor

Activity 1A – Understand the Electronics and Programming Required

- Read the '**micro:bit Programming**' section at the end of this unit
- **Decide** if you are going to use a **micro:bit and servo motor** to control your barrier
- **Decide** also if you are going to use the **sensor** option to trigger the motion

Design Option B – DC Motor, Electronics and Mechanisms

Activity 1B – Identify Possible Mechanisms for your Barrier

If you are lifting a barrier, name a mechanism that would not allow a heavy barrier to slip back down. Name two other **mechanisms** you could use to operate a barrier system.

Non-Slip Mechanism 1: _____

Mechanism 2: _____

Mechanism 3: _____

Activity 2B – Discuss Design and Manufacturing Options

Discuss the following in groups, or with your teacher and class:

1. Discuss and **choose** the **basic type of movement** you want to implement
2. Discuss, **select** and **justify** the type of **mechanism** you want to use, if any
3. Discuss, **choose** and **justify** the **type of motor** you wish to use
4. Look at the *Reversible DC Motor Circuit with Limit Switches* circuit in the Electronics section later in this unit. Discuss **how the circuit works**, and where **limit switches could be physically placed** in your design to control the barrier opening and closing
5. Discuss your **choice of materials** – from at least two metals and two plastics. **Choose** your materials and **justify** your choices
6. Discuss the type of **surface coatings** you could use in your project

Design Option C - Sensor Activation with Option B

Activity 3C – Discuss Additional Sensor Option

- Look at the *Reversible DC Motor Circuit with Limit Switches and Sensor* circuit in the Electronics section of this unit
- **Decide** if you wish to use this option. (It will take longer to get this circuit working)
- Discuss the **impact** of the additional electronics on the **physical design** of your barrier
- You may decide to **first build and get Option B working**, and then later re-wire to add the sensor elements of the circuit (bearing in mind they may impact on the physical design)

Design Drawings and Planning

Activity 4 – Draw Your Chosen Electronic Circuit

Based on your chosen Design Option (A, B or C), **draw your chosen electronic circuit** in the Design Drawings section in the working drawings area. *Use a rectangle to represent any micro:bit.*

Activity 5 – Concept Design Sketches

- Based on the Design Option you have chosen (A, B or C), free-hand **sketch some concept ideas** for the **look** and **operation** of your barrier, in the *Concept Designs* section of the working drawings area in this unit
- Consider how the barrier will be **stopped and held** at the end of its travels
- Consider how to **integrate** the chosen electronics and mechanisms, and how to assemble all the parts
- Consider **different concepts** for the movement for the barrier (you can always change the mechanisms required)
- Indicate the **materials** chosen on your concept designs
- Check that your designs **satisfy the project brief**
- Ask your teacher or peer to **evaluate** your chosen design(s), and make any **improvements**

Activity 6 – Planning - Manufacturing

Make a **list** of all the **materials**, **components**, **tools** and **equipment** you will need for your project. Ask if they will be available when you need them.

Activity 7 – Planning – Create a Gantt Chart

Create a **Gantt Chart** for the **remaining tasks** in the project: e.g. completion of design, manufacture and assembly of all the mechanical parts, integration and testing of the circuit, and micro:bit programming if required.

Activity 8 – Final Design Drawings

In the *Design Drawings* section of the working drawings area in this unit, accurately **draw to scale with dimensions all the mechanical parts** (including mechanisms) required for your barrier. Indicate on the drawings how the parts will be **joined** and **surface-finished**.

Manufacturing

Activity 9 – Manufacture and Test Your Car Park Barrier

Build and **test** the **electronic circuit**. If using a micro:bit, first create and test the program.
Mark out and **manufacture** the **mechanical parts**.
Assemble the **mechanical parts** and **mechanisms**.
Integrate the **electronics** with the mechanical parts.
Test, and **improve**. Make note of **all changes made** and **reasons**.

Project Assessment

Student Self-Assessment

In this project, I gained the following new **skills** and **knowledge**:

1. _____

2. _____

3. _____

I **evaluate** my project to have **turned out well** in the following areas:

_____

_____

If I were to carry out this project again, I would **modify** or **improve** the following aspects:

_____

_____

_____

_____

On a scale of 1 to 10, I would give my project a **score** of…

Peer Assessment

I felt the following aspects of the project were **good**:

_____

_____

_____

I felt the following project aspects could be **improved**:

_____

_____

_____

Teacher Feedback

Teacher comments on student's project:

Not Graded	Partially Achieved	Achieved	Merit	Higher Merit	Distinction

---

Learning Topics for Unit 11

Processes and Principles

Surface Finishing of Metals

Surface Coatings

A **surface coating** is a **thin layer of another material** applied to a material **surface**

Surface coatings are applied to **metals** to **improve** their:

  (a) **visual appearance**,

  (b) **tactile feel / touch**   *(for example, to remove a feeling of coldness or slippiness)*

  (c) **resistance to corrosion**   *(i.e. rusting)*

Common surface coatings used on metals are: (a) **another metal** - see below, (b) **plastic**, (c) **glass** (enamelling), and (d) **paint** (including varnishes and lacquers).

Metal Plating

Plating means to coat a metal with a **thin layer of a different** (usually non-ferrous) **metal**

- **Plating** is usually carried out for the following **reasons**:
  - to improve the **look** (aesthetics) of a metal - for example in **jewellery** and **ornaments**
  - to **protect a ferrous metal from corrosion**
- Common plating metals are: **tin, zinc, silver**, and **gold** *(all non-ferrous metals)*
- The main ways to carry out plating are: **dip-coating** and **electroplating** *(see next page)*

Examples of Metal Plating

TIN PLATING	• Plating sheet **steel** with **tin** makes **tinplate** • Used for **food and drinks cans** as tin is **non-toxic** and **does not corrode** easily • Can be **hot-dipped** or **electro-plated** (*see below*)
SILVER PLATING	• Used for **jewellery, cutlery, ornaments** • Used to create **high-quality electrical connections** BEFORE PLATING AFTER PLATING
GALVANISING	• Plating steel or iron with **zinc** • Carried out using the **hot-dip** method • Provides **high protection against corrosion** • Used for steel that is **exposed outdoors**, e.g. metal **roofs**, outdoor **nails**

Metal Plating Processes

HOT-DIPPING	ELECTRO-PLATING
• The object to be plated is dipped in a bath of **molten plating metal** • Hot-dipping is used for **galvanising** as it produces a thicker layer than electro-plating	• Uses **electricity, two electrodes** and a **bath of electrolyte solution** • The object to be plated is connected to the **negative side** of the power supply and placed in the bath. The object to be plated becomes the **negative electrode** • A **positive electrode** is made out of a **block of the plating metal**, is connected to **positive side** of the power supply, and is dipped in the bath • The electric field between the two electrodes causes the plating metal to come out of the bath solution and **deposit on the negative electrode**, coating the object with a fine coat of the plating metal

Plastic Coating

Metal objects can be coated in **plastic** to protect them against **corrosion** and to improve their **tactile feel** (i.e. how they feel to human hands). This is very useful for metal products that need to be **handled** frequently, and/or metal products that come in contact with a lot of **water** or **moisture**.

PLASTIC COATING	• **Protects against corrosion** • **Safe, easy-clean** and **comfortable touch** • Used on **dishwasher trays, fridge trays, shopping baskets, kitchen utensils** • Carried out using a **plastic dip coating tank** (see below)

PLASTIC DIP COATING TANK	• The tank contains **powdered plastic** • It has a **porous membrane** in the **floor** • The cleaned **metal product** is **heated** in an **oven** until it is very **hot** • **Air is blown up through the porous membrane** causing the plastic **particles to swirl** around in the tank (called *fluidising*) • The **hot metal** is **dipped** into the tank • The **plastic melts** onto the hot metal • The product is taken out to **cool** 
SAFETY PRECAUTIONS	• Do not **overheat the metal** as it can burn the plastic or surrounding items • Wear a **face mask** to protect against inhaling **fumes** and plastic **particles** • Wear **protective clothing**, gloves and safety glasses

Enamelling (Glass Coating)

ENAMELLING	• **Powdered glass** is **melted** onto the metal surface using a **blow torch** or **oven** • Used for **jewellery** and **artwork** to provide an **attractive, hard, brittle, colourful finish** 

Painting and Lacquering

*Paint can be applied to materials other than metal too, but most materials require a special **primer** before.*

SPRAY PAINTING	• Spray painting can achieve a smoother finish that brushing or rolling • Work in a **designated painting area** that is **well-ventilated** • Place your object in a cut-out **cardboard box** to prevent paint getting everywhere • Wear **protective clothing, disposable gloves** and a **face mask** • Clean the metal surface with **white spirits** • Optionally, the surface of the metal can be **warmed** with a **heat gun** • **Shake** the aerosol repeatedly before using • Spray lightly and evenly - **keep the aerosol constantly moving** while spraying, do not let drips build up, do not apply too much paint • You may need **more than one coat** / painting session to cover all the surfaces • Leave aside to **dry** • When the paint has dried, an improved finish can be achieved by applying a **second coat**, and/or by applying a coat of clear **lacquer** *(like paint without the colouring)*

Engraving

ENGRAVING	**Engraving** means **cutting designs or text into metal surfaces** with **sharp tools**. Differently-shaped manual and power tools are available for engraving letters and numbers on ornamental objects. 

Mechatronics

Electronic Components

Input Components – Sensors

> A **sensor** is an electronic **input component** that detects **changes in environmental conditions** and converts that information into an output **electrical signal**

Sensors detect changes in the environment around them - such as the amount of **light**, **temperature**, **pressure**, **sound**, **moisture**, or **movement**.

The electrical signals representing these environmental conditions are fed as **inputs** into an electronic **circuit** or computer which **processes** that information to create useful **outputs**.

> The BBC **micro:bit** computer contains a number of **built-in sensors**, e.g. for light, temperature and movement, some of which we have used in previous units.

Common Sensor Components

Component	Senses	Description	Picture	Symbol
LDR (Light-Dependent Resistor)	The amount of light	• The electrical resistance of an LDR is **high in darkness** and **low in brightness** • Used to **detect light levels** - for example to turn on **street lights** when it gets dark		
THERMISTOR (Heat-Dependent Resistor)	Temperature	• The electrical resistance of a thermistor is **high in the cold** and **low in heat** • Used to detect **temperature** in **ovens**, heating systems, and safety control systems		

Process Components

> **Process components** receive electrical signals from **input components** and **transform** them into signals that are suitable to be sent to **output components**

INPUT Components → PROCESS Components → OUTPUT Components

e.g. Switches, Sensors — e.g. Transistors, Computers — e.g. Motors, LEDs, Speakers

Common process components are **resistors**, **transistors**, **capacitors** and **integrated circuits** (chips).

> A **transistor** is a **process component** that **amplifies** a small or weak input signal to create a larger **more powerful output signal**

Transistors and **diodes** are **semiconductors**, i.e. made from a semiconducting material like **silicon**.
Integrated circuits (chips) can contain millions of transistors on a **single piece of semiconductor**.

Common Process Components

Component	Description	Images
DIODE	• A **diode** is a **semiconductor** device that **only allows current to flow in one direction** (in the direction of the arrow on the symbol) • Diodes are **polarised** components - they must be connected the right way around to work • Used in **rectifier** circuits, which convert **AC** (alternating current) into **DC** (direct current)	
TRANSISTOR	• A **transistor** is a **semiconductor** device that is used to **amplify** (increase) **an electrical signal** • A **small current** going in to the **base** of the transistor is transformed into a **large current** flowing from **collector** to **emitter** • **Transistors** can also be used as **electronic switches** in circuits and in **computers**	 collector base emitter
CAPACITOR	• **Capacitors** store small amounts of electrical **charge** (electrons) • Capacitors are used in **timer circuits** because they take some time to charge up • Some capacitors are **polarised** - they have a **positive connection** and **negative connection,** and only work when connected the right way. The polarity is indicated on the symbol and on the physical component	

Relays

A **relay** is an **electrically-operated switch**. Similar to a transistor, a small input electrical signal can turn on the relay, which can then conduct a **large amount of current** to power large output devices like motors.

RELAY	• A **relay** is an **electrically-operated switch** • When a small current flows between **A and B**, it powers a coil which magnetically attracts and **pulls the relay switch closed**, which allows current to flow between **C and D** • When the current between A and B is stopped, the coil stops attracting the relay switch and a **spring** returns the relay switch to its previous open position, cutting off the current flowing between C and D • SAFETY: There are **two separate circuits** in a relay: one containing A and B, and the other containing C and D. This makes a **relay** a very **safe** way of switching on and off a **high-voltage circuit** connected between C and D, using a safe low-voltage DC circuit connected between A and B.	COIL ARMATURE CONTACTS A B C D A C B D

Output Components

Servo and Stepper Motors

We've seen **DC motors** in Unit 7 Jitterbug, Unit 9 'Tis the Season and Unit 10 Motorised Vehicle. With a **DC** motor, you just connect the power and it turns. However, it is difficult to control **how much it turns**. With **servo** and **stepper** motors, you can send them **instructions** to tell them **what angle to rotate to**.

Stepper Motor

STEPPER MOTOR	<ul><li>A **stepper motor** can rotate in **small precise steps**</li><li>You send **electrical pulses** to it to tell it to 'click' along to the next position</li><li>Controlled by a **microcomputer** which sends it the right number of pulses to rotate to the desired angle</li><li>Unlike a servo motor (see below), a **stepper motor** does **not use sensors** or feedback to measure and control the position of the motor</li><li>**Simpler** and **less expensive** than a servo motor</li></ul> <u>APPLICATIONS:</u><ul><li>Controlling movement of **CNC machine tools** such as CNC **lathes**</li><li>Moving **paper** and **ink** feeds on a **printer**</li></ul>

Servo Motor

SERVO MOTOR	<ul><li>A **servo motor can be positioned accurately** by sending it **instructions** in the form of electrical pulses</li><li>A **servo motor** contains a built-in **electronic control system** which measures and controls the position of the motor</li><li>A **sensor** called an **encoder measures the angle** of the motor spindle</li><li>The **control unit** rotates the motor spindle until the **measured angle** of the motor spindle **matches the desired angle** that you instructed it to rotate to</li><li>If you push the motor spindle out of the desired position, this **feedback control system will move it back again** to the desired position</li><li>Servo motors are more **accurate**, **faster** and more **powerful** than other motors, but they are also more **expensive**</li></ul> <u>APPLICATIONS:</u><ul><li>Accurate positioning of **robot** arms</li><li>**CNC** control of machine tools like **lathes**</li><li>**Auto-focus** of camera lens</li></ul>

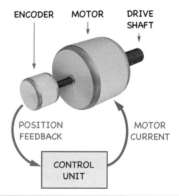

Useful Electronic Circuits

Reversible DC Motor Circuit with Limit Switches

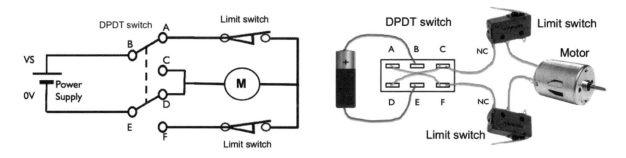

This circuit adds **two limit switches** to the **reversible motor circuit** you saw in Unit 10.
The limit switches are physically placed where they will **stop the motor** when the motor reaches its desired end positions.

APPLICATION – OPENING AND CLOSING A BARRIER

- A **DC motor** moves a barrier in a linear or rotary direction using a **mechanism**

- **Limit switches** are placed at either end of the barrier travel

- When the moving **barrier reaches the limit switch**,
  it pushes open the limit switch, which **cuts off the current** to the motor and **stops** the barrier

- When you **reverse the DPDT switch**, the motor turns on again but in reverse, which **moves the barrier back** to where it came from. This also releases (closes) the limit switch so that it can be used again

- When the barrier touches the **other limit switch**, the current is cut off and the **barrier stops** again at that point. The cycle can be repeated by reversing the DPDT switch again

---

Reversible DC Motor Circuit with Limit Switches and Speed Control

This more complex circuit, using a **variable resistor and a transistor**, works better at controlling the motor speed than using a variable resistor **in series** with the motor (as used in Unit 10 working drawings).

This is because this circuit can supply lots of current to the motor as well as a wide range of voltage.

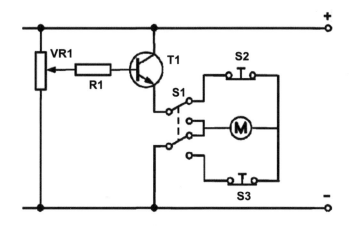

Light Sensor Circuit / Light Beam Detector Circuit

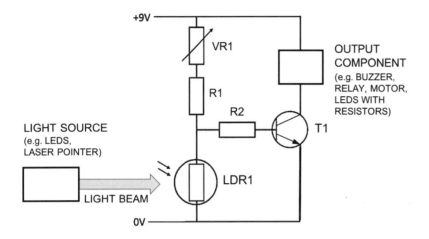

If the **light beam** shining on the **LDR** is cut off by an object coming between the light source and the LED, the **resistance of the LDR** and the voltage across it **rises** - this **turns on the transistor** which supplies **current** to the output component – for example a buzzer or motor.

- The **variable resistor** is needed to **adjust** the amount of darkness that will cause the transistor and the output to turn on

- If you **swap** the positions of LDR1 and (VR1 + R1) in the circuit, the circuit will work the other way round – i.e. the output will turn on when light shines on the LDR

If you wish to build this circuit you can try these values:

Component	Value
VR1	47KΩ
R1	1KΩ
R2	2.2KΩ
Transistor	BC108

Reversible DC Motor Circuit Triggered by a Light Sensor

The circuit below joins a **reversible motor circuit** to the **light beam detector circuit** above. The DPDT relay reverses the current to the motor depending on whether the light beam is broken or not. This circuit could be used to **open and close a barrier** triggered by an object crossing a light beam.

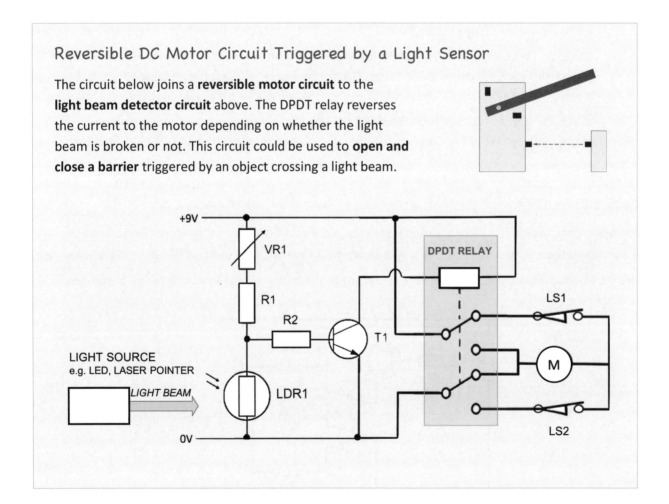

Mechanisms

Gears

Mechanism	Description	Picture	Usage
GEAR TRAINS *and* **IDLER GEARS**	• A **gear train** is **two or more gears** meshed together • In a **simple gear train**, all gears except the first and last are **idler gears**	Idler Gear	• **Idler gears only change the direction of motion**, they have **no effect on the speed** of the gear train
COMPOUND GEARS	• A smaller gear and a larger gear **rotate on the same axle** • Compound gears enable greater speed and power changes		• **Reducing speed of electric motors** - when smaller gears drive the larger ones • Individual **gear ratios are multiplied**
WORM DRIVE	• **Non-reversible gear system:** the worm can turn the worm wheel, but *the worm wheel cannot turn the worm* • **High gear ratio:** one full turn of the worm rotates the worm wheel by one tooth	Worm Worm Wheel	• **Raising heavy loads without slipping** • Guitar string tuners • Tightening ropes • **Reducing motor speed** e.g. used in inline motors
RATCHET AND PAWL	• The ratchet gear can **only rotate in one direction** • The **pawl** prevents the ratchet gear **slipping back** and turning the other way		• **Turnstiles** • **Ratchet spanners** • **Bicycle rear axle**: allows the wheel to turn while not pedalling • **Tensioning** clothes lines, sports nets

Gear Ratios

The **Gear Ratio** is the no of teeth in the **driven gear divided by** the no of teeth in the **driver gear**

$$\text{Gear Ratio} = \frac{\textbf{number of teeth} \text{ on the output } \textbf{driven gear}}{\textbf{number of teeth} \text{ on the input } \textbf{driver gear}}$$

The **gear ratio** tells you the **speed difference** between the input and the output gear:

$$\textbf{Speed} \text{ of the output } \textbf{driven gear} = \frac{\textbf{speed} \text{ of the input } \textbf{driver gear}}{\text{gear ratio}}$$

For example, if there were **twice as many teeth** in the **driven gear** than in the **driver gear**:
- the **gear ratio** would be 2
- the **speed** of the output gear would be **half** the speed of the input gear
- the **torque** (turning power) delivered by the output gear would be **twice** that of the input gear

Mechatronics Activities

Mechanisms Activity

(a) Name the **type of mechanism** being used when a chuck key is turned in a chuck:

_____

(b) **Why** is the gear on the chuck key **smaller** than the gear on the chuck? What advantage does this bring? *(Hint: think of torque)*

_____

_____

Mechatronics Activities – Motor Drives

In engineering, the system used to **create motion** from a motor or engine is often referred to as a **drive** or **drive system**. Consider the following types of **motor drives**:

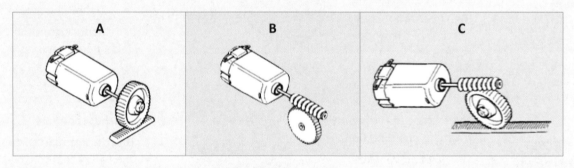

| A | B | C |

1. Name the **mechanism** used at **A**: _____

2. Name the **mechanism** used at **B**: _____

3. With the same motor speed, which mechanism (**A** or **C**) produces the **fastest** motion?

   _____

4. Give an **application** for **A**: _____

4. Give an **application** for **B**: _____

5. Give an **application** for **C**: _____

Mechatronics Activities – Apply Your Knowledge of Mechanisms

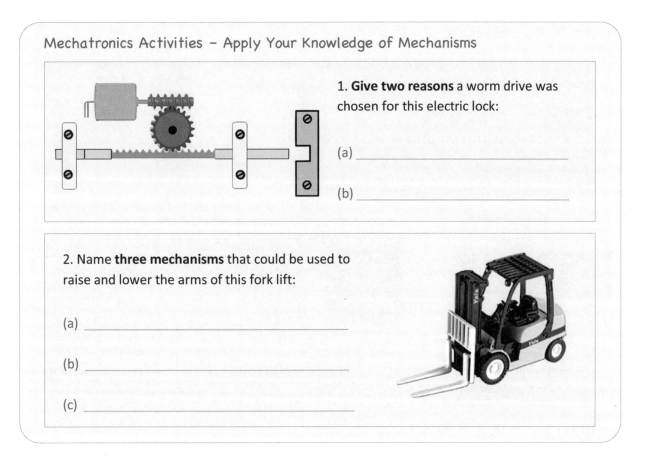

1. **Give two reasons** a worm drive was chosen for this electric lock:

(a) _____

(b) _____

2. Name **three mechanisms** that could be used to raise and lower the arms of this fork lift:

(a) _____

(b) _____

(c) _____

Example Mechatronics Application

Hoist - Using a Worm Drive and Pulley System

Many machines need to be able to lift heavy weights without slipping. The example below shows how an electric **motor**, a **worm drive** and a **pulley system** can be used to lift heavy weights without slipping.

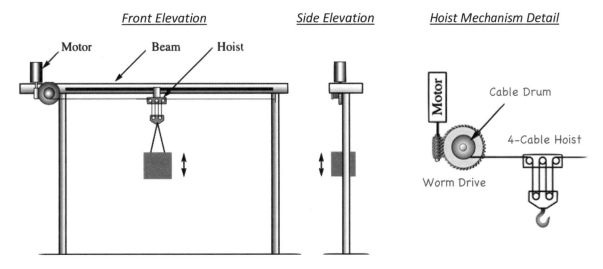

Front Elevation *Side Elevation* *Hoist Mechanism Detail*

Motor Beam Hoist

Motor

Cable Drum

4-Cable Hoist

Worm Drive

The 4-cable pulley system provides a speed reduction (and a corresponding gain in lifting force) of 4.

Activities

1. Give **two reasons** why a **worm drive** is used for **lifting or pulling heavy loads**:

(a) _____ (b) _____

micro:bit Programming

This section describes how to use a **micro:bit** to control a **servo motor**. This control system can be used for the barrier project in this unit.

> *If you wish to control a **DC motor** with a micro:bit, see Unit 9 page 238*

Servo Motors

A servo motor allows you to **control its position accurately** by sending instructions to the motor.

Servo Motor Connections

Unlike a DC motor, a servo motor has **three connections**:

Servo Motor	Connection	Wire Colour	Description
POWER / CONTROL / GND	**POWER**	Red	*Power Connection e.g. 3V, 6V*
	GROUND	Black/Brown	*Ground / Zero Volts Connection*
	CONTROL	Orange or Yellow	*Controls how the motor spindle rotates (see below)*

Types of Servo Motor

A micro:bit can control a **servo motor** that is **rated between 3V and 6V**. For the purposes of this unit, we need to use a **180 degrees rotational micro-servo**, not a continuous rotational servo.

Connecting a micro:bit to a Servo Motor

Connecting a Servo Motor rated at 3V

It is possible to supply power to a 3V micro servo directly from the 3V and GND pins on the micro:bit as shown opposite.

Connect the servo control wire to any micro:bit output pin e.g. Pin 1. *(Use jumper wires to plug into the servo connector block, or even cut off the servo connector block and bare the three wires, and use crocodile clips to connect them to the micro:bit pins).*

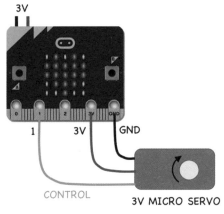

For more reliable operation, however, it is recommended to **connect a separate power supply to your servo motor** as shown below.

Connecting a Servo Motor rated 3V, 4.5V or 6V to a micro:bit

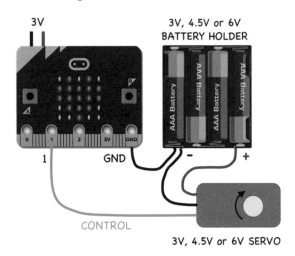

To supply sufficient current to a servo motor, connect its power lines to a **separate DC power supply** such as a populated battery holder. Note the servo motor is a **polarised component** – the **red** power wire must be connected to the **positive terminal** and the **black ground** wire must be connected to the negative side.

Connect the **control wire** to one of the micro:bit output pins e.g. Pin 1.

Also connect the **micro:bit GND pin** to the negative side of the battery holder, so that both circuits share the common ground / 0V voltage reference.

Do not connect the red wire from a 4.5-6V battery pack to the micro:bit as you may permanently damage it.

Programming a Servo Motor

Controlling a servo motor from a micro:bit is very simple, using the **servo write pin** makecode code block shown below.

Useful Code Blocks

Code Block	Description
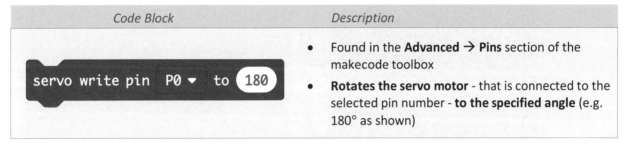 servo write pin P0 ▼ to 180	• Found in the **Advanced → Pins** section of the makecode toolbox • **Rotates the servo motor** - that is connected to the selected pin number - **to the specified angle** (e.g. 180° as shown)

Programming Activities – Raising and Lowering a Barrier

The following activities can be used to open and close the **barrier** project in this unit.

Activity 1 - Raise a Barrier when Button A is pressed

Task

Set the servo arm to **horizontal** when the micro:bit is first powered up.

Rotate the servo arm to **vertical** when micro:bit **button A** is pressed.

Solution

- Go to the micro:bit **makecode editor** at https://makecode.microbit.org
- Create a **new project**
- Create the **code** below

micro:bit simulator

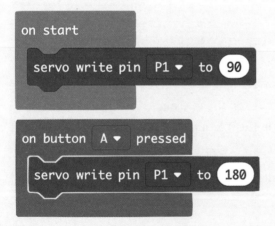

*Note – because your physical servo motor can be mounted in different orientations, you will have to **experiment** to find the programmed **angle values** that work best for your application. Test before mounting the motor.*

Testing

- Click on **button A** on the micro:bit **simulator** and observe what happens
  (click on the refresh symbol on the simulator to restart the simulation)

- Don't download to the physical micro:bit yet, until we are able to lower the barrier as well - see next activity

Activity 2 – Raise and Lower the Barrier when Button A is pressed

Task: **Modify** the program from Activity 1 to **lower the barrier 5 seconds after raising it**

Solution: Update the **code** in your '**on button pressed**' code block to the following:

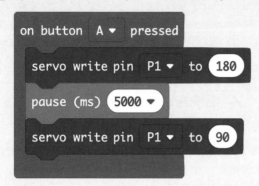

Test using the Simulator

- Click on **button A** on the micro:bit **simulator** and observe what happens

Download and Test

- **Connect** the **servo motor** to your **micro:bit** as described earlier
- **Do not connect** the servo motor to your barrier yet
- **Download** the program to your micro:bit. Test by pressing button A
- Depending on how you are going to orient your motor, **determine the angles you need to use in your program** to correctly open and close your barrier

Note: Do not mount your servo motor into your barrier until you know which angles in your program will correctly move the barrier to the desired physical open and closed positions.

Activity 3 – Add User Instruction Messages to your micro:bit Barrier

Task

1. **Modify** the program used in Activity 2 as follows:
   - On start-up, display (scroll) the text "**Press A**" on the micro:bit LEDs
   - After lifting the barrier, display "**ENTER**" on the micro:bit LEDs, followed by an arrow ↑
   - After the dropping the barrier, display "**Press A**" again

2. **Test** the program using the **simulator**, then **download** and test on your **micro:bit** barrier

Activity 4 – Add Red and Green STOP/GO LEDs to your micro:bit Barrier

Task

1. Physically **connect** a **red LED** and a **green LED** to two unused output **pins** on your micro:bit (e.g. Pin 0 and Pin 2). Don't forget they will need to be protected by resistors *(see Unit 6)*

2. **Modify** the program used in Activity 3 as follows:
   - On start-up, **turn on** the **red LED**
   - After lifting the barrier, **turn off** the **red LED** and **turn on** the **green LED**
   - Just before dropping the barrier, **turn off** the **green LED** and **turn on** the **red LED**

2. **Test** using the simulator, then **download** and test on your physical **micro:bit**

Raise and Lower your Barrier using a Light Sensor (LDR)

These activities allow you to use an LDR to detect the presence of an object and then open the barrier.

Useful Code Blocks

Code Block	Description
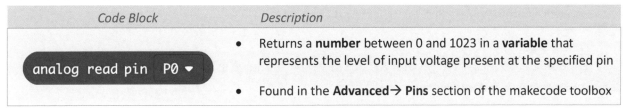 analog read pin P0 ▼	• Returns a **number** between 0 and 1023 in a **variable** that represents the level of input voltage present at the specified pin • Found in the **Advanced → Pins** section of the makecode toolbox

Reading the Light Level from an LDR

Activity 5 – Reading the Light Level from an LDR

Connect an LDR to Pin 0 of your micro:bit as shown below.

(If you have carried out Activity 4, connect your LED to a different pin. If you have a servo motor connected to Pin 1, you can leave it connected)

- Connect one leg of the **LDR** to the **3V** pin, and the other leg to **Pin 0**

- Connect a **10KΩ** resistor between the **GND** pin and the **LDR** leg that is connected to pin 0

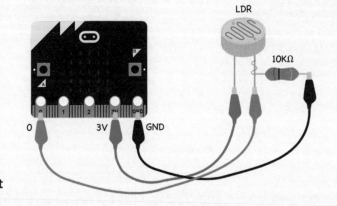

- **Create a new makecode project** and create the program below

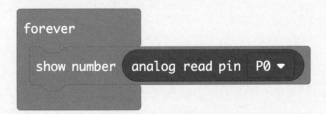

```
forever
    show number  analog read pin P0 ▼
```

- **Download** the program to your micro:bit and test

Testing

1. The built-in **LED screen** on the micro:bit should **display a number** between 0 and 1023 representing the amount of light currently being detected by the LDR light sensor

2. **Cover the LDR** with your finger and you should see the displayed light value **decrease**

3. **Shine a bright light** on the LDR (e.g. using a phone or torch) and you should see the displayed light value **increase**

Extension Activity: If you have time and want a challenge, change your program to display a **bar chart** of the light value on the micro:bit LEDs, instead of the number value.
(Hint: search for a 'plot' code block)

Activity 6 – Open and Close the Barrier based on the LDR Light Sensor

Task

Raise the barrier when an object (like a model car or person) **blocks light** to the LDR.
Lower the barrier again when the object **moves away**.

Connections

- Connect your **LDR** and **resistor** to your micro:bit as shown in **Activity 5** on previous page
- Connect your **servo motor** to your micro:bit as shown on **page 294**

Programming

1. **Modify** the program from Activity 5 (or create a new makecode program) as follows:

2. Explain in your own words what this program does:

_____

_____

_____

3. **Enhance** this program to **lower the barrier when the light level is greater than 300**
   (Hint: you don't have to test the condition again, you can extend the 'if-then' code block...)

NOTES

1. *We have used 300 as an example light value to trigger the opening of the barrier. In your project, and with your light conditions, you will need to **experiment** to find the light value that will work best to trigger the opening and closing of your barrier.*

2. Before you physically mount the servo motor into the barrier, make sure you have found and tested the right **values to use for the angles** in your program, so that the servo will open and close the barrier when you mount the servo motor into its final orientation in the barrier.

You can use the table below to record your progress with these activities

Activity Number	Too Difficult	Partially Completed	Completed
1			
2			
3			
4			
5			
6			

Unit (11) Revision

Unit 11 Revision Questions

1. (a) Give two reasons for applying surface coatings to metals.
   (b) Name three surface coating techniques.

2. (a) Describe the steps required to spray paint metal.
   (b) Give three safety precautions that should be taken when spray painting.

3. Name the two primary methods used to plate metal.

4. (a) Identify the steps required in the plastic dip coating process.
   (b) Name one tool in the workshop which has a plastic-dip-coated finish.

5. (a) Explain what galvanising is.
   (b) Explain why galvanising is not carried out on non-ferrous metals.

6. Explain the term gear ratio.

7. (a) Sketch and explain the principle of a ratchet and pawl.
   (b) Give two applications for a ratchet and pawl.

8. Give one advantage and one disadvantage of using a solar cell as a means of powering a mechatronic system.

9. (a) Describe what an electronic sensor component is and does.
   (b) Give two examples of a sensor component

10. Describe what happens to the resistance of an LDR as light levels change.

11. (a) What causes the resistance of a thermistor to fall?
    (b) Give one application for a thermistor.

12. (a) Describe the basic principle of operation of a servo motor.
    (b) How many electrical connections are there to a servo motor?
    (c) Give one advantage of a servo motor over a DC motor.
    (d) Comment on the accuracy of servo motors.
    (e) Give two applications of servo motors.
    (f) Give one disadvantage of a servo motor.
    (g) Why can't a 6V servo motor be powered directly from a micro:bit?

13. Describe the basic principle of operation of a stepper motor.

14. (a) Does a worm drive have a high gear ratio or a low gear ratio?
    (b) Give two advantages of a worm drive over other gear types.

15. Explain the difference between a simple gear train and a compound gear train.

Unit 12 – Engineering In Our World

Unit Objectives

- Appreciate the wide **applications of engineering** across society, homes, schools, industry
- Explore the **impact** of engineering and mechatronics on **society** and **environment**
- Understand **computer-based technologies** such as **ICT** (Information and Communications Technologies), **robotics**, **CNC machine control** and their relevance to engineering
- Appreciate the contribution of **inventors** and **inventions** to engineering and mechatronics

Content

PROCESSES AND PRINCIPLES	**Applications**	• Engineering in homes, businesses, transport, shopping, communications, food, manufacturing, materials
	Impacts	• Negative impacts of engineering, energy and waste • Measures to reduce environmental damage
DESIGN APPLICATION		• Design application in everyday products and green technologies • Inventors and Inventions • Design software
MECHATRONICS	**ICT**	• Structure of computer systems, input and output devices, peripherals, computer software, networks, internet
	Robotics	• Types, applications, pros and cons
	CNC control	• Computer control of machine tools like lathes

Learning Outcomes from this Unit

PROCESSES AND PRINCIPLES	DESIGN APPLICATION	MECHATRONICS
1.5, 1.6		3.4, 3.5

Suggested Timeframes

This unit may be studied independently of other units. We feel it will be of more benefit if studied later in the Junior Cycle, when greater engineering knowledge and context is understood.

Applications of Engineering

Engineering in the Home

Engineering is involved in the design, manufacturing, supply, maintenance and recycling of the following:

- **Building materials** for our houses like concrete, steel, glass and plastic
- **Electrical lighting** to light our homes; modern **heating and insulation systems** to keep us warm
- **Water**, **electricity**, **gas**, **phone**, and **internet connections**
- **Washing machines**, **dryers**, **ovens** and **fridges** to make our lives easier
- Most of our domestic appliances have integrated **computer control**
- **Home automation** - such as the automatic and remote control of heating, lights, food restocking, and voice control, are examples of **smart technology**

Engineering in Communications and Entertainment

- Engineers design **computers**, **phones**, **Wi-Fi** and **internet connections** which give us access to information all over the world
- **Telecommunications networks** are built using **engineered materials, structures** and **machines** – including, satellites, cables and communications masts
- **Websites**, **social media channels**, **internet-based film services**, **podcasts**, **radio**, **TV**, **computer games** and **subscription-based music services** provide entertainment and communication services
- **Drones** are a cost-effective way of carrying out high-altitude **filming**

Engineering in Retail and Shopping

- Engineering provides the ability to construct large **steel-framed buildings** like supermarkets and shopping centres to provide many shops and food outlets in one building
- **Checkout, security** and **payment systems** allow us to shop, transfer money and track purchases
- **Drones** can be used for **delivery** of food, medicine and goods, and for **security** surveillance

> ### Research Activity – Explore the Use of Drones
> Research and document the uses of **drones**, and their **advantages** and **disadvantages**

Engineering in Transport

- Engineering provides the **engines** and electric **motors** that power our cars, ships, trucks, buses, airplanes and trains
- Engineering provides the **materials** and **technology** to build our vehicles from materials like **steel**, **aluminium** and **plastics**
- Engineering-designed **safety features** include seat belts, air bags, warning systems, rear- view cameras and crumple zones
- **GPS systems** help us map routes, and estimate journey times
- **Energy-saving features** include LED lights, low weight, low emissions and electric engines
- Modern technologies used in **bicycles** include quick-release wheels, disc brakes, very light composite materials used for frames and wheels, improved safety features, drive system and shock absorbers

Engineering in Manufacturing

- Engineering is used to develop **machines and tools** that can be used to manufacture other products
- **CAM software** (see ICT section), **CNC machines**, **automation** and **robots** are used to manufacture and transport products in factories
- **Computer systems** are used to track components and orders as they move through factories

> ### Research Activity 2
> Research and report on the uses, benefits and disadvantages of **robots**.

Engineering in Materials

- Materials like **alloys, plastics and composites** are **engineered** to provide **specifically-designed properties** such as lightness, strength, toughness, hardness, durability and corrosion-resistance
- **Smart fabrics** are materials that have one or more properties that can be changed in response to their environment. They can also have anti-allergy or antiseptic properties

Engineering in Food Production

- **Farm machinery** is used to plant, spray, water and harvest crops, milk cows and feed animals
- **Artificial fertilisers** and **growth additives** increase production
- Food is **processed** and **packaged** using **machines** and **robots**
- Food is **preserved** using chemicals, vacuum-packing, drying and freezing
- **Trucks, ships** and **planes** move food around the world

Engineering in Health and Medicine

Engineering has contributed greatly to human health, not only through more efficient and safer food production, but also through great advances in **medical technology**: developing life-saving machines and products like ventilators, life-support machines, X-ray machines, MRI scanners, artificial limbs, heart valves, dental products, virus protection equipment, wheelchairs, pharmaceutical products and drugs.

Impacts of Engineering

Positive and Negative Impacts

Engineering has undoubtedly made our lives more comfortable and healthier, but there are **negative side-effects** too - engineering has produced machines and products that use **vast amounts of energy**, create large amounts of **waste**, and release **greenhouse gases** that cause **climate change**.

However, engineering can be part of the **solution** to this, by developing **environmentally-friendly (green)** products, **renewable** sources of energy, and **recycling** solutions.

Sources of Environmental Damage

- **Burning fossil fuels** in our vehicles, factories, houses, and electrical power plants creates **air pollution** (smog) and releases **greenhouse gases** (like carbon dioxide) into the atmosphere - which causes **global warming** and **climate change**

> **Carbon footprint** is the **amount of carbon dioxide** released into the atmosphere by a person, a community, an activity or a product

- **Mining** for ores and the **destruction of forests** causes **environmental damage**
- **Rivers** and **seas** are polluted by disposal of **sewage**, **fertilisers chemicals** and **plastics**
- **Disposing waste in landfills** causes damage to land, animals and birds

Reducing Environmental Impact

- Replace polluting **fossil fuel** power plants with non-polluting, green **renewable energy sources** like **wind** turbines, **solar** panels, **wave** and **geothermal** technology.
- **Replace fossil fuel engines** with **electric motors**
- **Insulate** houses and buildings to reduce energy usage and waste
- **Recycle** – make new products out of old products to reduce waste and energy usage. **Metals, glass, thermoplastics, rubber and paper** can be melted down or processed to make new products.
- **Upcycling** means using a discarded product to create a product of **higher value** than the original
- Use **LED lights** rather than incandescent bulbs
- Use **rechargeable batteries** to reduce the damaging chemical waste contained in batteries
- Separate organic waste to make **compost** which can re-used as safe fertiliser
- **Incineration** of non-recyclable waste **reduces the amount of landfill waste** and can **generate electricity** from the heat produced. However it also generates some chemical gas emissions

> Research Activity 3
>
> Research and report on initiatives in your area where **engineering** is involved in providing **solutions that promote a better environment** or quality of life.

ICT – Information and Communciations Techology

> **ICT** (Information and Communications Technology) is the use of **computer-based technologies** to **capture**, **process** and **transmit information**

Impact of ICT in Engineering

Computers and ICT are **centrally important** to **engineering work**, in the following ways:

1. **Computer (CAD) software** is used to create, communicate and test new **designs**
2. **Computer-controlled machine tools** and **robots** are used to **manufacture** and **test products**
3. **Computer technology** is **integrated** into **engineered products** to control their operation

Computer Hardware

> **Hardware** means the **physical parts** of a **system**

Types of Computers

DESKTOP	• A **desktop computer** has a separate processor unit, keyboard, mouse and screen • Contains **ports** to connect to other devices
LAPTOP	• A **laptop** is a **portable computer** with a **built-in screen**, **keyboard**, **trackpad** and **wifi connection** • Contains ports to connect to other devices
TABLET	• A **tablet** is a portable, light battery-powered computer • Use a **touchscreen** instead of a keyboard and mouse • They are easy and fast operate
SMARTPHONE	• A **smartphone** is a **portable battery-powered mobile phone** that also performs many of the functions of a **computer** and also has **internet access** • Contains built-in wifi, camera and recording functionality, and uses a **touchscreen**
MICRO-COMPUTERS	• **Microcomputers** or **microprocessors** are small embedded computers that are **built in** to industrial and domestic **appliances** to **control** their operation and to **communicate** with users • Examples include dishwashers, washing machines, microwaves, ovens, cars, calculators and smartphones
ROBOTS and CNC MACHINE TOOLS	• Computers are integrated into industrial machinery such as **robots** and **CNC machine tools** like CNC lathes - to **control** the operation of these **mechatronic** systems and to **communicate** with users
micro:bit	• The **micro:bit** is a microcomputer used to teach **programming**, build interesting stand-alone **projects**, and act as a **control system** for mechatronic projects

Integrated Circuits

INTEGRATED CIRCUIT	• Affordable and small computers would not be possible without **Integrated Circuits** (ICs) or 'chips' • One IC contains **thousands** (or even millions) of **electronic components** on a single piece of semiconductor material

Parts of a Computer System

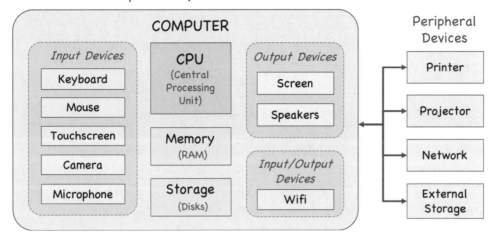

Basic Computer Components

CPU and Memory are electronic components called **Integrated Circuits** (ICs) or 'chips', which are made from **semiconductors.** They typically contain millions of **transistors** *(see Unit 11).*

CPU	• The **Central Processing Unit** chip is the **'brain'** of the computer, where the programs are run • It is a **process component,** rather than an input or output component	CPU chip

MEMORY	• **Memory** is a process component that is used to **store programs and data** for fast access by the CPU. There are two main types:
	
	  • **RAM** *(Random Access Memory)* is temporary fast read-able and write-able memory. Data in RAM is **lost** when the computer is powered off
	
	  • **ROM** *(Read-Only Memory)* – holds permanent pre-programmed instructions for the computer (e.g. to start it up)
		Memory chips on a PCB

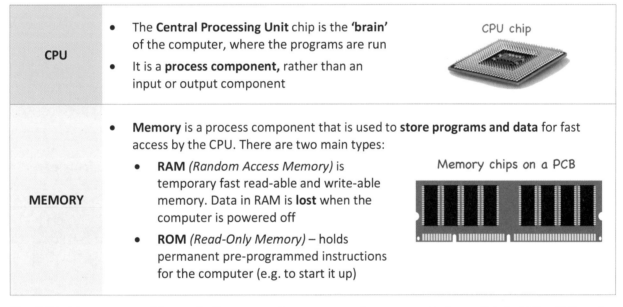

The CPU chip, memory chips and other computer components are mounted on a **Printed Circuit Board** (**PCB**) - *see Unit 6, page 143 -)* which makes the electrical connections between all the components.

Data

DATA

Digital **data** is the **Information** stored in, and used by computers.

The quantity of data is measured in:

    o **megabytes (MB)** - approximately one **million bytes**

    o **gigabytes (GB)** - approximately one **billion bytes**

One **byte** is equal to **eight bits** of information

One **bit** of information is represented by a **1 or a 0**, or a high or low voltage in a computer

Classification of Computer Devices

Device	Description
INPUT DEVICES	• Input devices **gather information** from the real world and **send it to the computer** e.g. **keyboard, mouse, trackpad**
OUTPUT DEVICES	• Output devices **receive data from the computer** and cause something to happen change in the real world e.g. **screens, speakers, printers, robot arm**
INPUT and **OUTPUT**	• Some devices are **both input and output devices** – e.g. a touchscreen, disk drives
INTERNAL / EXTERNAL	• **Internal** devices built-in to the computer - **inside** the computer casing • **External** devices are **outside** the computer casing, separate from the computer • External devices are often called **peripherals**

Some Common Computer Input and Output Devices

STORAGE DEVICES	• **Storage devices** are used to **store large quantities of data for a long time**, also when the power is switched off. They are write-able and slower than RAM memory • **Magnetic disks** - called hard disks • **Optical discs** - like CDs and DVDs • **Flash Memory / Solid State Drives** – these are fast permanent writeable memory chips. These are also used in **USB drives** / memory sticks and **SD cards**

Optical disk

USB drive / Flash memory

TOUCH-SCREEN	• A **touchscreen** is a **touch-sensitive screen** that is both an **input** and an **output device**. It replaces the need for a keyboard and mouse, so it is ideal for **devices** like **smartphones** and **tablets** • Surfaces are made from **scratch-resistant glass** with **sensors** underneath the screen to detect finger pressure • **Disadvantages:** Screens can get smudged. May be difficult for elderly and visually impaired people to use
PRINTER	• A **printer** is an **output** device that takes **digital data** from a **computer** and prints it on **paper**
SCANNERS	• A **scanner** is an **input** device that can scan a **paper page** and send it as **image data** to a **computer**
3D PRINTER	• A **3D printer** is an **output** device that physically **builds plastic or metal objects** using data from a computer
USB (Universal Serial Bus)	• **USB is a standardised way of connecting an external input or output device** to a computer • Many devices such as keyboards, printers, cameras and mice connect to computers over USB

Activity 4 – Brainstorm Input, Output and Storage Devices

In **pairs**, in a 3-minute race against the clock, list of as many computer devices as you can think of under the following headings:

- Input Devices *(supplies data into computers)*
- Output Devices *(takes data from computers)*
- Storage Devices *(stores data permanently)*

Computer Software

Software is the set of **instructions** that a computer carries out – the **programs**

A piece of software with a specific purpose is called a software **program**, an **application** or an **app**.

Common Types of Computer Software

Software	Description
OPERATING SYSTEM	• The operating system **communicates with all the hardware,** and **allows multiple application programs** to run on the same computer • Common operating systems are **Windows, Mac OSX, IOS** and **Android**
OFFICE SOFTWARE	• **Office software**, like **Microsoft Office**, is a collection of software used to carry out common tasks like **email**, creating **documents**, **spreadsheets** and **presentations**
MOBILE APPS (Applications)	• **Apps** are **software applications** that run on **mobile devices** • Apps carry out specific tasks such as **email**, **navigation**, **sending messages**, **banking**, **social media**, etc.
CLOUD COMPUTING	• **Cloud computing** means r**unning computer programs on the internet** (on computers called servers on the internet) rather **than on your own personal computer** • Examples are **cloud storage** services such as **Google Drive**, and software services like **Google Docs**
VIRUS	• A **virus** is a **malicious (bad) program** that attaches itself to another program or file to gain access to your computer • Viruses can **delete files**, **access accounts**, **steal data**, **block access** and more
CAD (Computer-Aided Design) **SOFTWARE**	• **CAD software** creates accurate **technical drawings** for **design** and **manufacture** • Also includes software for designing and testing **electronic circuits** • **SolidWorks** and Circuit Wizard are common CAD packages used in schools
CNC MACHINE PROGRAMS	• **CNC programs** are created on a computer and downloaded to a CNC-controlled **machine tool** such as a **lathe**, to get the machine to carry out specific operations automatically

Computer Networks

> A **computer network** is set of **inter-connected computers**
> and related devices that can **communicate with each other**

The **Wi-Fi** in your house forms a **network** because it connects computers, phones and printers to a **router**, which connects you to the **internet**.

INTERNET	• The **internet** is the **largest computer network in the world** • It is a **network of networks** – an international set of **inter-connected networks**

Wireless Technology

WIRELESS TECHNOLOGY	• **Wireless technology** is any technology that allows devices to communicate **without physical wires** • Wireless technologies can use **radio waves** – like **Wi-Fi** (see below) and the **micro:bit** – or can use **infrared waves** - like your **TV remote** control	
WI-FI	• **Wi-Fi** is a **wireless technology** that uses **radio waves** to allow computers and devices to **communicate with each other**	
BLUETOOTH	• **Bluetooth** uses **radio technology** to send information between devices that are close to each other, e.g. to allow **smartphones** to communicate with each other, and with wireless microphones and speakers	

Accessing the Internet

INTERNET SERVICE PROVIDER	An **Internet Service Provider** is a **company** (like eir, Vodafone, Sky etc) that provides customers with **internet access** via a phone line, cable or satellite dish
MODEM	A **modem** allows a digital network (like as a Wi-Fi network) to connect to and use a **wired phone line to connect to the internet**
WORLD-WIDE WEB (WWW)	The **world-wide web** is the set of all **web pages** on the internet. Web pages are inter-connected using **hyperlinks** called **URLs** (Uniform Resource Locators)
BROWSER	A **browser** is a **software program** e.g. Chrome, Safari, Firefox) used to access and **view web pages**
SEARCH ENGINE	A **search engine** is a cloud software program that searches for and **finds web pages** on the internet based on entered keywords, e.g. Google
ENCRYPTION	Encryption means to **encode information into a form that cannot be read**, until it is decrypted again by someone who has access to the secret code or key to read it. Data transferred via the internet is encrypted until it reaches its desired destination. This keeps our data private and allows us to **shop** and **bank safely online**.

Applications of Computers and ICT

COMMUN- ICATIONS	• Computers make modern communications possible: **internet messaging**, **phones**, **social media**, **internet video**, **TV, radio** • High-quality **microphones** and **webcams** are used for **video conferencing** using programs like **Zoom** and **Skype**
BUSINESS	• Businesses rely heavily on computers to operate efficiently. Computers are used to record and **manage all aspects of the business**: customers, orders, stock, shipments, payments in, payments out, manage company finances, staff, contracts and wages
NAVIGATION and MAPS	• **GPS (Global Positioning System)** uses a set of **satellites** orbiting the Earth to beam down **radio** signals to Earth • This allows our **smartphones** to figure out where we are and calculate routes for us, using **software** like **Google Maps**
ENTER- TAINMENT	• Computers are used for **reading**, **listening to music** and **watching videos** • Video and audio files are **streamed** over the internet
EDUCATION and RESEARCH	• The **world-wide web** provides **vast information** online for **learning** and **research** • Computers are used to **write reports and presentations** and **share videos** • There are lots of **online courses** and tutorials available online
SECURITY and HEALTH	• Computer, wifi and bluetooth technologies are used for **security systems**, house alarms, baby monitoring, CCTV, **patient monitoring systems**, and many **medical devices** and machines
ENGINEERING and AUTOMATION	• Computers and ICT are indispensable to the application of Engineering: ○ Computers are **built in to engineered products** ○ Computer **software** is used to **design**, model and **simulate** engineering solutions ○ Computers control **automated processes**, **robots**, and **CNC** machine tools in **factories** (see below)

Automation, Robotics and CNC Control

> A **robot** is a **computer-controlled machine** that performs actions **normally carried out by a person**

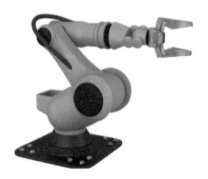

Automation means **using machines** to carry out work that humans previously carried out.

Robots, CNC machine tools, computers and **smartphones** are all examples of **automation**.

Automation enables work to be carried out **faster, more accurately** and for **less cost** than can be carried out by humans alone.

However, fewer people and **fewer jobs** are needed to carry out the tasks that have been automated.

EXAMPLES OF AUTOMATION AND ROBOTICS

- In **factories**, robots **assemble and paint cars**, and **pick up objects** on conveyor belts
- On **farms**, robots **milk cows,** and **drones** are used to find and **check on animals**
- **Houses** can be cleaned using **robot vacuum cleaners** that avoid obstacles and find their way back to their recharging station
- In an **engineering workshop**, a computer sends data to a **CNC lathe** and to a **laser cutter** to control their movements (see below)

> **CAM** (Computer-Aided Manufacturing) is the use of **computers** to control **manufacturing processes**

CNC Machine Tools (e.g. CNC Lathes)

CNC (Computer Numerical Control) is a particular way of programming and controlling the operation of a machine tool by sending it **numerical codes**.

- **G-codes** are used to control the movement of the cutting tool, **M-codes** are used for other machine commands like rotate the spindle, change the speed etc.
- A **canned cycle** is a **pre-programmed set of codes** to carry out a complex operation
- **Jog keys** can be used to move the tool position in order to teach / create the program
- The **tool park position** is where the cutting tool rests when it is finishing cutting

Activities - ICT

Activity 6 – Computer Usage Presentation

Working in **groups** or **alone**, using **presentation software**, and using a **cloud-based search engine** for secondary research, create a short presentation "Changes in Computer Usage since the Invention of the Internet"

Activity 7 – Use Photo Editing Software

Using a digital camera, e.g. on your phone, take a photo of a machine or tool in your Engineering room. Use **photo editing software** to crop (cut off) the edges. Send the photo to a peer using email, an internet messaging service, or a cloud-based file sharing system

Activity 8 – Identify Computer Input and Output Devices

Identify whether the following devices are input or output devices, or both, by ticking the boxes in the appropriate columns:

Device	Input	Output		Device	Input	Output
Motion Sensor				Robot arm		
Keyboard				Headphone set		
Drone Controller				Mouse		
3D Printer				Laser Cutter		
Virtual Reality Goggles				Scanner		
Computer Speakers				CNC Lathe		
Printer				Webcam		
Touchscreen				Projector		

Inventors and Inventions

TRANSPORT	
James **Watt**	Steam engine with separate condenser
John **Dunlop**	Pneumatic tyre
Nicolaus **Otto**	Internal combustion 4-stroke engine
Henry **Ford**	Assembly line manufacture and model T car
Wright Brothers	First aeroplane
Dugald **Clerk**	Two-stroke engine
Frank **Whittle**	Turbojet engine
Rudolph **Diesel**	Diesel engine
John P. **Holland**	Submarine
Harry **Ferguson**	Modern tractor and its 3-point linkage system, 4-wheel drive Formula 1 car
Heinrick **Focke**	Developed the helicopter
Enzo **Ferrari**	Built the first Ferrari car, founded the Ferrari company and Formula 1 team
COMMUNICATIONS	
Steve **Jobs**	Founder and CEO of apple computers, Pixar animation film company
Guglielmo **Marconi**	Inventor of the radio, the telegraph system, worked on long-distance radio
John **Logie Baird**	Television
Alexander **Graham Bell**	Telephone
Bill **Gates**	Founder of Microsoft
Tim **Berners Lee**	World Wide Web
Mark **Zuckerberg**	Co-founder of Facebook
Elon **Musk**	Founder of SpaceX and Paypal, CEO Tesla, designed the Hyperloop system
Neil **Papworth**	Software developer who sent the first text message
Jack **Dorsey**	Twitter
COMPUTERS AND OFFICE EQUIPMENT	
Steve **Jobs**	Co-founder of Apple: iMac, iPod, iTunes, iPhone
Chester **Carlson**	Photocopier
Bill **Gates**	Co-founded Microsoft
Charles **Hull**	3D printing
Charles **Babbage**	First mechanical computing device for performing calculations
George **Boole**	Created a mathematical language used to design digital devices
OTHER	
Thomas **Edison**	Invented phonograph, motion cameras, some motors, voting recorder, typewriter, magnetic ore separator, pre-cast buildings, electric light bulb
James **Dyson**	Bag-less vacuum cleaner, Airblade hand dryer
Jeff **Bezos**	Founder of Amazon
Henry **Maudslay**	The lathe, standard screw threads
Robert **Boyle**	Discovered the relationship between gas pressure and volume
Nikola **Tesla**	Contributed to the design of the modern AC electricity supply system
Eileen **Gray**	Furniture designer and architect
Isaac **Singer**	Singer sewing machine
Mary **Anderson**	Windscreen wipers
Alessandro **Volta**	Electric Battery

Appendix 1 – Unit 10 Motorised Vehicle – Default Design

Assembled View

Exploded View

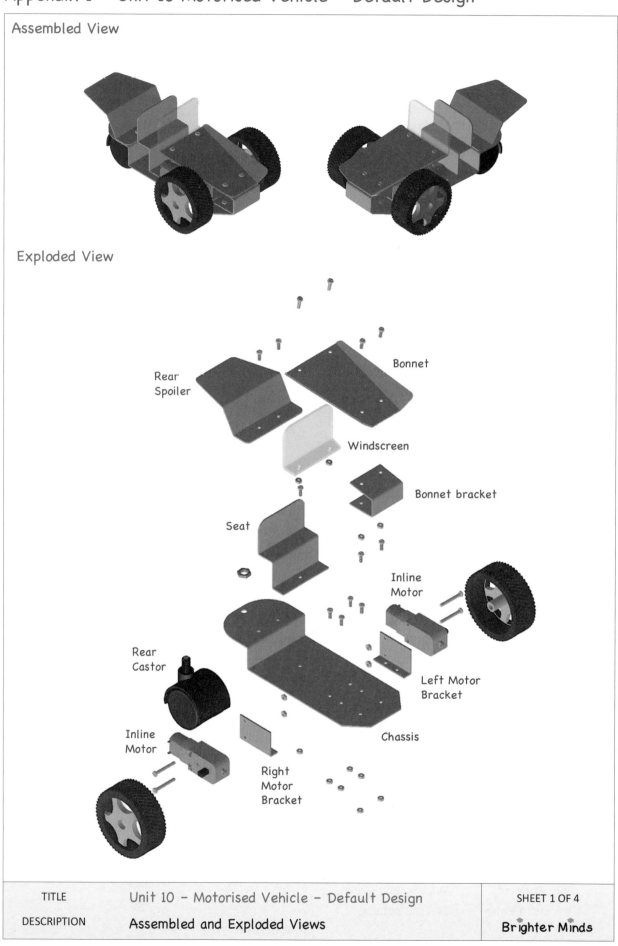

Rear
Spoiler

Bonnet

Windscreen

Bonnet bracket

Seat

Inline
Motor

Rear
Castor

Left Motor
Bracket

Inline
Motor

Chassis

Right
Motor
Bracket

TITLE	Unit 10 – Motorised Vehicle – Default Design	SHEET 1 OF 4
DESCRIPTION	Assembled and Exploded Views	Brighter Minds

Chassis

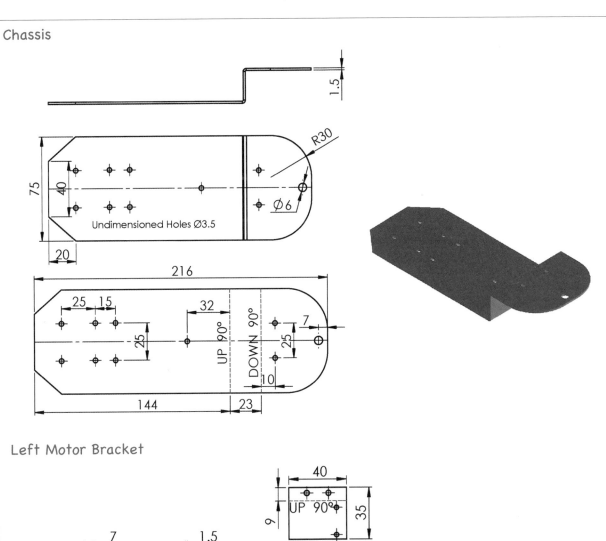

Left Motor Bracket

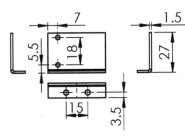

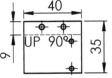

Undimensioned Holes Ø3.5

Right Motor Bracket

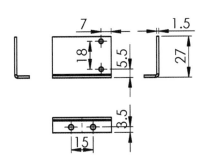

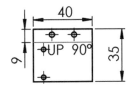

Undimensioned Holes Ø3.5

TITLE	Unit 10 – Motorised Vehicle – Default Design	SHEET 2 OF 4
DESCRIPTION	Chassis, Left and Right Motor Brackets	Brighter Minds

Bonnet Bracket

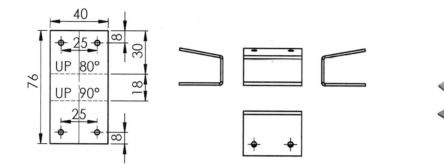

Undimensioned Holes Ø3.5

Bonnet

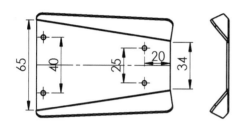

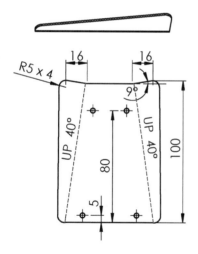

Windscreen

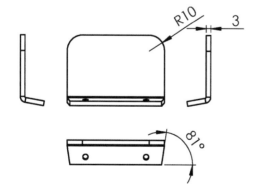
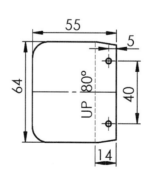

TITLE	Unit 10 – Motorised Vehicle – Default Design	SHEET 3 OF 4
DESCRIPTION	Bonnet Bracket, Bonnet, Windscreen	Brighter Minds

Seat

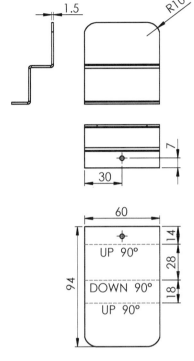

Rear Spoiler

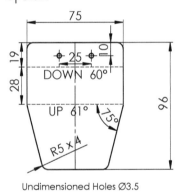
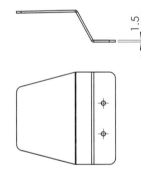

Undimensioned Holes Ø3.5

Bill of Materials

ITEM NO.	PART	DESCRIPTION	QTY.
1	CHASSIS	Aluminium 1.5mm	1
2	LEFT MOTOR BRACKET	Aluminium 1.5mm	1
3	RIGHT MOTOR BRACKET	Aluminium 1.5mm	1
4	MOTOR	Right-Angle Inline Geared Motor 3-6V 90rpm	2
5	MOTOR FIXING BOLTS	M3 x 30 Pan Head	4
6	FRONT WHEELS	68mm Diameter, D-Shaft fitting	2
7	BONNET BRACKET	Aluminium 1.5mm	1
8	BONNET	Aluminium 1.5mm	1
9	WINDSCREEN	3mm Transparent Acrylic	1
10	SEAT	Aluminium 1.5mm	1
11	REAR SPOILER	Aluminium 1.5mm	1
12	REAR CASTOR WHEEL	40mm diameter wheel, screw spindle + nut fitting	1
13	ASSEMBLY BOLTS	M3 x 10 Pan Head	13
14	ASSEMBLY BOLTS	M3 x 8 Pan Head	2
15	ASSEMBLY NUTS	M3 Hex Nut	15

TITLE	Unit 10 – Motorised Vehicle – Default Design	SHEET 4 OF 4
DESCRIPTION	Seat, Rear Spoiler, Bill of Materials	Brighter Minds

Appendix 2 – Unit 11 Car Park Barrier – Possible Starting Concept

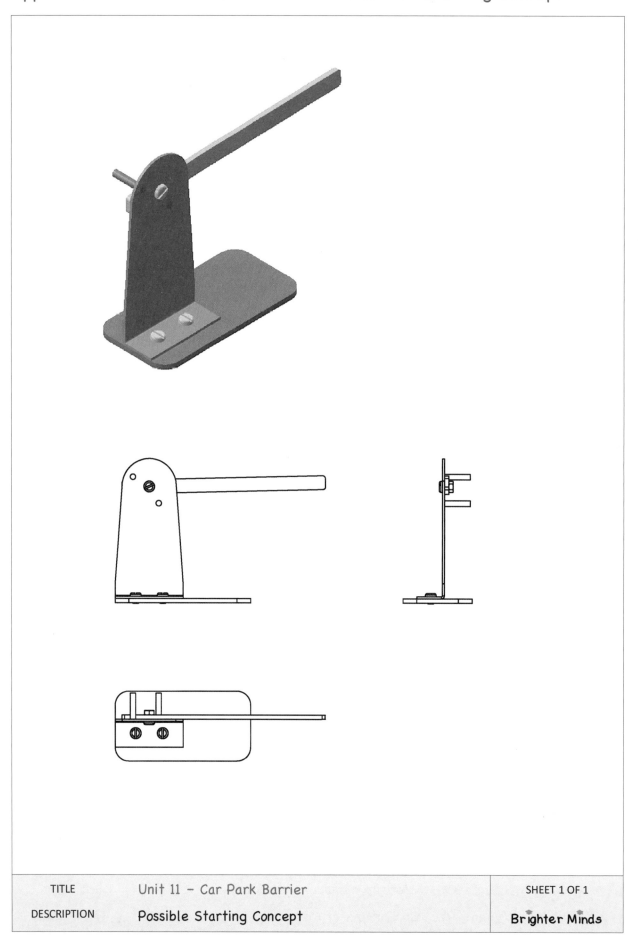

TITLE	Unit 11 – Car Park Barrier	SHEET 1 OF 1
DESCRIPTION	Possible Starting Concept	Brighter Minds

Notes

Notes

Notes

Notes

Notes

Notes

Index

Processes and Principles